# The ULTIMATE BOOK of CARD GAMES

D0896957

# The
# ULTIMATE
# BOOK of
# CARD
# GAMES

## The Diagram Group

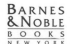

BARNES
&NOBLE
BOOKS
NEW YORK

Library of Congress Cataloging-in-Publication Data Available

2   4   6   8   10   9   7   5   3   1

Published 2004 by Sterling Publishing Co., Inc.
387 Park Avenue South, New York, NY 10016
© 1995 Diagram Visual Information Ltd.
195 Kentish Town Road, London NW5 8SY

Designed by StarGraphics Studio

*Printed in China*
*All rights reserved*

ISBN 0-7607-5480-2

# FOREWARD

Card playing has been popular for more than 500 years, and the greatest variety of card games in existence today reflects both this long history and the tremendous potential of playing cards as a source of entertainment. This illustrated encyclopedia brings together more than 250 card games and variations – old and new, easy and difficult, familiar and unfamiliar. Detailed rules of play are given step-by-step for each game in clear, concise language complemented by explanatory diagrams

The first four sections of the book place card games in one of four categories: general games, children's games, gambling games, and solitaire games. Obviously these divisions are somewhat arbitrary: some general games may be played for money; some children's games are popular with adults; some gambling games require high levels of card-playing skill; and some solitaire games require two players.

The order in which the games appear within each of the first four sections is basically alphabetical. In the gambling games section, for example, the games run literally from a to z, from Ace-deuce-jack to Ziginette. Alphabetical ordering, however, has not been applied to variants of games; these are included under the same main heading as the parent game (although they are also listed separately in the index). Thus Gin Rummy, for example, appears under the main heading for Rummy, not between Forty-five and Grand. Similarly, although the names are quite different, Black Maria appears under the heading for Hearts.

Obviously an important consideration when choosing a card game is the number of players. In the title bar for each game, a number indicates the number of players who can enjoy the game to best advantage.

Further useful informaton on finding a suitable game is to be found in section 5. This includes cross-referenced lists of games for different numbers of players, a list of variations, a list of alternative names, and a comprehensive index.

# TABLE OF CONTENTS

## SECTION 1

# General Card Games

| | | | |
|---|---|---|---|
| General rules | 10 | Kalabriasz | 102 |
| All fives | 18 | Knaves | 108 |
| Auction pitch | 20 | Loo | 110 |
| Bezique | 23 | Michigan | 113 |
| Boston | 33 | Napoleon | 116 |
| Bridge | 37 | Oh hell | 118 |
| Calabrasella | 52 | Pinochle | 120 |
| Canasta | 54 | Piquet | 127 |
| Casino | 60 | Pope Joan | 135 |
| Cribbage | 66 | Preference | 140 |
| Ecarté | 74 | Rummy | 142 |
| Euchre | 77 | Seven up | 147 |
| Five hundred | 81 | Skat | 150 |
| Forty-five | 84 | Solo whist | 158 |
| Grand | 89 | Spoil five | 162 |
| Hearts | 93 | Vint | 166 |
| Imperial | 98 | Whist | 170 |

# SECTION 2

# Gambling Games

| | | | |
|---|---|---|---|
| Introduction | 175 | Kentucky derby | 258 |
| Ace-deuce-jack | 177 | Lansquenet | 262 |
| Baccarat/Chemin de fer | 180 | Monte bank | 265 |
| Bango | 191 | Poker | 274 |
| Banker and broker | 193 | Polish red dog | 308 |
| Blackjack | 196 | Red and black | 311 |
| Blücher | 219 | Red dog | 313 |
| Brag | 221 | Skinball | 320 |
| Card craps | 229 | Slippery Sam | 324 |
| Card put-and-take | 236 | Stuss | 327 |
| Chinese fan-tan | 239 | Thirty-five | 329 |
| Faro | 242 | Thirty-one | 332 |
| Hoggenheimer | 250 | Trente et quarante | 335 |
| Horse race | 253 | Yablon | 339 |
| Injun | 256 | Ziginette | 342 |

# General Card Games

## GENERAL RULES

The origin of playing cards is a mystery. Chinese playing cards, it seems, grew out of a marriage between divinatory arrows and paper money. Such cards may have reached Europe via the Crusades or the China trade. Alternatively Western playing cards may have had a separate European origin – seeming to have appeared quite suddenly, around 1370, in almost their present form.

## THE CARDS

The deck The standard international deck of playing cards consists of 52 cards, divided into four suits of 13 cards each. Many decks also contain two jokers, sometimes used as wild cards.

The suits are named hearts, diamonds, spades, and clubs, and each card of the suit bears the appropriate symbol, as shown. Hearts and diamonds bear red symbols, spades and clubs black symbols.

The cards in any one suit are all of different denominations: nine are numbered from 2 to 10; three are "face" cards (jack, queen, king); the remaining card is the "ace," which is the "1" but is often the most powerful card of the suit.

The denomination of numbered cards is shown both by numbers and by the appropriate number of suit symbols.

The ace is shown by an "A" and a single large suit symbol.

Face cards are shown by stylized drawings and by initial letters, which vary according to the country of origin of the deck. In English language countries these letters are "J" (for jack), "Q" (for queen), and "K" (for king).

The rank of cards is usually either: 2 (low), 3,4,5,6,7,8,9,10, j,q,k,a (high); or a (low), 2,3,4,5,6,7,8,9,10,j,q,k (high).

In either list, a card beats any card listed before it.

# Complete deck of cards

## Hearts

 and the remaining Hearts cards J, Q, K and Joker

## Diamonds

## Spades

## Clubs

These rankings are referred to in the text as "cards rank normally, ace high," and "cards rank normally, ace low."

A meld is a scoring combination of cards in certain games. It is usually either:

**a** three or more cards of the same denomination; or

**b** three or more cards in consecutive order of rank and of the same suit.

Trumps In games with tricks (see p 16), it is often ruled that certain cards are made trump cards (trumps). If so, any trump card ranks above any other card.

Usually, all the cards of one suit are chosen as trump cards (trump suit). But in some games only some cards of one suit are the trump cards; or in many other games there are other trump cards in addition to the trump suit.

Within a trump suit, cards rank in the standard order for the game being played.

Choice of trump suit The method depends on the game being played.

Some games use a permanent trump suit, chosen by agreement or convention at the beginning of the game. But usually a suit has the role of trump suit for only one deal at a time. In this case, the trump suit for a deal is decided in one of the following ways, depending on the game being played:

**a** by competitive bidding among the players;

**b** by chance, i.e., turning a certain card face up, the suit revealed becomes trumps;

**c** by set order of rotation among the suits.

## PREPARING AND DEALING

Choice of partners for partnership play is usually by an initial draw. Each of the four players draws one card from the deck; the two players with the highest ranking cards form one partnership and the other two players form the second.

Choice of the first dealer

a By high cut. Any agreed player acts as temporary dealer and shuffles the cards. Any other agreed player cuts them.

Shuffling

Each player then cuts the deck, beginning with the player to the temporary dealer's left, going clockwise, and ending with the temporary dealer.

Each cut consists of lifting a section of cards from the top of the face-down deck. The card cut by the player is that at the bottom of this section.

The section is held up so all players can see this card.

After each cut, the two sections of cards are restacked in their original order, before passing to the next player.

The player cutting the highest denomination card becomes the first dealer. Cards rank normally; ace ranks high or low according to the game played. Players who cut equal-highest, cut again until a decision is reached between them.

b By deal of cards. Any agreed player acts as temporary dealer and shuffles the cards. Any other agreed player cuts them. The temporary dealer then deals one card face up to each player, including himself, beginning with the player to his left and going clockwise, until the first card of a specified denomination is dealt (e.g., the first ace). The player receiving this card becomes the first dealer.

Shuffle and cut are often required before every deal. The

dealer shuffles. Any other player also has the right to shuffle, but the dealer has the right to shuffle last.

The procedure of shuffling is not governed by rules – providing that an adequate shuffle is given to the cards in some way. One simple and satisfactory procedure is illustrated on the previous page.

The player to the dealer's right is offered the cards to cut. If he declines the player to his right is offered the cut, and so on. If no player wishes to cut, the dealer must cut.

A cut consists of lifting a section of cards from the top of the deck, placing it on the table, and placing the other section on top of it.

Cards remain face down and unexposed throughout.

There must be at least five cards in each section.

**Winning a trick**

Trumps

Lead

King wins

Trump wins

The deal Unless otherwise stated, the dealer gives one card at a time to each player, beginning with the player to his left and going clockwise. This rotation is repeated until each player has the required number of cards. The deal must be from the top of a face down deck.

Deal in packets is a deal in which each player receives more than one card at once. It is required for certain games.

On the deal, the dealer gives each player a specified number of cards (e.g., three cards), before going on to the next player.

Otherwise the deal follows normal procedure.

Sometimes the number of cards specified changes during the deal. For example, in solo whist: when the dealer goes round the circle of players for the first, second, and third times, he gives each player three cards each time; when he goes around the fourth (last) time, he gives each player one card, as in a normal deal.

A widow is a batch of cards dealt in addition to the players' hands. Its role varies from game to game.

The stock is, in certain games, the part of the deck which remains undealt after the deal is complete but which becomes available to players in the course of play.

## ROTATION OF PLAY

Unless otherwise stated, play begins with the player to the dealer's left, and continues with the other players in clockwise rotation.

## TRICKS

A trick signifies, in certain games, one round of cards during play – one card being contributed by each active hand. It also means the cards themselves when gathered together.

On each trick one player plays first ("has the lead"), and the

The winner of the last trick takes the last stock card, and the loser takes the exposed trump card.

During this stage the players are not obliged to follow suit. A trick is taken by the higher card of the suit led or by a trump card. If cards of equal value are played, the card that led takes the trick.

The second stage begins when the stock is exhausted.

The players must follow suit for these last eight tricks, except they may trump if they cannot follow suit. A player must win a trick if he is able to.

The winner of the last trick scores 10 points.

Declarations may be made after winning a trick.

The cards of each meld must be laid face up in front of the player, but they may be played to tricks as if they were still in the hand.

**Declarations**

Trumps

**a**
20 points

**b**
40 points

**c**
40 points

**d**
40 points

**e**
60 points

**f**
80 points

**g**
100 points

**h**
250 points

**i**
500 points

**j**
10 points

The possible declarations are as follows:

a  common marriage: king and queen of the same suit, except trumps, 20 points;

b  royal marriage: king and queen of the trump suit, 40 points;

c  bezique: queen of spades and jack of diamonds, 40 points (when spades or diamonds are trumps, some players prefer to make "bezique" the queen of clubs and jack of hearts);

d  any four jacks, 40 points;

e  any four queens, 60 points;

f  any four kings, 80 points;

g  any four aces, 100 points;

h  sequence: a,10,k,q,j of the trump suit only, 250 points;

i  double bezique: both queens of spades and both jacks of diamonds, 500 points;

j  exchanging the 7 of trumps for the face-up card, 10 points (the holder of the other 7 of trumps scores 10 points when he plays it, which does not count as a declaration).

A player may make only one declaration after winning a trick. But if his exposed cards show a second possible declaration, he can announce that he will declare it when he next takes a trick. No card may form part of a second similar declaration. For example, a queen of spades in "four queens" cannot form part of a second declaration of "four queens," but can form part of a "bezique," "double bezique," "royal marriage," or "sequence."

The cards used to form a "bezique," can be used again to form part of a "double bezique," but neither card can be used with a fresh partner for a second "bezique."

Brisques are every ace and every 10 taken in tricks, and they count 10 points each.

The brisques are counted up by each player examining his tricks at the end of the game.

Game is either 1000 or 2000 points up.

Penalties If a player draws out of turn, his opponent scores 10 points.

If a player holds more than eight cards, his opponent scores 100 points provided he himself has the right number of cards. A player who plays to the next trick without having drawn a card during the first stage forfeits 10 points to his opponent. A player who revokes (fails to follow suit although able to) during the last eight tricks, or fails to take a trick if he is able to do so forfeits all eight tricks to his opponent.

Scoring is most easily done using special bezique markers; but it can also be done with pencil and paper, counters, or with a cribbage board (each hole on the board counting as 10).

## THREE-HANDED BEZIQUE

Three-handed bezique is the same as ordinary bezique except that 96 cards (three piquet decks) are used. Each player plays for himself. Triple bezique scores 1500 points.

## RUBICON BEZIQUE

Rubicon bezique is a popular two-player variation of the standard two-handed game. It is similar to standard bezique, with the following differences.

The deck consists of 128 cards, or four piquet decks.

The deal consists of nine cards to each player, dealt either singly or in threes.

Trumps are established by the first sequence or marriage declared by either player. No stock cards are turned up, and the 7 of trumps has no value.

## Rubicon: declarations

Trumps

**a**
50 points

**b**
150 points

**c**
1500 points

**d**
4500 points

Play is the same as for standard bezique, except that the last trick counts 50 points.

Declarations are as in standard bezique, with the following additions.

a  Carte blanche: worth 50 points, and scored if either player is dealt a hand not containing a face card. The hand must be displayed. (See diagram overleaf.)

  If, after drawing a further card, the player's hand still does not contain a face card, carte blanche may be scored again, and this continues until a face card is drawn.

  Once a player has held a face card, carte blanche cannot be scored.

b  Ordinary sequence/back door: a sequence not of the trump suit, 150 points.

c  triple bezique: three queens of spades and three jacks of diamonds, 1500 points.

**d** quadruple bezique: four queens of spades and four jacks of diamonds, 4,500 points.

Cards may be reused to form the same combinations. For example, if "four queens" are declared and one queen is played, a fifth queen may be laid down to form "four queens" again. Two marriages of the same suit may be rearranged to form two more marriages.

Brisques are only counted if there is a tied score, or to save a player from being "rubiconed," i.e., failing to reach 1000 points. If one player chooses to count brisques, the other player's brisques are also scored.

Game is a single deal. The player with the higher score wins 500 points plus the difference between his and the loser's score. If the loser is rubiconed, the winner gets 1000 points, plus the sum of his and the loser's scores, plus 320 points for all his brisques.

(This applies even if the winner himself has scored fewer than 1000 points).

If the loser fails to score 100 points, the winner scores an extra 100 points.

Any fractions of 100 points may be ignored in scoring, except if the player's scores are very close.

## SIX-DECK BEZIQUE

Six-deck bezique, also known as Chinese bezique, is a variant of rubicon bezique. The rules are the same as for rubicon bezique, with the following changes.

The deck is 192 cards (six piquet decks shuffled together).

The deal is 12 cards to each player, dealt singly or in threes.

Trumps are indicated by the first declared marriage or sequence.

Brisques do not count at all.

Declarations can be made as in rubicon bezique, reusing

## Six-deck: declarations

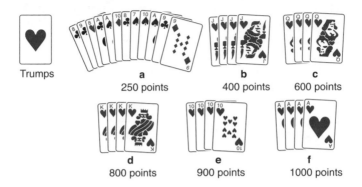

Trumps

**a**
250 points

**b**
400 points

**c**
600 points

**d**
800 points

**e**
900 points

**f**
1000 points

cards in similar scoring combinations.

In six-deck bezique, carte blanche (a) is worth 250 points, as is winning the last trick. Declarations in addition to those in rubicon bezique are, in the trump suit only:

b four jacks, 400 points;
c four queens, 600 points;
d four kings, 800 points;
e four 10s, 900 points;
f four aces, 1000 points.

Bezique varies according to which suit is trumps, as follows: hearts, queen of hearts and jack of clubs; diamonds, queen of diamonds and jack of spades; clubs, queen of clubs and jack of hearts; spades, queen of spades and jack of diamonds.

Game is a single deal. Scores are calculated as for rubicon bezique, except that: the winner gets a game bonus of 1000 points instead of 500; and the rubicon point is 3000 instead of 1000.

## EIGHT-DECK BEZIQUE

Eight-deck bezique is played like six-deck bezique, with the following variations.

The deck consists of 256 cards, or eight piquet decks.

The deal is 15 cards to each player.

Declarations are as in six-deck bezique, with the following changes and additions:

**a** bezique, 50 points;

**b** quintuple bezique, 9000 points.

In the trump suit only:

**c** five jacks, 800 points;

**d** five queens, 1200 points;

**e** five kings, 1600 points;

**f** five 10s, 1800 points;

**g** five aces, 2000 points.

A player is rubiconed if he fails to score 5000 points.

### Eight-deck declarations

Trumps

**a**
50 points

**b**
9000 points

**c**
800 points

**d**
1200 points

**e**
1600 points

**f**
1800 points

**g**
2000 points

**Four-handed declarations**

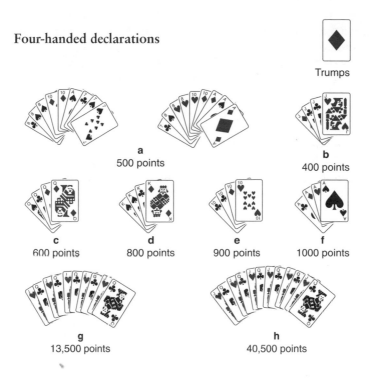

Trumps

a
500 points

b
400 points

c
600 points

d
800 points

e
900 points

f
1000 points

g
13,500 points

h
40,500 points

## FOUR-HANDED BEZIQUE

Four-handed bezique is similar to rubicon bezique, but the game is played with 192 cards (six piquet decks). The players play in partnership, two against two.

The deal is nine cards to each player, the player on the dealer's left leads to the first trick.

Declarations may be made by any player after winning a trick; alternatively he may allow his partner to make the declaration. A player may use both his own cards and any of his partner's declared cards to make a declaration.

Scoring is as in rubicon bezique, with the following variations and additions:

  **a** double carte blanche: both players in a partnership being dealt a hand without a face card, 500 points;

  **b** any four jacks, 400 points;

  **c** any four queens, 600 points;

  **d** any four kings, 800 points;

  **e** any four 10s, 900 points;

  **f** any four aces, 1000 points;

  **g** quintuple bezique, 13,500 points;

  **h** sextuple bezique, 40,500 points.

# 4 BOSTON

This game developed from whist and is itself an ancestor of the now more popular solo whist. It was very popular at the time of the American Revolution.

**Players** The game is for four players, each player for himself.

**Rank**

**Cards** Two standard decks are used: one in play and the other for determining the "preference" and "color" suits. (If the preference and color suits are determined before the deal the game can be played with only one deck). Cards rank normally, with ace high.

**Chips** A large number of chips are required for scoring purposes. (To make settlement simpler, players sometimes use chips of different values).

**Objective** Each player tries to contract and fulfill a bid.

**Choice of first dealer** is by high cut, with ace low.

**Pool** Before each hand, each player pays 10 chips into a pool. If the pool exceeds 250 chips, the excess is put aside for the next pool.

**Deal** The dealer deals out all the playing deck, beginning with the player to his left and going clockwise. The cards are dealt three at a time, with a final round of single cards.

If there is a misdeal, the dealer must pay 10 chips into the pool.

The deal then passes one player to the left.

**Determining preference and color suits** After the deal, the second deck is cut by the player sitting opposite the dealer.

The top card of the bottom section is turned face up and denotes the preference suit. The other suit of the same color is called the color suit.

**Bidding** Each player in turn, beginning with the player to the dealer's left, may make a bid or pass.

**The bids** are ranked in the following order, with each outbidding the one before:

a    "Boston," i.e., a bid to win five tricks with one of the plain suits as trumps;

b    six tricks;

c    seven tricks;

d    "little misery," i.e., a bid to lose 12 tricks, playing with no trumps and after each player has discarded one card face down;

e    eight tricks;

f    nine tricks;

g    "grand misery," i.e., a bid to lose every trick, playing with no trumps;

h    10 tricks;

i    11 tricks;

j    "little spread," i.e., a bid to lose 12 tricks, playing with no trumps and the hand exposed;

k    12 tricks;

l    "grand spread," i.e., a bid to lose every trick, playing with no trumps and the hand exposed;

m    "grand slam," i.e., a bid to win all 13 tricks.

**Trumps** There are no trumps for misery and spread bids. For other bids the player chooses his own trump suit, usually stating what it is only when his bid has been accepted.

However, if two or more players wish to make a bid for the same number of tricks, the bids are ranked as follows according to the proposed trump suit: preference suit (high), color suit, plain suits (low).

No bid hands If all players pass, each one throws in his cards
and pays 10 chips into the pool. The deal then passes one
player to the left.

Play The player to the left of the dealer leads to the first trick.
Play is as for whist (p 164).

A player who revokes loses the hand and must pay 40
chips into the pool.

Settlement If a player fulfills his bid he receives chips from
each of the other players, and if his bid was for seven
tricks or higher, he also receives the chips in the pool.

If a player fails to fulfill the bid he pays to each of the
other players and must also double the chips in the pool.

## Table A

| Tricks bid | 5 | 6 | 7 | 8 | 9 | 10 | 11 | 12 | 13 |
|---|---|---|---|---|---|---|---|---|---|
| Payment | 10 | 15 | 20 | 25 | 35 | 45 | 65 | 105 | 170 |

## Table B

| Tricks bid | Number put in for | | | | | | | | | | | | |
|---|---|---|---|---|---|---|---|---|---|---|---|---|---|
| | 1 | 2 | 3 | 4 | 5 | 6 | 7 | 8 | 9 | 10 | 11 | 12 | 13 |
| | Payment | | | | | | | | | | | | |
| 5 | 10 | 20 | 30 | 40 | 50 | | | | | | | | |
| 6 | 15 | 25 | 35 | 45 | 55 | 65 | | | | | | | |
| 7 | 20 | 30 | 40 | 50 | 60 | 70 | 80 | | | | | | |
| 8 | 25 | 35 | 45 | 55 | 70 | 85 | 100 | 115 | | | | | |
| 9 | 35 | 45 | 55 | 65 | 80 | 95 | 110 | 125 | 140 | | | | |
| 10 | 45 | 55 | 70 | 80 | 95 | 110 | 125 | 140 | 155 | 170 | | | |
| 11 | 70 | 80 | 95 | 110 | 125 | 140 | 155 | 170 | 185 | 200 | 220 | | |
| 12 | 120 | 130 | 145 | 160 | 180 | 200 | 220 | 240 | 260 | 280 | 300 | 320 | |
| 13 | 180 | 200 | 220 | 240 | 260 | 280 | 300 | 320 | 340 | 360 | 390 | 420 | 450 |

For misery and spread bids the bidder pays or receives chips as follows: 20 for a little misery; 40 for grand misery; 80 for little spread; 160 for grand spread.

If a player fulfills any other bid he is paid according to table A.

If a player fails to fulfill any other bid he pays according to the number of tricks by which he fails – as given in table B. A player is said to be "put in for" the number of tricks by which he fails.

# 4 BRIDGE

For many people bridge is the most fascinating of card games: it is played in homes, clubs, and tournaments throughout the world. Its origins can be traced back some 400 years to the development of whist in England, but it was only in 1896 that the game of bridge itself evolved.

## CONTRACT BRIDGE

**Rank**

This form of bridge was developed in 1925, and within a few years had become by far the most popular form of the game.

### GENERAL RULES

Cards A standard deck of 52 cards is used. By convention a second deck with contrasting backs is also used, so that while one player deals another can shuffle in readiness for the next deal.

The cards rank: ace (high) through 2 (low). The 2 is commonly called a "deuce," and the 3 a "trey."

Players As in whist, there are four players, each pair forming a partnership. Partners sit oppo site each other. One partnership is usually called North–South, the other East–West.

Objective Each partnership aims to win a "rubber," by winning the most points in the best of three games.

A game is won by scoring 100 points, earned by taking tricks that have been contracted for.

Honors are the high-ranking cards in the trump suit, from the ace down through and including the 10. In "no trump" games, the four aces are honors.

Suits For the purpose of bidding, the suits are ranked as follows: spades (highest), hearts, diamonds, clubs (lowest).

The draw At the beginning of a bridge game, one deck is spread face down on the table, and each player draws one card from the deck.

The two players who draw the highest cards form one partnership; the other two players form the second. The player with the highest card becomes the first dealer and chooses his seating position; his partner sits opposite him.

If cards of the same denomination appear on the draw, they are ranked according to suit, as for bidding.

**Rank of suits**

♠

♥

♦

♣

**Honors**

## Sample deal and bidding

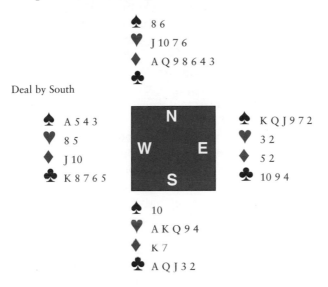

Deal by South

North:
♠ 8 6
♥ J 10 7 6
♦ A Q 9 8 6 4 3
♣ —

West:
♠ A 5 4 3
♥ 8 5
♦ J 10
♣ K 8 7 6 5

East:
♠ K Q J 9 7 2
♥ 3 2
♦ 5 2
♣ 10 9 4

South:
♠ 10
♥ A K Q 9 4
♦ K 7
♣ A Q J 3 2

Shuffle and cut The player to the left of the dealer shuffles the deck; the player to the dealer's right cuts the deck.

As the cards are being dealt, the alternate deck is shuffled by the dealer's partner.

The deal begins with the player to the dealer's left. The cards are dealt in a clockwise direction, one at a time and face down, until each player including the dealer has 13 cards.

## BIDDING

The auction begins once players have had a chance to study their cards. It opens with the dealer and continues in clockwise rotation. Each player, according to his hand, makes a "call," which may be a bid, pass, double, or redouble.

If a player passes, he may still make another call at a later stage in the bidding. But when a bid, double, or redouble is followed by three passes in succession, the auction ends.

If there are four passes at the opening of bidding, one from each player, the cards are "thrown in" to the center of the table and shuffled. A new hand is then dealt by the next dealer.

A pass indicates that a player does not choose to make any other call at that time in the bidding.

A bid is a statement of a number and a trump suit, e.g., "three clubs," or "five no trumps." It offers an undertaking that if that suit is trumps (or if there are "no trumps") the bidding player's partnership will take a number of tricks.

Bidding refers to the number of "odd" (i.e., additional) tricks that a bidder undertakes to make over six tricks.

A bid of "one club," for instance, means that a player thinks that his partnership can make seven tricks in all, if clubs are trumps.

**Bidding**

| S | W | N | E |
|---|---|---|---|
| 1 ♣ | double | 1 ♦ | 1 ♠ |
| 2 ♥ | 2 ♠ | 3 ♦ | double |
| 3 ♥ | pass | pass | 3 ♠ |
| 4 ♥ | pass | pass | pass |

*The contract is four hearts: North-South have bought the contract and South is declarer.*

A bid of "four no trumps" offers the undertaking to make ten tricks in all, if no suit is trumps.

Continuing the bidding As the auction continues, each successive bid must be higher than the preceding bid – either by calling a greater number of tricks or by naming a higher ranking suit.

For instance, a bid of "two spades" is higher than two hearts, diamonds, or clubs.

A no trump call ranks above all suits. So, for example, a bid of "two no trumps" is higher than two spades. The next player to bid would have to bid at least "three clubs."

The contract The highest bid of the auction becomes the "contract." The players in the partnership making that bid must, in play, make as many tricks as they have contracted for, or more. Their opponents have only to prevent them from doing this – it does not matter what they themselves have bid.

The first six tricks taken by the contracted bidders are commonly referred to as "making the book."

Slam The maximum number of tricks in any played hand is 13. This gives a maximum bid of "seven," when one side believes it can take all the tricks: the book (of six), plus seven odd tricks. If a side succeeds in bidding and winning 13 tricks, this is known as a "grand slam."

A "small slam" occurs if a side bids and wins a total of 12 tricks.

Doubling If a player says "Double" after any of his opponents' bids, it means that he believes he could prevent them from making their bid, if it became the contract.

A bid that has been doubled need not become the contract: it can be overbid in the usual way, by either partnership. If, however, it does become the contract and succeeds, the contracting players' score is doubled. Should the bidders "go down" (i.e., not make their contract) the side that doubled gets at least twice the score that it would otherwise have had.

Redoubling If a bid has been doubled either player of the bidding partnership may say "Redouble." This confirms his confidence in the bid, and – as in doubling – the scoring is affected whether or not the contract is made (see the section on scoring page 41).

A bid that has been redoubled can be overbid in the usual way.

The declarer The player in the contracting side who first made a bid in the trump suit of the contract (spades, hearts, diamonds, clubs, or no trumps), is referred to as the "declarer." He plays both hands of the contracting partnership's game.

## PLAY

A trick consists of four cards, one played from each player's hand, in clockwise rotation. The player who must play first is called the "lead."

The lead The opening lead is held by the player to the dealer's left. He plays the first card after the bidding ends. After this, the winner of each trick makes the next lead.

A player may lead any card, and the other three players must follow suit if possible. If a player cannot follow suit, he may play any other card in his hand.

Winning the trick If none of the four cards is a trump, the trick is won by the highest card played in the suit led. If one or more of the four cards is a trump, the trick is won by the highest trump.

No trump When a "no trump" bid becomes the contract, all suits have equal rank and the highest card in the suit led always wins the trick.

**Beginning
the play**

**Dummy**

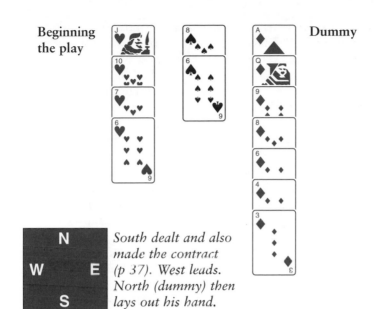

*South dealt and also
made the contract
(p 37). West leads.
North (dummy) then
lays out his hand.*

**Dummy** As soon as the opening lead has been made, declarer's
partner lays down his cards face up on the table, sorted
out by suit, with trumps to his right.

The exposed cards, and declarer's partner himself, are
referred to as "dummy" for that hand.

Only declarer can choose the cards to play for the
dummy hand. The dummy partner may not participate in
that hand, other than physically to play a specified card at
declarer's request. Plays from a dummy must be in correct
order of rotation, i.e., following a card played by the
player to declarer's left.

Declarer must play a card in dummy that he touches

(except when rearranging the cards or touching a card next to the one to be played).

Gathering won tricks is done by either player of the side winning the trick.

The four cards are gathered together and placed face down on the table.

All declarer's and dummy's tricks are placed in front of declarer; all the opponents tricks' are placed in front of one opponent.

The arrangement of gathered tricks must show clearly how many tricks have been won and in which order. Common procedure is to bunch the first six of the declarer's tricks into one group, so that it is clear how many odd tricks have been made.

A trick may be inspected by the declarer or by either opponent, until a player of the inspecting side has led or played to the following trick.

## SCORING

It is important to master the scoring in contract bridge as this strongly affects the game's strategy.

Both sides should keep score in case of disagreement.

A scoring pad has a central vertical line dividing "we" (one partnership) from "they" (its opponents).

A horizontal line is initially drawn across the scoring pad, and a partnership can score points either "below the line" or "above the line."

Trick points are entered below the line. Only declarer's side can score trick points on a hand, and only if the contract is made. Only the odd tricks contracted for can be scored below the line. Trick points show each side's progress toward winning the current game.

Premium points are scored above the line, and may be scored

## Scoring

| a | b | c | d |
|---|---|---|---|

## Explanation of scoring diagrams

a "We" score 70 trick points.

b "We" score 30 trick points and 150 premium points. "We" win first game and are now vulnerable.

c "We" go under by two tricks. "They" score 200 under-trick points.

d "They" score 60 trick points and 150 premium points.

by both sides in any hand. They are won for:

a overtricks;

b successful doubling or redoubling;

c bidding and making a slam;

d having a certain number of honors cards in one hand in the deal; or

e winning the final game of a rubber.

Undertricks If declarer's side fails to make the contract, the number of tricks it has failed by are known as "under-tricks." These are credited to the opponents' premium points and scored above the line.

Vulnerable A partnership is "vulnerable" if it has won its first game towards the rubber. (It is therefore possible for both partnerships to be vulnerable).

Winning a game The first side to reach a score of 100 or more, either in one or several hands, wins the game.

A horizontal line is then drawn below the trick scores of both sides. Trick scores for the next game are entered below this line, both sides beginning again from zero.

Winning the rubber When one side has won two games, the rubber ends.

This side earns 700 premium points if its opponents have won no game, and 500 premium points if its opponents have won one game.

All trick and premium points are then totalled, and the side with the higher total wins the rubber.

The back score indicates an individual player's standing. It is used in any competition in which partners rotate.

After a rubber, the difference between the two sides' final scores is calculated by subtracting the lower from the higher. This difference is rounded to the nearest 100 (50 and above become 100), and divided by 100. For example, 753 becomes 800, giving 8. Each player of the winning partnership is then given a score of plus 8 and each opponent a score of minus 8. In subsequent rubbers, with different partnerships, the same procedure is followed. The player with the highest plus score at the end is the overall winner.

## DUPLICATE CONTRACT BRIDGE

Duplicate contract bridge is very popular among advanced bridge players. It is the only form played in international tournaments. All groups of players are presented, in turn, with the same deal of cards. In this way, the game relies more on skill than on luck of the deal.

Equipment

1 one table for every four players in the tournament;

## Contract bridge scoring table

**Trick score: scored by declarer below the line**

|  | ♣ | ♦ | ♥ | ♠ | NT |
|---|---|---|---|---|---|
| First trick over six bid and made | 20 | 20 | 30 | 30 | 40 |
| Subsequent tricks bid and made | 20 | 20 | 30 | 30 | 30 |
| Doubling doubles trick score | | | | | |
| Redoubling doubles doubled score | | | | | |

**Premium score: scored by declarer above the line**

|  | Not vulnerable | Vulnerable |
|---|---|---|
| Small slam | 500 | 750 |
| Grand slam | 1000 | 1500 |
| Each overtrick undoubled | Trick value | Trick value |
| Each overtrick doubled | 100 | 200 |
| Each overtrick redoubled | 200 | 400 |
| Making a doubled or redoubled contract | 50 | 50 |

**Rubber, game, and partscore: scored above the line**

|  | Points |
|---|---|
| For winning rubber, if opponents have won no game | 700 |
| For winning rubber, if opponents have won one game | 500 |
| For having won one game in an unfinished rubber | 300 |
| For having the only partscore in an unfinished rubber | 50 |

**Honors: scored by either side above the line**

|  | Points |
|---|---|
| Four trump honors in one hand | 100 |
| Five trump honors in one hand | 150 |
| Four aces in one hand, no trump contract | 150 |

**Undertricks: scored by opponents above the line**

|  | Undoubled | Doubled | Redoubled |
|---|---|---|---|
| First trick, not vulnerable | 50 | 100 | 200 |
| Subsequent tricks | 50 | 200 | 400 |
| First trick, vulnerable | 100 | 200 | 400 |
| Subsequent tricks | 100 | 300 | 600 |

2 the same number of duplicate boards or trays as tables;
3 one deck of cards for each board.

Players Competing units may be individuals, pairs, or teams of four or six, depending on the nature of the tournament.

In individual events, partnerships change during the tournament; in team events, partnerships change at half-time; and in pairs matches, the same partnerships are preserved throughout.

A duplicate board is used at each table. Each board has four pockets, an arrow or label indicating North's side, and markers indicating the dealer and the vulnerability or otherwise of partnerships.

Before the tournament the boards are arranged so that a quarter have North-South vulnerable, a quarter East-West vulnerable, a quarter both pairs vulnerable, and a quarter neither pair vulnerable.

Within each category, the position of dealer is distributed equally between the pairs.

Basic procedure Each board maintains the same deal of cards throughout the tournament.

The boards and players move from table to table in a specified way.

The tournament ends, according to the system used, either:

a when all North-South players have met all East-West players; or

b when all players have played with and against all other players.

Deal For the first hand at each board, the designated dealer shuffles and deals the cards in the usual way.

Thereafter, following each hand, this original deal is preserved. Each player's cards are placed in the appropriate board pocket, in readiness for the next set of players.

The auction for any hand takes place in the usual way, commencing with the player indicated as dealer. If all players pass there is no redeal.

Play on any hand proceeds as in contract bridge, except that after each trick is completed the cards are not gathered together.

Each player takes back his card, and turns it face down on the table in front of him. He points the card lengthwise toward the partners who won the trick; this allows players to keep track of the number of tricks won by each side.

Scoring a hand No points are given for winning a rubber. If a side bids and makes a contract that gives it a game (100 trick points), it gets 500 premium points if vulnerable, 300 if not. Additional premium points for making a grand slam are 1500 if vulnerable, 1000 if not; and for a small slam, 750 if vulnerable, 500 if not.

If a side bids and makes a contract less than game, it gets 50 premium points.

A score made on one board cannot be carried forward to affect scoring on the next.

Unless cumulative tournament scoring is used, no premium points are given for holding honors in one hand.

Scoring the tournament

a Match point procedure is always used if the competing units are individuals. It can also be used for pairs.

The comparison is between scores made at the same board, i.e., success in playing the same deal.

Each score is given two points for each lower score made in the same position on that board, and one point for each exactly equal score.

Each individual in an individual event receives points for the score made by his partnership.

The individual or pair with the highest number of match points wins the competition.

b International match point (IMP) scoring is usually used for teams. Each partnership's surplus (or deficit) of points over its opponents is calculated for each hand,

and added together at the end to give a team total. This
is then converted into match points on the basis of an
established scale.

c Cumulative (total point) scoring is still sometimes used
for team competitions.

## AUCTION BRIDGE

A forerunner of contract bridge, auction bridge evolved
from the game of whist.

Except for the scoring – which greatly affects the strategy
of the game – its rules are as for contract bridge.

Major differences The two major differences in scoring are as
follows:

1 In auction bridge there is no concept of vulnerability.
   If one partnership has won a game there is no extra
   penalty (as in contract bridge) for failure to make a
   contract.

2 All odd tricks, whether contracted for or not, are scored
   "below the line." They contribute to winning the game,
   provided that declarer has succeeded in making the minimum number of tricks named in the contract.

Game The first side to score 30 points below the line wins a
game. A horizontal line is drawn across the scoring pad,
as in contract bridge, to indicate that a game has been
completed.

Rubber The first side to win two games out of three wins the
rubber and is awarded an additional 250 points.

Honors If either side has three or more honors in the trump
suit (or aces and no trumps) then – whether or not that
side is declarer – the following scores are given above the
line: three honors or aces, 30 points; four honors or aces,
divided, 40 points; five honors, divided, 50 points; four
honors, one hand, 80 points; five honors, divided four to

| Trick points | | | | | |
|---|---|---|---|---|---|
| | ♣ | ♦ | ♥ | ♠ | NT |
| Undoubled | 6 | 7 | 8 | 9 | 10 |
| Doubled | 12 | 14 | 16 | 18 | 20 |
| Redoubled | 24 | 28 | 32 | 36 | 40 |

one, 90 points; four aces, one hand, 100 points; five honors, one hand, 100 points.

Bonuses 50 points are given above the line if a doubled contract is bid for and made. In addition, declarer's side gets 50 points for each trick in excess of the contract.

If declarer succeeds in making a redoubled contract, both the bonuses mentioned above are raised to 100 points each.

Undertricks If declarer's side fails to make contract, the opponents are given the following points (above the line) for each undertrick: undoubled contract, 50; doubled contract, 100; redoubled contract, 200.

Slams If either side makes a small slam (12 tricks), it receives 50 points above the line – regardless of the bidded contract. If a grand slam (13 tricks) is won, 100 points are awarded.

# 3 CALABRASELLA

Calabrasella is an interesting and fast-moving card game for three players. Its characteristic features are a stripped deck, unusual rankings of cards, and the absence of a trump suit.

### Rank

Cards A standard deck of playing cards with the 8s, 9s, and 10s removed is used.

The cards rank 3 (high), 2, a, k, q, 7, 6,5,4 (low).

Players This is a game for three.

Objective Each player tries to take certain tricks.

Deal Players cut for the deal and the lowest card deals.

The dealer gives each player 12 face-down cards in packets of four. The four remaining cards are placed face down in a pile in the center of the table as the widow (extra hand).

Bidding Starting with the player to the left of the dealer, each player in turn may choose either to play or pass.

The first player to choose to play is opposed by the other two players in partnership for that round.

If none of the three players wishes to play, the hand is thrown in and the cards are redealt.

Widow The player who decides to play may discard, face down, up to four of his cards and replace them with cards from the widow, turned face up. The discarded cards, if any, and any remaining widow cards are then placed face down in a pile. These four cards will go to the winner of the last trick.

Play The player to the left of the dealer leads to the first trick with any card he likes. In turn, each of the other players must follow suit if possible, or discard if not.

The winner of each trick leads to the next.

Scoring Players score for taking cards in tricks as follows: aces, three points each; 3s, 2s, ks, qs and js, one point each.

The player who takes the last trick scores an extra three points, and also scores for the four spare (widow or discard) cards.

Thus the maximum possible score is 35 points.

Each side totals its score, and the difference between them is the final score for the hand.

Payoff If the single player wins, each of the opponents pays him the final score in counters or points.

If he loses, he pays each opponent the final score.

If one side scores the maximum of 35 points, the payoff is 70 points or counters.

Game is 100 points. Alternatively, play can continue until one player has lost all his counters.

# 4 CANASTA

Canasta is a partnership game of the rummy family.

Originating in Uruguay, it reached the United States in 1949 and in the early 1950s became one of the biggest fads in the history of card playing.

Cards Two standard decks of 52 cards and four jokers are used, shuffled together.

The cards are not ranked.

There are 12 wild cards: the four jokers and all eight deuces (2s). Wild cards can be given any denomination that the holder wishes.

Players In the standard game there are four players divided into two partnerships.

The objective is to be the first side to score 5000 points over a series of hands. Points are mainly scored by making melds.

A meld is a set of at least three cards of the same denomination. They can be all natural cards, or a mixture of natural and wild cards. But whatever the size of the meld, there must be at least two natural cards and not more than three wild cards.

Melds score according to the cards they contain (see table A, page 59).

Cutting for partners Each player cuts a card from the deck, and the two who cut the highest cards play against the other two. For this purpose, cards rank normally (ace high) and suits rank spades (high), hearts, diamonds, clubs (low).

Players cutting a joker or exactly equal cards cut again.

Player cutting highest becomes first dealer and has choice of seats.

Shuffle and cut are normal.

The deal begins with the player to the dealer's left.

The cards are dealt one at a time and face down in a

clockwise direction until each player including the dealer has 11 cards. The remaining cards are then placed face down on the table as the stock. The top card of the stock is turned face up alongside to start the discard pile.

Play starts with the players to the dealer's left.

In a normal turn a player first takes the top card of the stock. He then makes any melds that he can, or adds to those that he or his partner have already laid out on the table.

Finally he discards by placing one card from his hand face up on the discard pile.

The initial meld of a partnership after each deal must total at least a certain number of points – how many depends on their score so far (see table B, page 59).

Once either partner has made this first meld, both partners can make new melds of any value and can add to melds that they have already laid out on the table.

A player may add to either his own or his partner's melds.

**Wild cards**

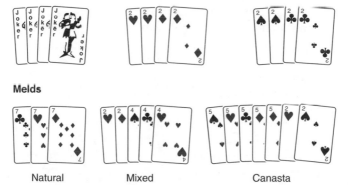

**Melds**

Natural     Mixed     Canasta

A canasta is a meld of seven cards.

A natural canasta consists of seven cards of the same rank and has a bonus value of 500 points on top of the card score.

A mixed canasta has natural cards and one to three wild cards, and has a bonus value of 300 points.

Once a canasta is completed, the cards are gathered into a pile.

A natural canasta has a red card placed on top for identification, and a mixed canasta has a black card.

Further cards may be added to a canasta. But a mixed canasta may not receive a fourth wild card and a natural canasta loses its value if a wild card is added.

Taking the discard pile In place of taking the top card from the stock, a player may in his turn take the upcard from the discard pile – but only if he has in his hand at least two natural cards of the same denomination.

He must lay the appropriate hand cards face up on the table and meld the upcard with them.

He then also takes all the remainder of the discard pile, and immediately uses as many cards as possible by adding to existing melds or laying out new ones. Any cards that he cannot use become part of his hand.

The player ends his turn by discarding one card to start a new discard pile.

Provided it is not "frozen," a player may also take the discard pile:

a if he can meld the upcard with one card of the same denomination and one wild card; or

b if the upcard matches an existing meld of his partnership.

Frozen discard pile The discard pile is frozen as follows.

1 It is frozen for a partnership that has not made its initial meld.

2 It is frozen for a player if a black 3 is the upcard. In this case it is no longer frozen after the player has drawn from the stock and discarded.

3 It is frozen for all players if the discard pile contains a red 3 or a wild card. In this case further discards are placed crosswise on top of the freezing card. The discard pile remains frozen until one player unfreezes it by melding the upcard or wild card with two natural cards from his hand.

Red 3s are bonus cards counting 100 points each (a). They cannot be melded.

If a player draws a red 3 from the stock, he must lay it face up on the table and draw another card from the stock.

If he is dealt a red 3 he must lay it face up on the table and draw a card from the stock in addition to his regular draw.

If a red 3 is taken as part of the discard pile, it must be laid face up on the table without any extra card being drawn from the stock.

If a partnership holds all four red 3s, these cards count 200 points each, i.e., 800 points in all (b).

All red 3 points count against a partnership if it has not made an initial meld when the play ends.

Black 3s may only be melded when a player is going out.

a

100 points

b

800 points

They can never be melded with wild cards. Their main use is as "stop cards" to freeze the discard pile.

Going out occurs when a player is able to meld all his cards, providing that when he has gone out his side has made at least one canasta. A player can go out without discarding if he wishes.

Concealed going out occurs when a player melds all his cards when he has not previously melded any cards.

Note that a player must always meld a canasta unless his partner has already melded one.

Permission is usually asked to go out, in the form of "May I go out, partner?" A yes or no answer is required and is binding. This procedure is generally used as a warning to a partner to meld as many cards as possible, so that the requesting player can go out in his next turn.

Scoring Each partnership receives the total of all bonus points earned in the hand (see table C), plus the total point value of all melded cards, less the value of any cards remaining in the hands of either player in the partnership at the end of play.

(Note that the low bonuses for going out make the completion of high-scoring melds more significant than being first to go out).

If one partnership has failed to meld at all, the value of any red 3s it has laid down count against it.

It is possible for a partnership to make a minus score on a hand.

Hands continue until one side has made a total of 5000 points and wins the game.

For each successive hand the deal passes clockwise.

Variant rules The following variations on the standard rules are widely accepted.

1 Even if the discard pile is not frozen, a player may not

## Table A

| Card | Points for each card in meld |
|---|---|
| Joker | 50 |
| Deuce (2) | 20 |
| Ace | 20 |
| 8,9,10,j,q,k | 10 |
| 4,5,6,7 | 5 |
| Black 3 | 5 |
| Red 3 | see text (p 53) |

## Table B

| Accumulated score of partnership | Value required for initial meld |
|---|---|
| Any minus score | 15 |
| 0-1495 | 50 |
| 1500-2995 | 90 |
| 3000 or more | 120 |

## Table C

| | Bonus points |
|---|---|
| Natural canasta | 500 |
| Mixed canasta | 300 |
| Going out | 100 |
| Concealed going out | 100 extra |
| Red 3s | See text (p 53) |

take the upcard to add it to a completed canasta of his own side.

2 When taking the upcard from the discard pile to make a new meld, a player must always have a natural pair to match it (i.e., not a matching card and a wild card).

## 2–4 **CASINO**

Casino can be traced back to the fifteenth-century gambling games of France. In the United States, its era of greatest popularity was eclipsed by the gin rummy boom of the 1930s.

Although appearing comparatively simple, casino is in fact a game of considerable mathematical skill.

### CASINO: BASIC GAME

Players The game can be played by two, three, or four players. A deck of standard playing cards is used.

Face cards have no numerical value; aces count 1; and other cards count their face value.

Objective Each player tries to "capture" certain cards during play and to score the most points.

Deal Players cut for the deal and the lowest card deals. If there are two players, two cards are dealt face down to the nondealer, then two cards face up to the center of the table, then two cards to the dealer. This procedure is repeated so that each player has four cards and there are four face-up cards in the center of the table.

If there are three or four players, the dealer deals two cards to each player including himself, two face-up cards to the center of the table, two more cards to each of the players, and then two more cards to the center.

Each time the players have played the cards in their hands, they are dealt a further four cards in packets of two – no more cards are dealt to the center.

Players take turns to deal the whole deck.

Play Beginning with the player to the left of the dealer, players take turns to play one card. Each player may "capture," "build," or "trail" with each card.

Capturing Cards are captured in the following ways. (See diagram overleaf.)

**a** Pairs: if a face up card has the same numerical value as a player's card, the player may capture the face up card. He does this by placing his card face down on the face up card, and then moving the pair toward him. For example, a 7 of spades may capture a 7 of diamonds.

If two or more face up cards match a single card in the

## Capturing

**a**

**b**

**c**

player's hand, he may capture them all at the same time.

**b** Groups: if the combined value of two or more face up cards is equal to the numerical value of a player's card, the player may capture all the face up cards involved. He puts the face up cards in a pile in front of him and places his own card face down on top of them. For example, a 9 could capture a 2, 3 and 4 from the center.

If one of the player's cards has the same numerical value as both a single face up card and a group of face-up cards, he may capture all the cards involved at the same time. For example, a 9 of spades could capture both a 9 of diamonds and a group of cards (e.g., 2,3 and 4) totalling 9.

**c** Court cards: if a player holds a face card he may either capture one matching face up face card, or alternatively three matching face up face cards if he holds the fourth.

This means that if, for example, he holds a queen and there are two face-up queens, he can only capture one of them in a turn (but had there been three face-up queens, he could have captured all of them in turn).

Building may be in either one of two ways: single or multiple.

Single build A player may build a card face up onto a central face up card provided;

**a** the combined numerical value of the cards does not exceed ten; and

**b** he holds another card that is of equal value to the build he is making, so that in his next turn he would be able to take that build.

For example, if a player holds a 4 and a 7, he may build the 4 onto a face up 3 (i.e., 4 + 3 = 7) and say "Building 7."

A build may be increased by either player with a card from his hand, provided that the total of all the cards in the build still does not exceed ten, and that he holds a card equal in value to the build he is making.

For example, if the opponent holds an ace and an 8, he may build the ace onto an existing build of 7, saying "Building 8."

Multiple build A single build can be changed to a multiple build by duplicating the single-build value with other cards.

For example, a player may add an ace from his hand to a build of 7 in order to make a build of 8 (i.e., 3 + 4 + 1 = 8), and add to that build another build of 8 (i.e., 2 + 6) and say "Building 8s."

Once a multiple build has been established, its stated value cannot be altered.

A multiple build is captured by a card equal in value to its stated value (8 in the example above).

Next turn If a player makes or adds to a build, unless his opponent plays to the build immediately, he must in his next turn either;

**Single build**

**Multiple build**

**a** capture it himself (placing the captured build face down in front of him):

**b** make a new build; or

**c** add to a build.

Trailing If in his turn a player cannot build or capture, he simply places one card from his hand face up on the table.

End of a round When all the cards have been dealt out, the last player to capture cards takes all the remaining face up cards for scoring.

Scoring Points are scored for capturing cards as follows: one point for the 2 of spades ("little casino"); two points for the 10 of diamonds ("big casino"); one point for each ace; one point for seven or more spades; three points for 27 or more cards.

In addition, one point is scored for capturing all the center face-up cards in any single turn during the course of play; this is known as "making a sweep."

Game Players may either: count each deal as a separate game (the player with the most points being the winner), or end the game as soon as one player (the winner) has made a set number of points (usually 21).

## ROYAL CASINO

This differs from casino in that the court cards are given numerical values and can be included in builds and captured in tricks like other cards.

A jack counts 11, a queen 12, and a king 13. Aces may count either 1 or 14 as the player chooses.

## DRAW CASINO

In draw casino only the first 12 cards are dealt. Thereafter, each player draws a card from the stock every time he plays a card.

Otherwise, play is the same as casino.

## SPADE CASINO

Spade casino is played like the basic game, but has additional scoring as follows: jack of spades, two points; 2 of spades, two points; other spades, one point each.

Game is 61 points.

## 2–4 CRIBBAGE

Cribbage is reputed to have been invented by Sir John Suckling, an English poet and courtier who lived in the early 1600s. Six-card cribbage for two players is the most popular form of the game today, but there are also five- and seven-card forms as well as adaptations for three and four players.

Cards All forms of cribbage are played with one single standard deck of 52 cards.

Card values Face cards count 10 each, and all other cards count their face value.

Cribbage board The score can be kept with pencil and paper, but it is easier to use a special cribbage board.

Most cribbage boards are made of wood and measure about 10 inch by 3 inch.

There are four rows of 30 holes, two rows for each player, and additional game holes at one or both ends of the board.

Each player has two pegs, usually red or black for one player and white for the other.

When there are four game holes, the players usually put their pegs in them for the start of play.

**Cribbage board**

A player marks his score by moving his pegs first along his outer row and then back along his inner row of holes.

Moving pegs Both pegs are used to score in the following way:

**a** a player marks his first score by moving one peg that number of holes from the start;

**b** his second score is marked by placing his second peg that number of holes beyond his first peg;

**c** his third score is marked by placing his first peg that number of holes beyond his second peg;

**d** scoring continues in this way until a player's forward peg has passed all the scoring holes to end in one of the game holes.

**Moving pegs**

## SIX-CARD CRIBBAGE

Players The basic game is for two players.

Objective The game is won by the first player to score 121 points, i.e., to go "twice around the board."

The deal Players cut for deal. The player with the lowest cut (with ace low) deals first, and then the deal alternates between players.

The deal is six cards, one at a time, to each player. The remaining cards are placed face down to one side.

**Scoring**

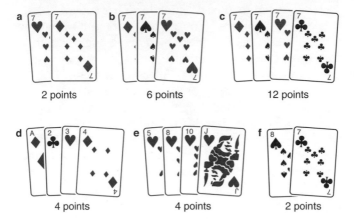

| | | |
|:---:|:---:|:---:|
| a | b | c |
| 2 points | 6 points | 12 points |
| d | e | f |
| 4 points | 4 points | 2 points |

The crib is an extra hand scored by the dealer. It is formed by each of the players discarding two cards and placing them, face down, to the dealer's right. Each player is thus left with a hand of four cards.

The cut After the discards the nondealer cuts the deck, and the dealer turns up the top card of the remaining stack.

This card is placed face up on the stack for the rest of the game.

It is known as the "start" or "starter."

If the start is a jack, the dealer scores "two for his heels."

Scoring Points are scored both during the playing of a hand and when the hands are shown after play.

Combinations of cards score as follows:

a A pair, two cards of the same rank, scores two points.

b A pair royal, three cards of the same rank, scores six points (two points for each of the possible pairs to be made).

c A double pair royal, four cards of the same rank, scores 12 points.

d A sequence or run is a series of cards in face order (ace low) and scores one point for each card. The cards do not have to be of the same suit.

e A flush is four or five cards of the same suit and scores one point for each card. If a flush is also a run, points are scored for both features.

f Fifteen is any combination of cards with a face value totalling that number. It scores two points.

Play begins with the nondealer. He places a card face upward in front of him and calls out its face value as he does so. Face cards are called as 10.

The dealer then places one of his cards face upward in front of himself and calls out its value.

Whenever a pair, pair royal, double pair royal, sequence or fifteen (but not a flush) is formed during play, the player putting down the card that forms it scores the appropriate points.

If the nondealer lays down a 5 and the dealer follows it with another 5, the dealer would say "ten for a pair" and score two points. If a third 5 is played, the nondealer

**Sample show**

Cards in hand

The "start"

**Scoring of sample show**

Total score: 24 points

8 points
for fifteens

4 points
for pairs

12 points for
sequences

would say "fifteen for eight," the eight points being made up of fifteen and a pair royal.

A sequence of cards scores regardless of the order in which it is played. Thus if cards are played in the order ace, 2,5,4,3, the player putting out the 3 can count on a run of five cards. Should the second player be able to add a 6 he can score a run of six cards, and so on.

When the count during play reaches 31, the cards are turned face down and the player whose card brought the total to 31 scores two points.

If a player at his turn is unable to play a card that is within the limit of 31, he says "Go." His opponent then plays any of his cards that are low enough to be within the limit. If they make 31 he scores two points; if less than 31 he scores one point and also says "Go."

Play then resumes with the remaining cards in hand, and proceeds until all the cards are played or 31 is again reached.

Playing the last card of a hand scores "one for the last."

**The show** After all the cards have been played, each player picks up his own cards from in front of him.

The nondealer shows and scores his hand first, which gives him an advantage if he is very near reaching 121. The start is taken into the reckoning as part of each hand.

A card may be ranked for scoring in any number of different combinations. Thus two 10s and two 5s would give a score of eight points for fifteens plus four points for pairs – giving a total of 12 points. The combination 4,4,5,6,6 scores eight points for fifteens, four points for pairs, and 12 points for sequences – giving a total of 24 points (see illustration).

If a player holds a jack of the same suit as the start, he scores "one for his nob."

A flush of four cards in a hand scores four points. If the start is of the same suit the player scores five points, but a flush of four cards including the start scores nothing.

After the nondealer has declared his score, the dealer

shows and scores his own hand. After that he shows and also scores for the crib.

The crib is scored in the same way as the hands, except that the only flush allowed is a five-card one.

Muggins If a player overlooks a score, whether in his hand or in play, his opponent may call "Muggins" and claim the score for himself. (This rule may be dropped).

Lurch If a player reaches 121 before his opponent is half-way around the board he scores a lurch and counts two games instead of one.

Errors If an error in dealing is noticed during the deal, there should be a redeal.

If an error in dealing is found after play has started, the non-dealer scores two points and the error is rectified either by a redeal or by drawing additional cards from the stack.

If after "Go" is called a player fails to play his additional cards, he may not subsequently play those cards and his opponent scores two points. Errors in counting during play are not penalized.

## FIVE-CARD CRIBBAGE

This is an earlier form of the game than six-card cribbage. Except as specified, the rules are as for the six-card game.

Objective Game is 61 points.

The deal is five cards to each player.

The crib consists of two cards from each player.

Play Nondealer pegs three points before play begins, to compensate for not having the crib.

Hands are not played out after 31 is reached or "Go" is called.

Hands are shown and scored; then there is a new deal.

## SEVEN-CARD CRIBBAGE

This version is played in the same way as six-card cribbage, except that:

a game is 181 points;

b the deal is seven cards each (of which two go to the crib).

## THREE-HANDED CRIBBAGE

The game is adapted as follows for three-handed play.

Game is 61 points.

The deal is five cards to each player and one to the crib. Each player then gives one card to the crib.

Play begins with the player to the left of the dealer, and passes to the left. The player who leads also has the first show.

## FOUR-HANDED CRIBBAGE

This is a partnership form of the game. Partners sit opposite each other, and play begins with the player to the dealer's left.

Game is 121 points.

The deal is usually five cards to each player (of which one goes to the crib).

# 2 ECARTÉ

Ecarté is a card game for two players that first became popular in France in the early 1800s. Its name is the French word for "discarded."

**Rank**

Deck A 32-card deck is used: a standard 52-card deck with 6s,5s,4s,3s, and 2s removed.

Cards rank: k (high),q,j,a,10,9,8,7.

Objective Each player tries to take tricks and to score points.

Deal Players cut for deal, highest card dealing first (the cards rank as in play). The dealer gives each player five face-down cards, in packets of either two then three, or three then two.

Whichever system is used must be kept throughout the game. The deal passes clockwise around the table.

Trumps The eleventh card is placed face up beside the stock and indicates trumps.

Exchanging cards The nondealer may propose an exchange of cards. To do this he says "Cards."

If the dealer accepts, the nondealer exchanges as many cards as he wishes for cards drawn from the stock. The dealer may then do likewise.

The nondealer may repeat the proposal, and players go on exchanging cards until the stock is exhausted.

**Deal**

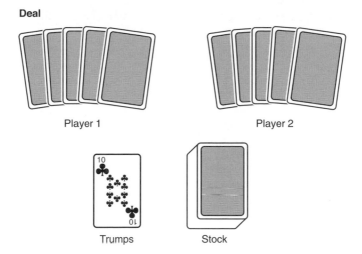

Player 1          Player 2

Trumps          Stock

But if the dealer refuses at any time by saying "Play," there is no more exchanging.

If the nondealer does not wish to exchange at any time, he says "I play."

The dealer cannot propose an exchange.

Play The nondealer leads first. Players must follow suit if they can and may trump if they cannot.

A player must always take a trick if he can. The winner of a trick leads to the next trick.

Scoring is as follows:

a "point" or "the trick" (three tricks won), scores one point;

b "the vole" (all five tricks won), scores two points;

c king turned up to indicate trumps, scores one point for the dealer; and

   **d** king of trumps held in the hand, scores one point if it is
     declared before the holder plays his first card.

   Game is five points.

**Penalties** If a player has refused to exchange and fails to make
   at least three tricks (point), his opponent scores an extra
   point if he makes a point.

   There is no penalty if the opponent scores vole.

## 2-6 EUCHRE

Euchre is a derivative of ecarté and dates back at least to the 1800s. For a time it was the national game of the United States. It is a game for two to six players depending on the version played; perhaps most popular is four-handed euchre.

**Rank in plain suits**

**Rank in trumps**

### FOUR-HANDED EUCHRE

Four people play in partnerships of two. Each player sits opposite his partner.

Deck A 32-card deck is used: a standard deck with the 6s,5s,4s,3s, and 2s removed. Ace ranks high, and 7 low.

Trumps The jack of trumps, called the "right bower," ranks as the highest trump. The other jack of the same color, called the "left bower," ranks second. For example, if diamonds are trumps, the jack of hearts is the left bower.

Thus the trump suit ranks: rb (high), lb,a,k,q,10,9,8,7 (low).

Objective Each partnership tries to win the most tricks.

Deal Players draw for first deal, lowest card dealing.

Each player is dealt five face-down cards, in packets of three and two. The dealer then turns the next card face up to indicate trumps. The deal passes clockwise around the table.

Nominating trumps Each player, beginning with the player to the dealer's left, has the option of accepting the suit of the face-up card as trumps, or refusing it in the hope of nominating a different suit.

To accept, the dealer's opponents say "I order it up": the dealer's partner says "I assist"; and the dealer says nothing but indicates his acceptance by discarding one card and adding the face up card to his hand.

To refuse, the nondealer says "I pass," and the dealer puts the face-up card under the stock.

Once one player has accepted, play begins.

If all four players refuse, there is a second round in which each player in turn has the right to nominate the trump suit or pass. Once a player has nominated a suit, play begins.

If all players pass, the hands are thrown in and the cards are dealt by the next dealer.

Play The player who nominated trumps is called the "maker." Before play begins, he may decide to play the hand without his partner, in which case he says "I play alone."

His partner then lays his hand face down on the table. Although he does not play the hand, he shares in any stakes. Rules of play are the same as in whist.

Scoring If the maker and his partner win all five tricks, this constitutes a "march," and scores two points. If the maker is playing alone, he scores four points for a march.

If the maker and his partner win four or three tricks, they score one point; if they win fewer than three tricks they are said to be "euchred," and their opponents score two points.

Players may use counters to keep the score, but it is customary to use a 3 or a 4 from the unused cards as markers, one card being face up, the other face down, as illustrated below:

a the 3 exposed with the other card across it signifies one point;

b the 4 exposed with the other card across it is two points;

c the 3 on top of the other card is three points;

d the 4 on top is four points.

Game is generally five points, but some players prefer to set a target of seven or ten.

**Keeping the score**

| a | b | c | d |
|---|---|---|---|
| 1 point | 2 points | 3 points | 4 points |

## RAILROAD EUCHRE

In this variation of four-handed euchre, the joker is used as an additional trump, ranking above the right bower.

## TWO-HANDED EUCHRE

The deck is reduced to 24 cards by discarding the 8s and 7s.

Rules are the same as for four-handed euchre, except that there is no need for a declaration to play alone.

## THREE-HANDED EUCHRE

In three-handed euchre (also called cutthroat euchre) the maker plays on his own, with the other two players in partnership against him. The maker scores three points for march; otherwise scoring is as in the four-handed game.

## CALL ACE EUCHRE

This is a version for four, five, or six players, each playing for himself. The rules are as in four-handed euchre, with the following differences.

Calling The maker has the right to decide whether to play on his own or with a partner. To choose a partner he says "I call on the ace of..." and nominates a suit. If a player holds the ace named, he plays as the maker's partner, but does not declare his partnership until he plays the ace. As the ace may in fact not have been dealt, the maker may find he is playing alone!

Scoring A lone maker wins points as follows:

**a** march, as many points as there are players;

**b** four or three tricks, one point.

A partnership wins points as follows:

**a** march, two points for each player if there are three or four players, and three points for each player if there are five or six;

**b** four or three tricks, each partner scores one point.

If the maker, with or without partner, is euchred, the other players score two points each.

# 3 FIVE HUNDRED

Five hundred is related to euchre and also has certain similarities to bridge and whist. The basic game is for three players.

**Rank in plain suits**

**Rank in trumps**

## THREE-HANDED FIVE HUNDRED

Deck 33 cards are used: a standard deck excluding the 6s,5s,4s,3s and 2s; plus a joker. Ace ranks high, and 7 low.

In the trump suit cards rank, in descending order, as follows: joker, right bower (jack of the trump suit), left bower (other jack of the same color), a,k,q,10,9,8,7.

In no-trump hands, there are no right and left bowers. The holder of the joker may then nominate it to represent any suit he pleases; the joker automatically ranks as the highest card of that suit and takes any trick to which it is led or played.

Objective Each player aims to make a contract by bidding and to win enough tricks to fulfill it.

Deal Players cut for the deal (king ranks high, ace low, and joker lowest): lowest card deals.

Ten face-down cards are dealt to each player, in packets of either three, two, three, two; or three, three, three, one.

The remaining packet of three cards constitutes the "widow" and is placed face upward on the table.

The deal passes clockwise around the table.

Bidding Each player in turn makes a bid, starting with the player to the dealer's left. Each player specifies the number of tricks he intends to take and his choice of trumps.

The lowest number of tricks that can be bid is six, and the highest ten. For bidding the calls are ranked: no-trumps (highest), hearts, diamonds, clubs, spades (lowest).

Any player who passes cannot make a further bid in that round of play.

Widow The player who wins the contract adds the three widow cards to his hand and discards face down any three cards of his choice.

Play Rules of play are the same as in whist.

If a player leads the joker in a no-trump hand, he cannot nominate it to a suit in which he has either declared himself void or that he has failed to follow when able.

The winner of the trick leads to the next trick.

Scoring The players opposing the contract play as partners, but each always scores ten points for each trick he makes.

The bidder scores points according to the table, provided he has made his contract.

If he fails to score sufficient tricks, he loses the value of the contract.

Bonuses There are no bonuses for overtricks (i.e., tricks over the number bid).

## Scoring table for five hundred

| Tricks bid | ♠ | ♣ | ♦ | ♥ | no trumps |
|---|---|---|---|---|---|
| 6 | 40 | 60 | 80 | 100 | 120 |
| 7 | 140 | 160 | 180 | 200 | 220 |
| 8 | 240 | 260 | 280 | 300 | 320 |
| 9 | 340 | 360 | 380 | 400 | 420 |
| 10 | 440 | 460 | 480 | 500 | 520 |

However, a player who has made a contract of less than eight clubs but has scored "grand slam" (all ten tricks), receives a total of 250 points.

(There is an optional system for when grand slam is scored after a bid of eight clubs or better. In this system, the successful player scores a bonus equal to the contract.

For example, a bid of eight diamonds that results in a grand slam is worth 280 points plus a bonus of 280.)

Players losing contracts may well find their scores going into minus figures.

Game is 500 points. If two players reach this total in the same deal, the player who reached 500 first wins.

## TWO-HANDED FIVE HUNDRED

This is played in the same way as the three handed game, except that a third hand, known as a "dead-hand," is dealt. It remains face down throughout the game, and adds a degree of uncertainty to the bidding and play.

## FOUR-HANDED FIVE HUNDRED

This game is also played like the three-handed game, but facing players act as partners. The deck is increased to 43 cards by adding the 6s, 5s and two 4s – one of each color.

## 2-4-6 FORTY FIVE

This game is related to loo and spoil five. Cards have the same unusual ranking as in spoil five, but in forty-five there is a different scoring system and no pool. It is a game for two, four, or six players, divided into two equal and opposing sides.

**Rank in plain suits**

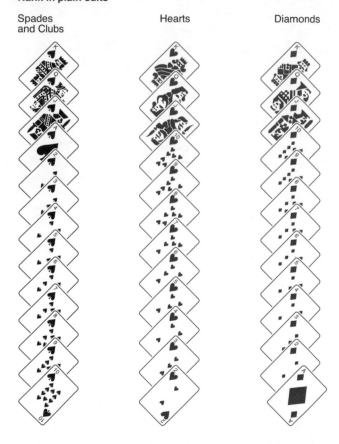

Spades
and Clubs

Hearts

Diamonds

Cards A standard deck of playing cards is used. The cards are ranked, in descending order, as follows. (See diagrams previous page and below.)

**Rank in trumps**

Spades
and Clubs                    Hearts                    Diamonds

### Spades and clubs

Plain suits (i.e., non-trump): k,q,j,a,2,3,4,5,6,7,8,9,10.

Trump suits: 5,j,a of hearts, a of spades or clubs, k,q,2, 3,4,6,7,8,9,10.

### Hearts

Plain suit: k,q,j,10,9,8,7,6,5,4,3,2.

Trump suit: 5,j,a,k,q,10,9,8,7,6,4,3,2.

### Diamonds

Plain suit: k,q,j,10,9,8,7,6,5,4,3,2,a.

Trump suit: 5,j,a of hearts, a of diamonds, k,q,10,9,8, 7,6,4,3,2.

**Objective** Players try to win tricks and to prevent their opponents from doing so.

**Deal** Players draw for deal, using standard ranking with ace high and 2 low. The player drawing the lowest card deals. Five face-down cards are dealt to each player in packets of two then three, or vice versa. The next card is turned face up to indicate trumps. The deal passes clockwise around the table.

**Exchanging** If the face-up card denoting the trump is an ace, the dealer may, before the first card is led, exchange this face-up card for any card in his hand.

Any player who has been dealt the ace of trumps has the option of exchanging any card in his hand for the face up card. If he does not exchange a card, he must announce that he has the ace at his first turn of play. Failure to announce that he has the ace of trumps means that this card becomes the lowest trump for the round.

**Play** Rules of play are as in whist, except as follows.

If a card of a plain suit is led, a player may choose either to trump or to follow suit; he may discard another plain suit card only if he can neither follow suit nor trump.

If a card of the trump suit is led, a player must usually

follow suit; he is not, however, obliged to play any of the top three trumps if the leading card was a lower trump.

Scoring Points are scored by the winning player or partnership. According to one scoring system, 5 points are scored for making three or four tricks and 10 points for making five tricks. An alternative scoring system gives 5 points for three tricks, 15 points for four tricks, and 25 points for five tricks.

Whichever scoring system is used, the game is won by the first side to score 45 points – a fact that gives the game its name.

## AUCTION FORTY-FIVE

Auction forty-five is very popular in parts of Canada. Its basic rules are the same as for spoil five, with the following variations.

Players Four or six people play in partnerships of two or three respectively. Each player sits between two players of the opposing side.

Bidding The player to the left of the dealer bids first, followed by each player in turn to his left.

The bids, indicating the number of points each side is contracted to make, are 5,10,15,20,25, and 30. Each bid must outbid the previous bid.

The dealer has the option of "holding," i.e., outbidding, the previous bid without increasing it. Each of the other players who bid may then bid again; but the dealer has the option of holding a second time.

Trumps are nominated by the highest bidder.

Discards Each player may exchange as many cards as he likes for cards drawn from the top of the stock.

Play The player to the left of the highest bidder leads first.

Scoring Each trick counts five points, and the highest trump in play scores five extra points for whichever side takes it.

If a side fulfills its contract it scores the number of points bid plus the points scored with its tricks.

If it fails, it loses the number of points bid.

The side that did not make the contract scores all the points it makes in play.

Game is 120 points.

## 4 GRAND

Grand is a combination of whist, euchre, and hearts. Each hand is played like one of these three games or according to rules for a fourth – "grand" – option, depending on the choice of the bidder.

Players Four people play, in partnerships of two.

Deck A standard deck of playing cards is used. The rank of the cards depends on the type of game being played.

Objective Each partnership aims to make and fulfill a contract.

Deal Players cut for the deal (ace ranks low), and highest card deals. Cards are dealt in a clockwise direction, one at a time and face down, until each player has 13 cards.

Bidding Each player in turn, starting with the player to the left of the dealer, has one chance to either bid or pass.

The bids are five and multiples of five, and indicate the number of points the bidder expects to score in that hand if he is the highest bidder.

At the end of bidding the highest bidder names which game (whist, grand, euchre, or hearts) will be played for that round. If the first three players pass, the dealer must make a bid.

General play Unlike whist, euchre, and hearts, the bidder always leads to the first trick.

### WHIST

If whist is chosen, the bidder names the trump suit. Play is the same as in whist.

Scoring Each trick more than six counts five points. For example, on a bid of 25 the bidding partnership needs to take 11 tricks to score.

If the bidding partnership makes a grand slam (winning all 13 tricks), it scores for all 13 tricks, making 65 points.

No points are scored for honors.

Setbacks If the bidding partnership fails to make its bid, the entire amount of its bid is deducted from its previous score. In addition, the opposing partnership wins five points for each trick that it takes above six tricks.

## GRAND

If grand is chosen, play is the same as in whist, except that there are no trumps.

Scoring Each trick more than six scores nine points.

A grand slam also scores 40 points for the first six tricks, making a total of 103 points. If either partnership makes a grand slam, it wins the game – regardless of its score.

Setbacks are scored in the same way as in the whist option, except that each trick counts nine points.

The opponents also win nine points for each trick they take over six tricks.

## EUCHRE

Euchre can only be chosen on a bid of 25 or less. The bidder names the trump suit. Each player then discards eight cards face down – he may not keep any trumps lower than 8.

Play is the same as in euchre with the following differences.

If the bidder calls less than 20 he cannot play alone. If he bids 20, he may choose whether or not to play alone. If he bids 25, he must play alone.

If playing alone, the bidder may exchange any one of his cards for the best card in his partner's hand. The bidder's partner puts his cards face down on the table.

Scoring Points are scored by either partnership as follows: three tricks, 5 points; four tricks, 10 points; five tricks if made in partnership, 20 points; five tricks if made by lone hand, 25 points.

Setbacks If the bidding partnership fails to make its bid, the
amount bid plus 20 points is subtracted from its score. If a
lone hand fails to make his bid, he loses twice the amount
bid.

## HEARTS

Hearts is only allowed on a bid of 50 or less. Play is as in
hearts.

Scoring If the bidding partnership does not take any tricks
containing hearts, it wins 50 points.

Setbacks If the partners do take tricks containing hearts, the
amount bid plus one point for each heart taken is subtracted from their score. The opponents are set back one
point for each heart they take.

Heart bid option If the first bidder passes when the dealer's
partnership has a score of less then 70, it is generally
regarded as an indication that he is prepared to play
hearts.

If the dealer's side has 70 or more points, the first bidder
may determine that hearts are played by leading a heart
and saying "Hearts."

Game is 100 points, but the game may finish at the end of a
time limit or after a set number of rounds. The scores at
the end of play are used to calculate the final result.

1 The difference between 100 and the lowest score at the
end of play stands as a separate score for the side with
the highest score at the end of play.

2 The difference between the number of times each side
has been set back is multiplied by ten. This stands as a
separate score for the side with the fewer setbacks.

3 The result of this final scoring indicates the winner.

For example, if at the end of play side A has a score of
80 with seven setbacks and side B has a score of 60 with

five setbacks, then the final result is calculated as follows:

1  100 − 60 = 40 (awarded to side A);
2  (7 − 5) x 10 = 20 (awarded to side B);
3  So side A wins with a total of 40 against side B's total of 20.

## 3-7 HEARTS

Hearts is one of the avoidance games – meaning that it is based on the principle of not taking penalty cards rather than of winning tricks. It evolved in the nineteenth century, since when many interesting variants have appeared.

**Penalty cards**

## HEARTS: BASIC GAME

Players Three to seven people can play. There are no partnerships.

Cards A standard deck of 52 playing cards is used.

2s are discarded as follows: one 2 with three players; none with four players; two with five players; three with seven players.

If possible, the 2 of hearts is not discarded.

The cards rank normally, with ace high. There are no trumps.

Choice of first dealer is by low cut.

Deal The dealer deals out all the cards one at a time and face down, beginning with the player to his left and going clockwise.

Play The player to the dealer's left leads to the first trick. Thereafter the winner of one trick leads to the next. Each player after the lead must follow suit if he can. If he cannot, he may play any card he likes.

A hand ends when all the hearts suit has appeared in play.

Revoking If a player fails to follow suit when he is able to, he may correct his mistake without penalty if he does so before the trick is picked up.

Otherwise he scores 13 penalty points and the hand ends. No other players can score penalty points on that hand.

Scoring Each player scores one penalty point for each card of the hearts suit contained in tricks taken by him.

Continuing play After each hand, the deal passes one player to the left.

The winner is the player with the fewest penalty points after an agreed number of hands.

Alternatively, the winner is the player with the fewest penalty points when one player reaches a set number of points (e.g., 50 points).

## SPOT HEARTS

Also called chip hearts, this game is played in the same way as basic hearts except that each heart card counts as many penalty points as its face value. The king counts 13, the queen 12, and the jack 11.

(Almost any hearts variant can be scored in this way.)

## BLACK LADY HEARTS

In this popular version the queen of spades is an extra penalty card, scoring 13 penalty points. Each heart card counts one penalty point.

Sometimes it is ruled that a player must take the first possible opportunity to discard the queen of spades.

## GREEK HEARTS

In this variant the penalties are the same as for black lady hearts, but play and scoring differ in the following ways.

Exchanging Before play begins, each player, after looking at his cards, passes three cards of his choice face down to the player to his right. No player may look at the cards he is receiving until after he has passed on his own cards.

13 points

Scoring Each heart is scored as in spot hearts, and the queen of hearts counts 50 penalty points, except that if one player takes all the penalty cards he does not score at all for this hand and instead all the other players score 150 penalty points each.

50 points

## DOMINO HEARTS

The penalty values are as in the basic hearts game, but play varies as follows.

Deal Six cards are dealt to each player, and the remainder are placed face down to form the stock.

Play If a player cannot follow suit he draws cards one at a time from the top of the stock until he can follow suit. Drawn cards of other suits remain in his hand to be played later. When the stock is exhausted players may discard as in the basic hearts game.

Each player drops out when he has played all his cards. The last player left in scores one penalty point for each heart card left in his hand as well as for those in his tricks.

If a player wins a trick with his last card, the lead passes to the next player to the left.

The winner is the player with the lowest score when one player reaches 31 points.

## JOKER HEARTS

In this hearts game, the 2 of hearts is discarded and a joker used.

The joker ranks between the 10 and jack of hearts, and wins any trick in which it is played, regardless of the suit led, unless a higher heart has also appeared in that trick – in which case the higher heart takes the trick.

5 points

A high heart played when the joker is not played is a discard as usual, unless hearts were led.

The joker counts five penalty points.

13 points

## HEARTSETTE

In this variant of hearts a widow hand is dealt face down in the center of the table.

The 2 of spades is not used if there are three or four players.

The size of the widow depends on the number of players: with three or four players, three cards; with five players, two cards; with six players, four cards.

10 points

All other cards are dealt out to the players.

Play and penalties are as in the basic hearts game except that the winner of the first trick adds the widow to it and scores penalty points for any penalty cards it contains.

7 points

## TWO-HANDED HEARTS

This is an adaptation of the basic game for two players.

It is played like basic hearts except that 13 cards are dealt to each player and the remainder are placed face down to form a stock.

After each trick the winner takes the top card from the stock and the loser takes the next card.

The game continues until all the cards have been played.

## BLACK MARIA

This very popular version of hearts is also known as Slippery Anne.

Play is as for basic hearts except as follows.

Penalty cards As well as hearts (one point for each card), there are three penalty cards: The queen of spades (Black Maria), 13 points; the king of spades, 10 points; the ace of spades, seven points.

Exchanging occurs before play as in Greek hearts.

Each hand ends when all penalty cards have been played.

## 2 IMPERIAL

This game resembles piquet, but there is a trump suit and the cards rank differently. It is a game for two players.

Cards A 32-card "piquet" deck is used – a standard deck with the 2s, 3s, 4s, 5s, and 6s removed.

Cards rank k (high), q,j,a,10,9,8,7 (low).

"Honors" are the k,q,j,a, and 7 of trumps.

**Rank**

Chips are used for scoring: 12 white chips and eight red. One red chip is worth six white. At the beginning of the game all chips are placed together in a central pool.

Objective The aim is to be the first to win five red chips.

Shuffle is normal.

Cut is by the nondealer. There need be only two cards in each section. Otherwise the cut is normal.

The deal is in packets of three cards, face down. When both players have 12 cards each, the 25th card is placed face up in the center of the table to denote trumps for the hand. The undealt part of the deck is placed to one side, out of use for the remainder of the hand.

Scoring procedure Scoring occurs before, during, and after each hand of play.

Whenever a player scores, he takes the appropriate chip or chips from the central pool. Whenever a player has

collected six white chips, he exchanges them immediately
for one red chip from the pool.

Whenever a player gains a red chip in any way, his opponent must put back into the pool any white chips that he
holds.

Scoring before play occurs in the following order:

1 the dealer scores one white chip if the turned up (25th)
card is an honor card;

2 either player scores one red chip if he has been dealt
carte blanche, i.e., a hand containing no king, queen or
jack;

3 players declare and score for combinations – point,
sequences, and melds – held in their hands;

4 players declare and score for sequences and melds that
use the turned up card in addition to cards in their
hands.

Declarations Combinations are declared in the order: point,
sequences, melds. A player may include any card in more
than one combination.

To avoid revealing more information than necessary,

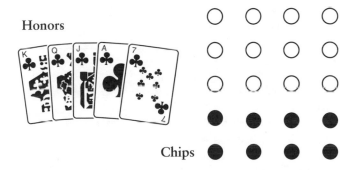

**Honors**

**Chips**

players use the same formal dialogue used in piquet (see Announcing the declarations, page 130). In imperial, all winning combinations must be declared and shown.

Point This term refers to a player's longest suit (i.e., the suit of which he holds most cards).

The player with the longest suit scores the point and takes one white chip for each card that he holds in that suit.

If players have suits of equal length, the point goes to the player whose relevant cards have the highest face value (counting ace 11, court cards 10 each, and other cards at their numerical face value). If players still tie, the nondealer scores.

Sequences These are consecutive cards belonging to the same suit. These may be of three or four cards but may contain only kings, queens, jacks, and aces. A four-card sequence beats a three-card sequence. Three-card sequences rank according to the top card. The player with the best sequence scores one red chip. If the players tie, the non-dealer scores.

Melds These are cards of the same rank. Only fours of kings, queens, jacks, aces and 7s are counted – ranking in that order, with king high. Threes do not count. The player with the best meld scores one red chip.

Combinations using the turned up card

1 Players declare any sequence that includes the turned up card. The higher ranking sequence wins one red chip.

2 A player declares if he has a meld of four using the turned up card. If so, he wins one red chip.

Play The nondealer leads to the first trick; thereafter the winner of each trick leads to the next one.

In every case, the second player to a trick must take it if he can. He must follow suit if possible. If he cannot follow suit he must use a trump if he has one; only if he has no trump may he discard.

Cards are not collected in tricks. Each player puts the cards he has played face up in front of him, and is free to examine them at any time.

### Scoring during play

1 A player taking the jack of trumps by leading the king or queen wins one red chip.
2 A player taking the ace also wins one red chip.
3 A player takes one white chip for each trump honor contained in tricks that he wins.

### Scoring after play

If one player takes more tricks in a hand than his opponent, he wins one white chip for every trick in excess of his opponent's total.

Thus if a player wins all 12 tricks – referred to as "capot" – he wins two red chips.

### The winner

is the first player to win five red chips. Hands continue until one player does this, with the deal alternating between players.

If a player gains five red chips in the middle of a hand, the hand is abandoned at once.

## 2 **KALABRIASZ**

This excellent game is also known as klaberjass, clab, and clobber. It is essentially the same as the French game, belote.

**Rank in plain suits**

**Rank in trumps**

Players The basic game is for two players.

Cards Play is with a standard deck of cards from which the 2s,3s,4s,5s, and 6s have been removed.

The cards rank as follows:

**a** in plain suits, a (high), 10, k,q,j,9,8,7 (low).

**b** in the trump suit, j (high), 9,a,10,k,q,8,7 (low).

Objective Players aim to meld sequences and to take certain scoring cards in tricks.

Choice of dealer for the first hand is by high cut, with ace low.

First deal The dealer gives each player six cards face down in packets of three. He then places the next card face up in the center of the table, and places the rest of the deck – the stock – face down in a pile beside it.

Determining trumps Players make bids to determine the trump suit.

1 The nondealer opens with a bid of "Accept," "Schmeiss," or "Pass."

   If he bids to accept, the suit of the central face up card becomes trumps for the hand.

   A bid of schmeiss is a proposal for a new deal. The dealer then has the opportunity of agreeing to a new deal or of accepting the suit of the central face up card as the trump suit.

   If the nondealer says "Pass," the dealer has a turn at bidding.

2 The dealer may now either: accept the suit of the central face up card as trumps; bid "Schmeiss," in which case the nondealer must agree to the new deal or accept the suit of the face up card as trumps; or pass, in which case there is a second round of bidding.

3 If both players pass in the first round of bidding, the nondealer may then either: nominate any trump suit that he wishes, in which case play will be with this suit as trumps; or pass, in which case the dealer may nominate trumps, or pass.

   If both players pass in the second round of bidding, the cards are thrown in and a new first deal made.

   The player who actually determines the trump suit is called "maker."

Second deal Once the trump suit has been established, each player is dealt three more cards, one at a time, and face down.

   The dealer then takes the bottom card of the stock and places if face up on top of the stock.

   If the suit of the central face up card was accepted as trumps, a player holding the 7 of that suit may exchange it for the central face up card if he wishes. The 7 of trumps is called the "dix."

Declaring sequences usually takes place before play begins, but may be after the nondealer has led to the first trick. By their declarations players establish who holds the highest sequence.

**Sequences**

20 points

50 points

Sequences All cards in a sequence must be consecutive and of the same suit. There are two kinds of sequence:

**a** a sequence of three cards, worth 20 points; and

**b** a sequence of four or more cards, worth 50 points.

For sequences cards rank in the order a (high), k,q,j,10,9,8,7 (low).

Sequences of equal value are ranked according to their highest card. Note that a sequence of four cards beats a longer sequence provided that the four-card sequence is headed by the highest card.

If sequences are of equal value and are headed by cards of the same rank, a sequence in the trump suit is higher.

If equal sequences headed by cards of the same rank are both in plain suits, some versions of the game rule that the nondealer's sequence is higher while others rule that the sequences are equal and neither player may score.

Declaration procedure The nondealer begins by announcing "Sequence of 50" if he has a sequence of four or more cards, or "Sequence of 20" if he has a three-card sequence.

The dealer then replies "Good" if he cannot beat it,

"Not good" if he can beat it, or "How high?" if he has a sequence with the same points value.

If the dealer replies "How high?" the nondealer states the rank of the card that heads his sequence, and then the dealer replies "Good" if he cannot beat it, or "Not good" if he can.

Scoring of sequences Only the player with the highest sequence scores any points at this stage of the game. He scores for his highest sequence after first showing it to his opponent. He also scores for any other sequences that he is prepared to show.

Play Nondealer leads to the first trick.

Players must follow suit if they are able, and if they cannot follow suit must play a trump if they have one. If a trump is led the opposing player must take the trick if he can.

The winner of a trick places it face down in front of him and leads to the next trick.

Bella is a meld comprising the king and queen of trumps. It is worth 20 points to any player who holds it, and is scored automatically when the second of these cards is played.

Scoring during play Players score points as follows for cards taken in tricks: (See diagram overleaf)

a "jasz" (jack of trumps), 20 points;
b "menel" (9 of trumps), 14 points;
c each ace, 11 points;
d each 10, 10 points;
e each king, four points;
f each queen, three points;
g each jack but jasz, two points.

The player who takes the last trick scores a further 10 points.

The final score for each hand is calculated as follows.

a If the player who determined the trump suit (the maker)

## Scoring during play

Trumps

| | |
|---|---|
| **a** 20 points | **b** 14 points |
| **c** 11 points | **d** 10 points |
| **e** 4 points | **f** 3 points |
| **g** 2 points | |

has a points total higher than his opponent, each player scores his own total.

**b** If the opposing player has a higher total, he scores both his own points total and that of the maker. This is called "going bate."

**c** If the players have an equal number of points, the maker scores no points and his opponent scores his own points total. The maker's opponent is said to have gone "half bate."

Game is usually 500 points. If both players reach the agreed game total in the same hand, the one with the most points wins.

## THREE-HANDED KALABRIASZ

In the three-handed game turns pass clockwise around the table. The maker must score more than both his opponents together, or go bate. Players score their own sequences and points won in play, but opponents share the maker's points if he goes bate.

## PARTNERSHIP KALABRIASZ

This differs from the basic game as follows.

All but the last card are dealt out so that the dealer has seven cards and the other players eight each.

The last card becomes the central face up card. Before play, the player with the dix exchanges it for a face up card and the dealer takes the dix to complete his hand.

After one player has established the highest sequence, his partner may also score for any sequences.

Partners keep their tricks together and score as a side.

## *3* KNAVES

This game combines the principles of trick-taking and of avoidance games. Players score points for taking tricks, but must then subtract points for any tricks containing jacks.

Players Knaves is a game for three players.
Cards A standard deck of 52 cards is used.
Object Each player tries to win tricks without taking any jacks.
Deal and play are as for whist (page 170).
Tactics Each player plays for himself, but if one player is winning, the other two often act as a temporary partnership to try to reduce his lead.
Scoring At the end of each hand, each player scores one point for each trick he has taken.

If he has taken any jacks, he then subtracts points as follows:
a  jack of hearts, four points;
b  jack of diamonds, three;
c  jack of clubs, two;
d  jack of spades, one.

A player may have a minus score.
The winner is the first to reach 20 plus points.

### POLIGNAC

This game is a French version of knaves. Players must avoid taking tricks containing jacks, especially jack of spades, which is given the name Polignac.
Players Four to six can play.
Cards For four players a standard deck without the 2s,3s,4s,5s, and 6s is used.

For five or six players the two black 7s are also removed.
Deal and play are as in whist (page 170), except without trumps.

**Scoring** At the end of each hand, each player scores 7 penalty points for each jack he has taken, as follows: one point each for the jack of hearts, diamonds, and clubs; two points for the jack of spades (Polignac).

**"General"** A player may decide to try and take all the tricks in a hand. This is known as general, and the player must announce his intention before the lead to the first trick.

   If he succeeds, all the other players score five penalty points.

   If he fails, he scores five penalty points and the jacks score penalty points in the usual way against the players who take them.

**The winner** is the player with the fewest points after an agreed number of hands.

**Penalty cards**

4 points

3 points

2 points

1 point

## 3–6 **LOO**

Loo, or lanternloo as it is sometimes called, was once one of the most widely played games in Europe. It has several variations but is always played for stakes.

### THREE-CARD LOO

Players Three or more people can play, but about six is best.

Deck A standard 52-card deck is used. Ace ranks high.

Objective Each player tries to win at least one trick.

**Rank**

Deal Players cut for deal, lowest card dealing.

Each player is dealt three face down cards, one at a time. An extra hand known as a "miss" is also dealt, as either the first or last hand of each deal. The top card of the remaining cards is turned face up and denotes trumps.

The deal passes clockwise around the table.

Pool In an optional opening deal called a "single," no miss is dealt, and only the dealer puts three counters into a pool. In subsequent deals, or if no single has been played, a miss is dealt and each player contributes three counters to the pool.

The choice Beginning with the player to the dealer's left, each player in turn chooses one of the following:

a to play with the cards he holds;

b to throw in his own cards and play with the miss; or

c to pass.

To indicate their choice, players say "I play," "I take the miss," or "I pass," as appropriate.

If a player passes, he throws in his cards and takes no further part in that deal. If everyone passes, the dealer takes the pool.

If only one player decides to play but has not taken the miss, the dealer must play him, using the cards in the miss. If the dealer loses, he does not pay, nor is he paid if he wins.

If only one player decides to play and has taken the miss, the dealer may either play him with standard scoring, or just let him take the pool.

Play The first player to choose to play leads to the first trick, with his highest trump if he has one.

Each player who did not pass plays a card to each trick. He must follow suit if he can, and if possible must play a higher card than any already played to that trick.

If a player cannot follow suit, he should trump the trick with a higher trump than any already played to that trick; if he cannot do this, he may discard.

The winner of a trick must lead with a trump if possible.

Scoring The winner of each trick takes one third of the pool.

Looing A player who has not won a trick is said to be "looed."

In limited loo, a looed player pays an agreed amount (usually three counters) into the pool.

In unlimited loo, he pays as many counters as there were in the pool at the beginning of the hand.

Penalties A player is also looed for:

a playing out of turn;

b looking at the miss without taking it;

c failing to take a trick when possible; and

d failing to lead the ace of trumps when holding it.

Variations

a The trump card is not turned up until a player cannot follow suit.

b If a player is dealt three trumps, he collects the pool. The hands are thrown in, and the cards are shuffled and dealt for the next round.

## FIVE-CARD LOO

This variant is played in the same way as three-card loo, except for the following changes.

Deal Each player receives five cards.

Pool Contributions to the pool are five not three counters.

Miss is never dealt.

Exchanges Each player may exchange up to five cards for the same number of cards drawn from the stock. A player who exchanges must then play his hand.

Pam The jack of clubs, called "pam," ranks as the highest trump regardless of suit. If a player leads the ace of trumps and says "Pam be civil," the pam cannot be played to that trick.

Flushes are five cards of the same suit, or four of the same suit plus pam. The holder of a flush exposes it before play and wins the pool. Each of the other players is then looed unless he also holds a flush or flush with pam.

If there is more than one flush, a trump flush wins over one in a plain suit, and if there is a clash between plain suit flushes, the highest card wins. If two or more plain suit flushes are equal, the pool is divided.

Blaze This is an optional winning hand, entirely made up of face cards. The same rules of precedence apply as with flushes, and a blaze outranks a flush.

## IRISH LOO

This is played like three-card loo, with the following changes.

a Miss is not dealt.

b Exchanging is carried out in the same way as in the five-card game.

c "Club law:" if clubs are trumps every player must enter the game.

## 3-8 MICHIGAN

Michigan is a popular and fast-moving game usually played for low stakes. It is easy to learn but can also be a challenging game for the experienced player. Other games by which Michigan is known are boodle, Newmarket, Chicago, and Saratoga.

**Boodle cards**

Players Any number from three to eight can play.

Cards In addition to one standard deck of playing cards, an ace, king, queen and jack – each in a different suit – from a second deck of cards are used. The four cards are called "boodle" cards and are placed face up in the center of the table.

Cards rank normally, with ace high.

Chips Each player is given a supply of betting chips or counters.

Objective Each player tries to play certain cards, thereby collecting chips, and to be the first to get rid of all his cards.

Ante Before each hand is dealt, every player must ante by putting one chip on each of the four boodle cards.

Deal Players cut for the deal, highest card dealing.

The dealer gives one face down card at a time to each player and an extra hand (widow) to the dealer's left.

Each player must have the same number of cards. Any card or cards left over at the end of the deal are placed face down on the table.

Auction Before the start of play the dealer has the right to exchange his hand for the widow. If he does so, he discards his hand face down.

If the dealer chooses not to take the widow, the other players may bid for it. The highest bidder pays the dealer in chips, discards his hand face down and takes the widow.

If no player wants the widow, it is left face down without being seen by any player.

Play begins with the player to the dealer's left. He places his lowest card in any suit face up in front of him.

The player with the next card higher in that suit (i.e., either the same or another player) plays it face up. This continues with cards played in sequence until either the ace is reached or nobody has the next card in the sequence.

Usually, players announce the rank and suit of cards as they play them.

Each player forms a pile of face up cards in front of him. Once a card is covered, it cannot be inspected.

Stopped play At the end of a sequence play is said to be "stopped." The last person to have played a card starts a new sequence with his lowest card in any other suit. If he cannot do this, the next player to his left able to lead with another suit does so.

If none of the other players can lead another suit, the first player may lead with his lowest card in the same suit as the previous sequence.

Boodle winnings Whenever a player lays down a card that matches one of the four boodle cards, he wins all the chips on that card.

If no player claims the chips on a boodle card during a hand, the chips remain on the card and carry over to the next deal.

Before each hand, each player antes one chip on each boodle card.

Play ends as soon as one player has got rid of all his cards.

Every other player must then pay him one chip for each card still in his hand.

Penalty If a player fails to play a card in sequence when able to do so, he must pay one chip to each of the other players. If by failing to play a card he prevented another player from winning boodle chips, he must make up the loss to the dispossessed player with his own chips. The chips on the boodle card remain and are carried over to the next deal.

The winner of a game is either:

a the first person to win an agreed number of chips; or

b the player with the most chips at the end of a set number of deals or on the expiration of a time limit.

## 2-7 NAPOLEON

Also called nap, this game is in some ways similar to euchre. Any number of players from two to seven may take part. There are no partnerships.

**Rank**

Deck A standard 52-card deck is used; ace ranks high.

Objective Each player aims to contract a bid and take tricks to fufill it.

Deal Players cut for deal, highest card dealing first. Each player is dealt five face down cards, one at a time. The stock is then placed face down on the table.

The deal passes in clockwise rotation.

Bidding Beginning with the player to the dealer's left, each player can either pass or bid two, three, four, or "Napoleon" – indicating the number of tricks he intends to win. (Napoleon signifies five tricks).

Each bid must be higher than the previous bid, and the player with the highest bid becomes the bidder.

There is only one round of bidding.

Trumps The bidder leads to the first trick, and the suit of his opening card denotes trumps.

Play is the same as in whist.

Scoring Napoleon is played for stakes, the usual ones being:

two units for a bid of two; three units for three; four units for four; and ten for Napoleon.

If the bidder wins his contract, each of the other players pays him the stake. If he fails to win his contract, he pays each of the other players the stake. If he fails on a bid of Napoleon, he pays only half the stake.

Optional bids The following optional bids are sometimes used.

a "Wellington" is a declaration to win all five tricks at double stakes. It cannot be called unless Napoleon has already been called.

b "Blücher" overcalls Wellington, and is for five tricks at triple stakes.

c "Misère" or "misery" is a declaration to lose every trick. In the bidding it ranks between three and four, and carries the same stakes as three. There are no trumps in this bid.

## PURCHASE NAP

The rules of purchase nap are the same as for Napoleon, except that each player may exchange any number of cards for fresh ones from the stock, on payment of one unit for each card.

The payments are put in a kitty, won by the first player to make a bid of Napoleon.

## SEVEN-CARD NAP

In seven-card nap, each player receives seven cards. Play is the same as for Napoleon, but bids of Wellington and Blücher are not permitted.

The order of bids with their stakes are as follows: three bids, a stake of three; four, a stake of four; nap and misère (optional), stake of 10; six, stake of 18; and seven, stake of 24.

Players losing nap, misère, six, or seven pay half stakes.

# 3+ OH HELL

Also known as blackout, this game has many features in common with whist. It is a game for three or more players, each playing for himself.

**Rank**

Cards A standard deck of 52 cards is used. Aces rank high.

Objective Each player tries to win the exact number of tricks he has bid.

Deal Each game involves a series of deals. Players cut for the first deal (highest card deals) and thereafter the deal passes in a clockwise direction around the table.

In the first deal, each player is dealt one card; in subsequent deals, the number of cards dealt to each player is increased each time by one card. When the size of the hand can no longer be increased by one card per player, the game is finished. Thus with four players, the cards will be dealt 13 times, and with five players ten times.

At the end of each deal, the dealer turns the top card of the stock face up to denote trumps. If in the final deal there is no spare card to turn face up, the hand is played without trumps.

Bidding Starting with the dealer, each player in turn bids the number of tricks he expects to win, or "nullo" if he expects to lose every trick.

In the first deal, possible bids are one or nullo; the number of possible bids increases with the size of each hand.

Play is opened by the player to the dealer's left. He leads with any card, and the other players must follow suit; if unable to do so they may trump or discard. The winner of a trick leads to the next.

Scoring Every player who fufills his bid exactly scores one point for each trick of his bid and a ten point bonus.

There is no standard score for making nullo; sometimes ten points are awarded, sometimes five, or five points plus the number of tricks in the deal. If a player wins more or fewer tricks than the number he bid, he neither scores nor pays a penalty.

Optional scoring A successful bid of small slam – winning all but one of the tricks in the hand – with a hand of more than five cards earns a 25 point bonus. Similarly, a successful bid of grand slam – winning all the tricks in the hand – earns a 50 point bonus.

The winner is the player with the highest cumulative score after all the deals have been played.

# 2 PINOCHLE

This game is derived from bezique and is widely played in North America. Its name is also spelled pinocle and sometimes penuchle.

**Players** The basic game is for two players.

**Rank**

**Cards** A 48-card deck is used: made from two standard decks excluding all the 2s,3s,4s, 5s,6s,7s, and 8s. Cards rank a (high),10,k, q,j,9 (low).

**Objective** Each player aims to take tricks containing certain cards, and to make melds.

**Choice of first dealer** is by high cut. Thereafter the deal alternates.

**Shuffle and cut** are normal (see p 14), except that the nondealer must cut.

**Deal** The dealer gives 12 cards to each player in packets of three or four.

The thirteenth card is then turned face up on the table, and its suit becomes trumps for that hand.

The rest of the deck, the "stock," is then placed face down on the table, half covering the trump card.

**First stage of play** This lasts as long as there are any cards in the stock.

The nondealer leads to the first trick. Thereafter the winner of one trick leads to the next.

In this stage, players may play any card to a trick. This includes playing a trump when holding a card of a plain suit led. Each trick is won by the highest trump, or, if no trumps appear, by the highest card of the suit led. If two cards of the same denomination and suit appear, the one

**Melds**
**Class A**

150 points

40 points

20 points

**Class B**

40 points

Trumps

**Class C**

100 points

80 points

60 points

40 points

played first wins. The winner of a trick places it face down in front of him. After each trick, the winner may make one meld (see the section on melding). Then, whether or not a meld has been made, the winner draws the top card from the stock and the loser draws the next card.

The winner then leads to the next trick.

Drawing after tricks continues until all the stock and the exposed trump card have been drawn. (It is often ruled that the player who draws the last face down card must also expose it.)

Melding After each trick in the first stage, the winner of the
trick may claim one meld.

A meld is claimed by placing the cards involved face up
on the table, and stating the score.

A player can only score for one meld in a turn – even if
the cards he exposes for that meld have also given him
another scoring combination.

Each card melded can also be used later to form another
meld of a different class (see the section on melds) or one
of a higher score in the same class. However, each new
meld formed in this way requires a new turn and the addition of at least one card from the player's hand.

Any card that a player uses in a meld may still be played
to a later trick, but once a card has been played to a trick
it cannot then be used in further melds.

Melds There are three classes of meld. Points are scored as
follows when the melds are put on the table. (See diagram
previous page.)

Class A: "sequence" (or "flush") – a,10,k,q,j of trumps – 150
points; "royal marriage" – k and q of trumps – 40 points;
"marriage" – k and q of any plain suit – 20 points.

Class B: "pinochle" – q of spades and j of diamonds – 40
points;

Class C: four aces, 100 points; four kings, 80 points; four
queens, 60 points; four jacks, 40 points; (Note that all
"fours" must contain one card of each suit.)

The second stage of play, or "play out," begins with each
player taking back into his hand any cards that he has
melded. The players then play for the remaining 12 tricks
to use up the cards in their hands. The winner of the last
trick in the first stage leads to the first trick in the second.

In this stage a player must follow suit if he can, and may
only trump if he cannot.

If a trump is led, the following player must play a higher trump if he can. (Usually it is made a general rule for this stage that a following player must win any trick he can.)

Tricks are won as in the first stage, and the winner of one trick leads to the next. No melds are made in this stage.

The "dix" is the name given to the 9 of trumps.

**The "dix"**

If the card turned up to decide trumps is a 9, the dealer scores 10 points immediately.

If a player holds a dix during the first stage of play,
he can declare it and win 10 points by placing it face
up on the table after winning the trick. (Most players rule that a meld can also be made in the same turn).

If the first dix to appear is one declared by a player, it is not left face up in front of him but is exchanged for the exposed trump card at the bottom of the stock pile. The player takes that trump card into his hand and puts the dix in its place.

**Scoring of tricks**

11 points

10 points

4 points

3 points

2 points

Scoring of tricks Points for cards taken in tricks are scored at the end of each hand. Cards are scored as follows:

a each ace, 11 points;

b each 10, 10 points;

c each king, four points;

d each queen, three points;

e each jack, two points.

The winner of the last trick in the second stage scores a further 10 points.

Points for tricks are rounded to multiples of 10 (only 7, 8, or 9 being rounded up) before being added to the players total score.

Game is usually 1000 points. If both players reach 1000 or more after the same hand, play continues until one player reaches 1250. If the same happens again, play continues to 1500, etc.

## AUCTION PINOCHLE

In this version, players bid on how many points they expect to score. Chips are collected by successful players.

Players Three people play. Usually the game is played at tables of four, with the dealer taking no active part.

Cards The deck and rank of cards are as in basic pinochle.

Deal 15 cards are dealt to each player in five packets of three. After each player has been dealt one packet, a widow of three cards is dealt face down.

Bidding Each player in turn, starting with the player to the dealer's left, may make a bid as to the number of points he expects to score.

Bidding must start at an agreed minimum (usually 300) and must rise 10 points at a time.

A player must bid or pass. If he passes, he may bid again in that hand. Bidding ends when two players have passed. The other player is then the "bidder," and his highest bid is his contract.

The other two players together try to prevent him making his contract.

Melding The bidder takes up the widow cards, shows them to
the other players, and then adds them to his hand.

He then names the trump suit and lays down his melds.
No other player is allowed to make melds at any time.

Melds and their scores are as in basic pinochle, except
that the dix counts as a Class A meld scoring 10 points,
and is scored only if the bidder places it on the table with
his other melds.

Starting play The bidder begins by discarding three cards face
down from those still in his hand. He then picks up his
meld cards and leads to the first trick.

He may change his mind about his melds, discards, or
trumps at any time before he actually leads to the first
trick. But if he discards a meld card that he has scored for,
he forfeits the game unless he corrects the mistake before
leading to the first trick.

Tricks are won as in basic pinochle. Each player must follow
suit if he can; and, if trumps are led, must try to win the
trick if he can.

If a player cannot follow suit he must trump rather than
discard. This still applies after a trick has been trumped,
but he need not trump higher if he does not wish to.

The winner of each trick leads to the next.

Scoring of tricks may be as in basic pinochle.

Alternatives are:

**a** 10 points for each ace or 10, and 5 points for each king
or queen; or

**b** 10 points for each ace, 10, or king.

Whatever the points system, the bidder scores for any
scoring cards contained in the three cards he discards, and
there is a bonus of 10 points to the bidder if he wins the
last trick.

Game Each hand is a complete game. If the bidder makes or

exceeds his contract, he wins chips from each player. Typical amounts are:

a 300-340 bid, three chips;

b 350-390 bid, five chips;

c 400-440 bid, 10 chips;

d 450-490 bid, 15 chips;

e 500-540 bid, 20 chips;

f 550-590 bid, 25 chips;

g 600 or more, 30 chips.

These amounts are doubled if spades are trumps.

A kitty usually features in auction pinochle. The following are typical rules.

1 Each player must put three chips into the kitty before play begins.

2 If all players pass on a deal, all pay three chips into the kitty.

3 If a bidder makes, or fails on, a contract of 350 or more, he collects from, or pays to, the kitty, as well as each other player. Amounts are the same as for settlements between players.

# 2 PIQUET

Piquet is a card game for two players that allows great opportunities for skill. It has been known, under various names, since the middle of the fifteenth century. The present French name and terminology were adopted in English during the reign of Charles I of England, as a compliment to his French wife, Henrietta Maria.

Players The game is for two.

Objective Each player aims to score points, both with certain combinations of cards in his hand and by playing for tricks.

Cards A deck of 32 playing cards is used, commonly called a piquet deck. This is a standard 52-card deck from which all the 2s,3s,4s,5s, and 6s have been removed.

Usually two decks are used alternately, one being shuffled in readiness for the next hand while the other is being dealt into play.

**Rank**

The cards rank normally, from 7 low to ace high.

Choice of first dealer is by low cut (see page 13).

The first dealer also has choice of seats.

Shuffle is normal (see pages 13-14).

Cut is by the nondealer.

There need be only two cards in each section. Otherwise the cut is normal.

The deal is in packets of two cards, face down. The dealer gives two cards to his opponents, then two to himself, until each has 12 cards.

The remaining eight cards form the stock, which is placed face down in the center of the table. The stock is divided so that the upper five cards rest at an angle to the lower three.

Discards The dealer has the chance to discard first. Under American rules, he need not discard;

under English rules, he must discard at least one card. In either case, the most cards he can discard is five.

If he is discarding, he places the discards face down beside him, and draws an equal number from the stock. (Players must draw cards in the order in which they are stacked in the stock.) Even if the dealer does not draw, or does not draw all five, he may look at the cards that he could have drawn, and then replace them without showing them to his opponent. Then the nondealer discards at least one card and at most as many cards as remain in the stock.

He places his discards face down beside him and draws an equal number of stock cards, beginning with any left by the dealer. The nondealer may look at any cards in the stock that remain undrawn. But in this case the dealer may turn these cards face up for himself to see also. (Sometimes it is ruled that the dealer may do this only after leading to the first trick.)

A player may inspect his own discards during play.

Scoring Points are scored in two ways. Some points are scored by "declaration," which occurs immediately after discarding and before play. Other points are scored during play.

Declarations Each player declares certain combinations of cards held in his hand, and scores points if his declaration ranks higher than his opponent's.

A player does not have to declare a potentially winning combination if he prefers not to – but he cannot then score points for it. This is called "sinking."

A player may include any card in more than one combination.

Scoring combinations

Point The player with the most cards of one suit scores one point for each card he holds in that suit.

If both players have long suits of the same length, the

better point is the one with the higher face value. (Face value is calculated by counting the ace as 11, face cards as 10 each, and other cards as their numerical face value). If the players tie, neither scores.

A player can only score for one point – even if he has more than one suit longer than his opponent's longest.

Sequences The player with the most cards in rank order in one suit scores as follows: tierce (three cards), three points; quart (four cards), four points; quint (five cards), 15 points; sextet or sixième (six cards), 16 points; septet or septième (even cards), 17 points; octet or huitième (eight cards), 18 points.

The holder of the highest sequence can also score for any other sequences he holds.

If players tie for the longest sequence, the sequence with the higher top card wins. If both sequences have the same top card, neither scores for any sequences.

Meld The player with the highest ranking meld, of three or four cards of a kind, scores as follows: trio or "three" (three cards of the same denomination), three points; quatorze or "fourteen" (four cards of the same denomination), 14 points.

**Sequence**

**Meld**

But only aces, kings, queens, jacks, or 10s may be declared for melds (and sometimes it is ruled that 10s only count if a quatorze is held).

If both players have sets of equal length, the one with the higher ranking cards wins.

The winner also scores for any other melds he holds.

Announcing the declarations is by a formal dialogue, designed to reveal no more information than necessary.

The nondealer makes the first declaration in each category of combination, following the order point, sequence, meld.

Declaring a point Nondealer says "A point of _____ ," stating whatever number of cards he holds in his longest suit.

Dealer replies:

"Good," if he concedes the point;

"Not good," if he holds a longer suit – stating its length;

"How many?" if he holds a suit of equal length.

If the reply is "How many?" the nondealer must then declare the face value of his point. The dealer then replies "Good," "Not good" (stating the value of his point), or "Equal" (in which case no one scores).

Whoever has won the point then states the length of his point again (adding the face value if that also had to be declared), and announces his score.

Declaring a sequence Nondealer says "A sequence of _____ ," (or "A tierce," etc.), stating the number of cards in his longest sequence.

The procedure then follows as in declaring a point – except that when the dealer holds a sequence of equal length his reply is "How high?" The nondealer then declares the top card of his sequence, and the dealer states "Good," "Not good," or "Equal."

Declaring a meld nondealer says "A three (or fourteen) of _____ ," naming the denomination.

(Alternatively he can use the words "trio" or "quatorze.") The dealer cannot hold a meld of the same length and denomination, and so must reply "Good" or "Not good."

## A sample declaration

Nondealer: "A point of five."

Dealer: "Good."

Nondealer: "A point of five. I score five." Then he names his best sequence: "A sequence of four" (or "A quart").

Dealer: "How high?"

Nondealer: "Queen."

Dealer: "Not good. Ace. Also a tierce. I score seven."

Nondealer (naming his best meld): "Three kings" (or "A trio of kings").

Dealer: "Not good. Fourteen queens" (or "quatorze of queens"). I score 14. I start with 21."

Nondealer (playing the lead to the first trick and automatically adding one point to his score – see next page): " I start with six."

## English style declaration

In this, the dealer only names his combinations after the Nondealer has led to the first trick. For example:

Nondealer: "A point of five."

Dealer: "Good."

Nondealer: "A point of five. I score five. A quart."

Dealer: "How high?"

Nondealer: "Queen."

Dealer: "Not good."

Nondealer: "A trio of kings."

Dealer: "Not good."

Nondealer (playing first card): " I start with six."

Dealer: "A quart to the ace. Also a tierce. Seven And a quatorze of queens: 14. I start with 21."

Showing combinations Sometimes it is ruled that all winning combinations must be shown before they score. More usually, winning combinations are shown only at the opponent's request. A combination that is shown is replaced in the holder's hand as soon as the opponent has seen it.

Play The nondealer leads to the first trick. Each player must follow suit to a lead if he can. If not he may discard any card. The winner of a trick leads to the next.

Scoring during play A player scores for tricks; also players may score additional points in various ways.

Scoring for tricks Each player scores as follows:

**a** one point for leading to a trick;

**b** one point for taking a trick that his opponent led to;

**c** one point for taking the last trick; and

**d** 10 points for taking seven or more tricks.

   Each time a player scores he announces his total score so far.

Variation Sometimes it is played that:

**a** a player scores for leading to a trick only if the card led is higher than a 9;

**b** a player scores for winning a trick only if the winning card is higher than a 9.

Additional scoring Points may also be scored in the following ways.

**a** Carte blanche is a hand devoid of face cards, and scores 10 points. It must be claimed by a player immediately before he discards after the deal. (Under English rules, it must be claimed before either player discards.)

**b** Pique is scored by the nondealer if he scores 30 points before the dealer scores anything. It scores 30 bonus points.

**c** Repique is scored by either player if he scores 30 points on declaration, i.e., before the lead to the first trick. It is worth 60 bonus points.

**d** Capot is scored by either player if he captures all 12 tricks in play. It is worth 40 bonus points, but the 10 standard points for taking a majority of tricks are not scored.

A game is known as a partie. It consists usually of six deals, though some players prefer to have a partie of four deals, with scores for the first and fourth deals counting double.

The turn to deal alternates between the two players.

Scoring the partie

**a** The scores for the individual deals are added together to give a total for each player.

The procedure then depends on whether these totals exceed the "rubicon" of 100 points.

**b** If both players have 100 or more points, the player with the higher total wins by the difference between the two totals plus 100 points bonus for the partie.

For example, if the dealer has totalled 120 and the nondealer 108, the dealer wins and scores 112 points (120–108+100).

**c** If either or both players have less than 100 points, the player with the lower total is said to be "rubiconed." The player with the higher total wins by the sum of the totals plus 100 points bonus.

For example, if the scores are 125 and 92, the player with 125 wins and scores 317 (125+92+100); if the scores are 98 and 92, the player with 98 wins and scores 290 (98+92+100).

## PIQUET AU CENT

This version has different final scoring. Deals continue until one player totals 100 points or more. At the end of the deal, the player with the higher total scores the difference between his own and his opponent's totals – or double that difference if his opponent's total was below 50.

## AUCTION PIQUET

This piquet variation puts more emphasis on the play of the hands.

Bidding takes place before the discard. The nondealer bids or passes first. If both pass, the cards are dealt again by the same player. Once a bid has been made, bidding continues until one player passes.

The minimum bid is seven. A bid may be either "plus" (winning the stated number of tricks) or "minus" (losing that number). Plus and minus bids rank equally: to continue the bidding a player must bid a greater number of tricks.

The final bid is the "contract" as in contract bridge.

Other rules are as for basic piquet, with the following exceptions.

Discards Players need not discard at all.

Declarations may be made in any order.

Sinking is not allowed on minus contracts.

Pique is scored after 29 points in plus contracts and 21 points in minus ones.

Repique is scored after 30 points in plus contracts and 21 points in minus ones.

Scoring for tricks Each player scores one point for each trick that he takes (whoever led to that trick).

Players do not score for leading to a trick or for taking the last trick.

Scoring the contract If the contracted player exceeds his contract, he scores 10 points for every trick won (on plus contracts) or lost (on minus contracts) in excess of his contract. If he fails to make his contract, every trick by which he fell short scores 10 points for his opponent.

Doubling and redoubling are allowed, as in bridge, but affect only the scores for overtricks or undertricks.

Scoring the partie Rubicon is 150 points, and bonus for the partie is also 150 points.

# 3+ POPE JOAN

Pope Joan is a card game for three or more players and was invented by combining two earlier games, commit and matrimony. Contestants try to play their cards in such a way as to win as many counters as possible.

Cards A standard deck of 52 cards is used, but with the 8 of diamonds removed.

The cards are referred to in the usual way, except for the 9 of diamonds which is called Pope Joan. Aces count low.

Counters At the start of a game, each player should have an equal number of counters.

Betting layout A board or other betting layout is required for the game.

Layouts are usually circular or square, and are divided into sections labelled ace, jack, intrigue, queen, matrimony, king, Pope Joan, and game. Some traditional Pope Joan boards comprise a circular tray revolving on a central stand.

A layout can easily be drawn on a sheet of plain paper or material. Each section should be large enough to hold at least 20 counters.

Objective Each player aims to win as many counters as possible by playing certain cards. Counters are also won by the first contestant to use all his cards.

Bet and deal Players decide upon a dealer.

Each player, including the dealer, then places counters in the different sections of the betting layout. This may be done in one of two ways, either:

a each player, including the dealer, puts out the same agreed number of counters, dividing them equally between the different sections; or

b each player, including the dealer, puts four counters in

**Layout**

**Betting**

the pope section, two in matrimony, two in intrigue, and one in each of the other sections.

The dealer then deals one hand to each player including himself, and one extra hand.

He deals by giving one card to each player in a clockwise direction, beginning with the player to his left. The card for the extra hand is dealt just before he deals to himself.

All cards are dealt face down. The deal continues in this way until all the cards but one have been dealt; this card is placed face upward on top of the extra hand.

The exposed card If the card dealt face upward
is Pope Joan (the 9 of diamonds), the dealer
wins all the counters in the pope and the game
sections. (In an alternative version of play the
dealer wins all counters on the layout.)

Pope Joan

The round ends and the player to the dealer's
left becomes the new dealer.

If any other card is dealt, its suit determines trumps for
that hand.

If the card dealt face upward is an ace or a face card, the
dealer wins the counters on the section with the same name.

Play Each player examines his own hand, but no player may
look at the extra hand.

The player to the dealer's left begins. He plays any
one card from his hand face up onto the middle of the
playing area and says its name, e.g., "3 of hearts."

The player with the 4 of hearts then plays it, followed
by the player with the 5, the 6, and so on.

This continues until no player can add to the sequence
because either:

a the sequence has been completed by reaching the king;
b the next card needed is the 8 of diamonds; or
c the next card needed is hidden in the extra hand or has
   already been played.

At this point the cards already played in the sequence are
turned face down, and whoever played the last card begins
a new sequence by playing any card of his choice.

Claiming counters Anyone who plays the ace, jack, queen, or
king of trumps receives all the counters in the section
marked with the same name (a).

If a player plays the jack and queen of trumps in
sequence, he wins all the counters in the intrigue section, as
well as those on jack and queen (b).

## Claiming counters

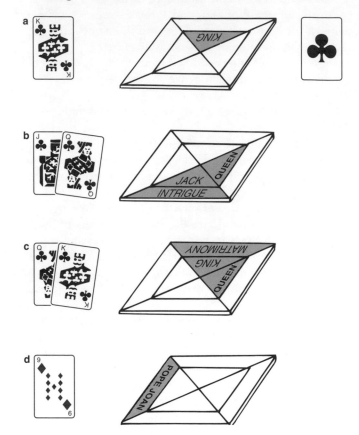

If anyone plays the queen and king of trumps in sequence, he receives all the counters in the matrimony section, as well as those on queen and king (**c**).

A player putting out Pope Joan wins all the counters on that section (**d**).

It should be noted that these cards only win counters when played in the correct way, i.e., by starting or adding to a sequence. They win nothing if they are still unplayed at the end of a round.

**Ending the round** The round continues until any one player has played all his cards, when he may take all the counters in the game section.

All the other players have to give him one counter for every card still in their hand, with the exception of any one holding the unplayed Pope Joan, who is exempted from paying for the cards left in his hand.

**Unclaimed counters** Any counters that are not won in a round remain on the betting layout until won in subsequent rounds. New counters are added as usual to all sections at the beginning of each round.

Any counters left at the end of a game are distributed by redealing the cards, face up, without an extra hand.

The players who receive the ace, jack, and queen of diamonds and the Pope Joan take any remaining counters in those divisions. And counters in the matrimony section are divided between the holders of the king and queen, and those in the intrigue section between the holders of the queen and jack.

# 3 PREFERENCE

This is a fairly straightforward game usually played for small stakes. Three players take part, each playing for himself.

**Rank**

Cards A standard deck with all the 2s,3s,4s,5s, and 6s removed is used.

The cards are ranked: ace (high), k,q,j,10,9,8,7 (low).

The suits, in descending order, rank: hearts (known as "preference"), diamonds, clubs, spades.

Objective Each player tries to be the highest bidder and to fufill the contract.

Preliminaries Before the start of play, each player puts an equal agreed number of chips into the pool.

Players must also decide:

a how much a successful bidder should receive from the pool, depending on the rank of the trump suit; and

b the payment to be made into the pool by an unsuccessful bidder.

Deal Any player may deal the first hand; thereafter the deal passes clockwise around the table.

The dealer gives ten face-down cards to each player, and also deals two cards face down in the center of the table as the "widow," making the deal as follows.

He first deals a packet of three cards to each player, then

he deals the widow, then another packet of four cards to each player, and finally a packet of three cards to each player.

Bidding Each player in turn, beginning with the player to the dealer's left, either bids a suit or passes.

By bidding a suit, the player indicates that he intends to win at least six tricks of the possible ten, with the named suit as trumps.

Each player is permitted one bid only, and each bid must be in a higher ranking suit than the previous bid.

If all three players pass in the first round of bidding, there is a second round in which each player can either pass or put chips into the pool. The player putting most chips into the pool then wins the right to name the trump suit; he may also discard any two of his cards and take the widow into his hand.

If a player bids in the first round, the widow is not used.

Play The player to the left of the successful bidder leads to the first trick.

Every other player must follow suit if he can; if he cannot he may play a trump card or discard any card.

The highest card in the suit led or the highest trump played takes the trick.

The winner of a trick leads to the next trick, and the game continues until all ten tricks have been taken.

Settlement If the bidder fufills his bid (takes at least six of the ten tricks) he wins the agreed number of chips from the pool, depending on the rank of the trump suit. If the bidder fails in his contract, he pays the agreed number of chips into the pool.

## *2-6* RUMMY

Rummy is one of the most commonly played of all card games, second only to poker in popularity. Formerly known as rum poker, rummy developed in the saloons and gambling houses of late nineteenth-century America. Although its rules are easily learned, it nonetheless offers plenty of scope for skilful play.

### RUMMY: BASIC GAME

Cards A standard deck of 52 cards is used.

In play, the cards rank normally with ace low.

For scoring, the jack, queen, and king are each worth 10 points; all other cards are worth their face value.

Players Two to six may play. There are no partnerships.

Objective Each player attempts to be the first to go out through having "melded" all his cards. Cards are melded in either groups or sequences.

A group is three or four cards of the same rank (e.g., 4 of hearts, 4 of spades, and 4 of clubs).

A sequence is three or more cards of the same suit falling in numerical order (e.g., 9, 10, and jack of diamonds).

Starting the game The player with the lowest cut or draw becomes dealer. The dealer shuffles, and the player to his right cuts the deck. The cards are dealt in a clockwise

**Group**

**Sequence**

direction. The number of cards dealt varies according to the number of players: two players, 10 cards each; three to four players, seven cards each; five to six players, six cards each.

After the deal, the remaining cards are turned face down to form the stock. The top card from the stock is turned face up beside it to start the discard pile (this card is called the upcard).

Play Players take their turns in a clockwise direction, beginning with the player to the dealer's left.

The player starts his turn by drawing the top card from either the stock or the discard pile. He may then meld a group or a sequence face up on the table.

He may also "lay off" (add) as many cards as possible to any matched sets already melded on the table, whether the original melds were his own or an opponent's.

He ends his turn by rejecting one card from his hand and placing it face up on the discard pile. If he began his turn by drawing a card from the discard pile, he is not permitted to end the turn by discarding that same card.

If the stock is used up before any player goes out, the discard pile is turned face down (unshuffled) to form a new stock.

Going out A player goes out – and wins the hand – if he succeeds in getting rid of all his cards, with or without a final discard.

Going rummy A player "goes rummy" if he goes out by melding all his cards in one turn without having previously melded or laid off any cards.

Scoring If a player goes out, the numerical value of all the cards then left in his opponents' hands is totalled to give the winner's score for the round. This score is doubled if the player went rummy.

Continuing play The deal passes to the next player to the left if there are more than two players. If there are two players, the winner of one round deals the next.

Game The first player to reach a previously agreed total wins the game.

## GIN RUMMY

This is probably the most popular of all rummy variations.

Cards Two standard decks of 52 cards are used. While one player deals, the other shuffles the second deck ready for the next deal.

The cards rank normally, with ace low. They are valued as for basic rummy.

Players Basic gin rummy is for two players. It can be adapted for any larger even number by dividing players into two equal sides, and holding separate but simultaneous games between pairs of players.

Objective As in rummy each player tries to meld his cards in groups or sequences. Unlike basic rummy, however, it is possible for a player to win a hand without melding all his cards.

Choice of first dealer The player cutting the higher card has the choice of seat, deck of cards, and whether he wants first deal.

Shuffle and cut are normal.

Deal The dealer deals 10 face down cards to each player, beginning with his opponent and dealing one card at a time. The twenty-first card is then turned face up and becomes the first card on the discard pile (the upcard).

The remaining cards are played face down on the table alongside the upcard to form the stock.

Start of play The nondealer then decides whether or not he wants the upcard. If he decides not to take it, the dealer has the option of taking it.

If the dealer does not want it, then the nondealer must draw the top stock card.

Whichever player takes a card must then discard one.

Turn of play In subsequent turns a player takes the top card from either the discard pile or the stock, and then discards. Players do not lay melds on the table until one player ends the hand by "going gin" or "knocking."

Going gin A player goes gin if he can meld all 10 of his cards in matched sets. He declares this when it is his turn, and lays all his cards face up on the table.

His opponent may then lay down his own melds, but he may not lay off any cards on to the winner's melds.

Knocking is an alternative way of going out. It may be done if the unmatched cards – deadwood – in a player's hand add up to 10 points or less.

A player can knock only when it is his turn. He draws a card in the usual way, knocks on the table, and discards one card face down. He then lays out all his remaining cards face up on the table, grouping them into melds and unmatched cards.

His opponent must then, without drawing, lay out his cards on the table. Cards should be grouped into melds and unmatched cards, but the player also has the opportunity of laying off cards onto the knocker's melds.

Each player's deadwood cards are then totalled, and the totals compared.

Scoring a hand

1 If a player goes gin he gets a 25 point bonus in addition to the value of his opponent's deadwood.

2 If a player knocks and his deadwood count is less than his opponent's the knocker wins the hand and his score is the difference between the two counts.

3 If a player knocks and his opponent's deadwood count is

lower than or the same as his own, the opponent has "undercut" the knocker and wins the hand. For this he scores a 25 point bonus as well as any difference between the dead-wood counts.

"No game" The last two cards in the stock may not be drawn. If the player who draws the fiftieth card is unable to go gin or knock, the hand is a tie and no points are scored. The same dealer deals for the next hand.

Box (or line) A running total is kept of each player's score. When a player wins a hand, a horizontal line called a box (or line) is drawn under his score.

Game score The first player to score 100 or more points ends the game and has 100 points added to his score.

If his opponent has failed to win a hand, the winner then doubles his score (including the 100 point bonus).

Finally, for every hand a player has won – as shown by the boxes in his running score – he receives an additional 25 point bonus.

## 2-3 SEVEN UP

Seven up is a card game for two or three players and origi-nated in England in the seventeenth century. Other names by which it is known are all fours, high-low-jack, and old sledge.

### SEVEN UP: BASIC GAME

Deck A standard deck of cards is used. Ace ranks high.

Objective Each player tries to score seven points and so win the game.

Deal Players cut for the deal, highest card dealing. Each player is dealt six face down cards in packets of three.

The next card is turned face up and denotes trumps, and if it is a jack the dealer scores one point.

The deal passes clockwise around the table.

Trumps If the player to the dealer's left is happy to play with the trump suit shown, he says "Stand" and play begins. Should he prefer to play another trump suit he says "I beg," and the dealer can choose whether or not to change trumps. If the dealer chooses to keep the same trump suit he says "Take one" to the player, who scores one point. Play then starts. If the dealer agrees to change the trump suit, he sets aside the face up card, deals a further three cards to each player, and turns the next card face up to denote trumps.

If this card shows a different suit from the first face up card, play begins with this suit as trumps – and if it is a jack, the dealer scores one point.

Should the face up card be the same suit again, however, another three cards are dealt to each player and a third card is turned face up.

This procedure is repeated until a new trump suit is determined, and the dealer scores one point for each jack that is turned up, provided it is not of the same suit as the suit initially rejected.

If the deck is exhausted before a new trump suit is turned up, the entire deck is shuffled and redealt.

Discarding If the trump suit has been changed, each player discards face down a sufficient number of cards to reduce his hand to six.

Play is the same as in whist.

Scoring At the end of each round the tricks are turned face up for scoring. Points are scored as follows: "high," one point for the player dealt the highest trump; "low," one point for the player dealt the lowest trump; "jack," one point for the player who takes the jack of trumps in a trick; "game," one point for the player who takes the highest total value of cards in tricks. The cards are valued as follows: four for each ace; three for each king; two for each queen; one for each jack; ten for each 10.

Game The first player to make seven points wins the game. If more than one player reaches seven points in the same hand, the points are counted in the following order so as to determine the winner: high, low, jack, game.

## FOUR-HANDED SEVEN UP

In this version four people play in partnerships of two. Each player sits opposite his partner.

Play is the same as in the basic game, except that the two players to the right of the dealer do not look at their cards until after trumps has been determined.

## CALIFORNIA JACK

This variant of seven up is sometimes called draw seven or California loo. It is played by two people and differs from seven up in the following ways.

**Trumps** The first card turned face up denotes trumps. After each trick, first the winner and then the loser of that trick take a card from the top of the stock. The next card of the stock is then turned face up and denotes trumps for the next trick. When the stock is exhausted, each player's remaining cards are played out using the last trump suit, and with the winner of each trick leading to the next.

**Scoring** One point is scored for taking each of the following in tricks: the highest trump, the lowest trump, and the jack of trumps. The first player to make 10 points wins.

## 3–5 SKAT

Skat developed in Germany in the early 1800s and its rules were codified in 1896. It has since flourished on both sides of the Atlantic, being one of the most skilful of all card games. The simplified variant described here – Rauber Skat – is gradually replacing the original game.

**Rank with no trumps**

All suits

Players Three to five people can play, but only three play on any one deal.

With four players, the dealer sit out. With five, the dealer and the third player to his left sits out: the first, second, and fourth play.

The first player to the dealer's left is called "forehand," the next "middlehand," and the last player with cards "endhand."

Cards Skat is played with a standard deck from which all the 2s,3s,4s,5s, and 6s have been removed.

Rank of cards Most contracts require trumps.

The highest trumps are always the four jacks, which rank in the order clubs (high), spades, hearts, diamonds (low).

In addition there may also be a trump suit. If so, the rest of that suit rank below the lowest jack, in the order a (high),10,k,q,9,8,7 (low).

When play is with trumps, cards in plain suits also rank a (high),10,k,q,9,8,7 (low).

When there are no trumps, all suits rank a (high), k,q,j,10,9,8,7 (low).

Objective Each player tries to win the right to choose the game that will be played, and then successfully to complete that game.

Choice of first dealer is by high cut. Thereafter the deal passes one player to the left after each game.

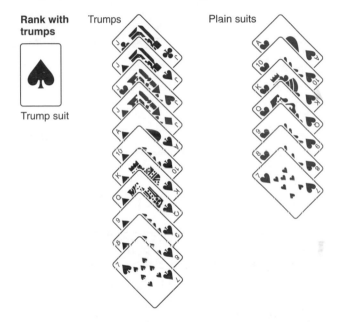

**Rank with trumps**

Trump suit

Trumps

Plain suits

Deal A packet of three cards is dealt to each active player. Then a "skat" of two face-down cards is set aside. A packet of four is next dealt to each active player, and finally a further packet of three.

This gives three hands of ten cards each, and two cards in the skat.

Bidding The player who makes the highest bid wins the right to name the game. He then tries to fufill his bid and the other two players try to prevent him.

A bid states only the number of game points that the player believes he can make if he wins the right to choose the game. The lowest permitted bid is 18; the highest practicable bid is about 100.

Bidding follows the deal.

Middlehand bids first, or passes.

If middlehand bids, forehand must reply. He must state either "Pass" or "Hold."

"Hold" means that he makes the same bid as middleman.

By bidding hold, he retains the right to name the game, because a player cannot lose this to a player to his left unless that player has bid higher.

This continues with forehand holding bids and middlehand raising bids until either player passes.

Then endhand must either raise the bid or pass; and if he bids, the survivor of the first pair replies by passing or holding. This continues as between the first pair, until one bidder gives in.

If both middlehand and endhand pass without bidding, forehand may make a bid or may pass. Once a player has passed, he may not make a bid.

The player who survives in the bidding will now be referred to as the "bidder."

The skat The bidder begins by deciding whether or not to pick up the two cards that form the skat.

If he picks up the skat, he must then discard any two cards from his hand. These discards will eventually count toward his final score.

If he does not pick up, this is referred to as "handplay." The skat is then set aside for the duration of play. At the end of the hand, the fate of the skat depends on the game that has been played.

If the bidder chooses to pick up the skat, this limits his choice of game for the hand (since for certain games it is ruled that the skat may not be picked up).

**The games** The bidder then chooses which game will be played in that hand. His choice is between "suits," "grand," "simple null," "open null," and "reject."

(A bidder who has picked up the skat is not permitted to choose simple null, open null, or reject.)

To fufill his bid, he must not only successfully complete the game he chooses (for example, by making sufficient trick points if that is required), but must also score sufficient "game" points to equal or exceed his bid.

**Suits** In this option, the bidder names a suit. All the cards in that suit become trumps, together with the jacks.

The bidder's aim is to make at least 61 trick points by taking tricks containing scoring cards.

**Grand** Only the four jacks are trumps. The bidder's aim is as in suits.

**Simple null** There are no trumps. The bidder aims to lose every trick.

**Open null** As in simple null, but the bidder must play with all his cards exposed. He lays them face up on the table before the opening lead.

**Reject** This game may only be chosen by forehand, and he may choose it only if middlehand and endhand have both passed without a bid. He does not make a numerical bid, but simply states "Reject."

Only the four jacks are trumps.

Each player tries to take fewer trick points than any other player.

**Open** If the bidder has opted for handplay, and names suits or grand, he may increase the value of his game by declaring "Open."

The bidder must then play with all his cards exposed, laying them face up on the table before the opening lead.

Schneider or schwarz If the bidder has named suits or grand, he may, before the opening lead, declare:

a "Schneider," i.e., he aims to win at least 91 trick points; or

b "Schwarz," i.e., he aims to take every trick.

He need not declare either – in which case his goal remains 61 trick points.

Play Forehand leads to the first trick. Thereafter the winner of one trick leads to the next.

Other players must follow suit if possible. If unable to follow suit they may trump (if there are trumps in the game) or they may discard.

The highest trump played, or the highest card of the suit led if no trumps appear, wins the trick.

Scoring of trick points Cards taken in tricks score as follows: each ace, 11 points; each 10, 10 points; each king, four points; each queen, three points; each jack, two points.

Scoring the skat After the last trick has been taken, the skat is allocated as follows:

a at suits or grand, to the bidder (if he took the skat before play, he is given the cards he discarded);

b at reject, to the winner of the last trick;

c at null, to no one – the skat is discarded.

Whoever receives the skat (or discards) counts trick points for any scoring cards it contains.

Making the game Except at reject (see separate section on reject play, page 156), the bidder makes the game if he achieves that game's object (i.e., 61 trick points, 91 trick points, all tricks, or no tricks.)

He must, however, then consider if he has made the number of game points that he bid.

Making the bid Except at reject, a bid is made if the bidder's game score equals or exceeds the number of game points stated in his bid. Game points are scored as follows:

a At null games, the game value is fixed: 23 game points for making simple null, and 24 for making open null. Provided that the player's bid was not higher than this, he makes his bid.

b At suits or grand, the game value has to be calculated – by multiplying a base game value by various multipliers. A player does not know how many multipliers he will qualify for until after play ends. The player makes his bid if the total game value (base x all multipliers) equals or exceeds his bid.

Base values for the games are: diamonds, nine game points; hearts, 10 game points; spades, 11 game points; clubs, 12 game points; grand, 20 game points.

The multipliers are as follows:

a automatic multiplier for having made game, one;

b for holding "matadors" (see separate section), the multiplier varies but is at least one;

c for choosing handplay, one;

d for making schneider or schwarz (see separate section), the multiplier varies but is at least one.

The player adds all his multipliers together. The total will be between two and 14. He then multiplies the base value for his game by this total.

Matadors The jack of clubs and all other trumps in unbroken sequence in the bidder's hand (including the skat, whether or not it is used in play) are called matadors.

When the bidder holds the jack of clubs, his hand is said to be "with" a number of matadors.

When he does not hold the jack of clubs, his hand is said to be "without" a number of matadors.

The multiplier is the number of matadors that the bidder is with or without (it does not matter which).

Two examples are shown (right).

**a** Spades are trumps, the player is with three matadors (the missing jack of diamonds breaks the sequence before the ace of spades). The multiplier is three.

**b** Hearts are trumps, the player is without two matadors (the top two trumps are missing). The multiplier is two.

Multipliers for schneider and schwarz The bidder may only count one of the following multipliers:

**a** schneider made but not predicted, one;

**b** schwarz made but not predicted, two;

**c** schneider predicted and made, three;

**d** schneider predicted and schwarz made, four;

**e** schwarz predicted and made, five.

Scoring Except when reject is played (see separate section), scoring is as follows. Only the bidder scores.

If he has made his bid, he scores the total of his game points (which may be higher than his bid).

If he has not made his bid:

**a** at suits or grand, he loses the amount of his bid at hand-play – or twice that amount if he took the skat;

**b** at null, he loses the absolute game value.

Scoring of reject In this game, there is no bidder and no bid.

Normally the player who makes the fewest trick points scores 10. But:

**a** if he takes no tricks he scores 20;

**b** if two players tie for fewest trick points, the one who did not take the last trick receives the score of 10;

**c** if one player takes all the tricks, he loses 30 and the others score nothing;

**d** if all players tie with 40 trick points, forehand alone scores 10 for naming the game.

Winning The scores are recorded on a piece of paper and totalled at the end of a session.

The winner is the player with the highest score.

Often, an average score is worked out - players above the average then collect money accordingly, while players whose score is below average must make the payments.

## Matadors

Cards in hand

Trumps

Three matadors: the
multiplier is three

Two matadors: the
multiplier is two

# 4 **SOLO WHIST**

Temporary partnerships are formed in solo whist, but each player scores for himself. Basically play is as for whist, but the game has its own bidding and scoring systems.

Players Solo whist is a game for four players. At the start of each hand each player is on his own.

Cards A standard deck of 52 playing cards is used. Cards rank normally, with ace high.

**Rank**

Objective Each player tries to contract and fufill a bid.

Choice of first dealer is by high cut, with ace low.

Shuffle and cut are normal.

Deal The dealer deals out all the cards, beginning with the player to his left and going clockwise. The cards are dealt three at a time, with a final round of single cards. All but the last card are dealt face down; the last card, dealt to the dealer, is dealt face up and indicates trumps for some bids. Rules for misdeals are the same as for whist.

Bidding Each player in turn, beginning with the player to the dealer's left, may make a bid or pass without making a bid. In certain circumstances players may have a second chance to bid.

The bids are ranked in the following order, with each outbidding the one before.

a Proposal and acceptance, or "prop and cop," involves a temporary partnership of two players. A call of "I propose" or "Prop" indicates that the player will try to win eight tricks in partnership with any of the others.

Play is with the trump suit indicated at the deal. In his turn, a subsequent bidder may call "Accept" or "Cop" to become the partner.

**Rank in three-handed solo**

b "Solo" is a bid to take five tricks playing alone against the other three. Play is with the trump suit indicated at the deal.

c "Misère" or "nullo" indicates that the player will try to lose every trick, playing with no trump suit.

d "Abondance" is a bid to take nine tricks, playing with trump suit nominated by the bidder. He does not announce the trump suit until all the remaining players have passed.

e "Royal abondance" or "abondance in trumps," is a bid to take nine tricks, playing with the trump suit indicated at the deal.

f "Misère ouverte" or "spread" indicates that a player will try to lose every trick, playing with no trumps and turning his remaining cards face up on the table after the first trick has been taken.

g "Abondance declarée" is a bid to take 13 tricks, playing with no trump suit.

Second bids may be made in the following cases:

a by the player to the left of the dealer to accept a proposal;

b by any player who has been overbid and wishes to make a higher bid;

c by a proposer who has not been accepted and wishes to amend his proposal to a higher bid.

No bid hands If all players pass, the cards are thrown in and the deal passes to the left.

Play The player to the dealer's left leads first, unless the bid is abondance declarée in which case the bidder leads.

The rules for making tricks and trumping are as for whist.

It is not always necessary to play a hand right out. For example, after a misère bid the hand ends once the bidder takes a trick.

Revoke A revoke (see page 172) loses or wins three tricks depending on the bid and on which player made the error. A hand is always played out after a revoke, and a bidder who revokes must pay for the three tricks even if he makes his bid without them.

Scoring Chips are usually used for scoring: red ones worth five points each and white ones worth one point. Alternatively a written record may be kept.

Scores are as follows. For a successful proposal and acceptance bid, one partner receives five points from one opponent, and the other partner the same from the other opponent. For an unsuccessful bid, partners pay instead of receiving the points. For all other bids, the bidder receives points from each of the other players if successful, or pays each of them if unsuccessful.

The number of points varies with the bids: solo, 10 points; misère, 15 points; abondance, 20 points; royal abondance, 20 points; misère ouverte, 30 points; abondance declarée, 40 points.

In addition, for bids other than misère, misère ouverte, or abondance declarée, one extra point changes hands at each payment for each overtrick (trick in excess of the bid) or undertrick (trick fewer than the bid).

## THREE-HANDED SOLO

The game can be adapted for three-handed play as follows.

Cards There are two alternative changes:

**1** A 40-card deck is used – obtained by stripping the 2s,3s, and 4s from a standard deck. 39 cards are dealt out and the 40th indicates the trump suit.

2 A 39-card deck is used – obtained by stripping out the whole of one suit. The trump suit is indicated by the last card dealt.

Bids There is no proposal and acceptance bid. Misère overbids abondance, and misère ouverte overbids abondance declarée.

Scoring Misère is worth 20 points, abondance 15 points, misère ouverte 40 points, and abondance declarée 30 points.

## 2-6 SPOIL FIVE

Spoil five is similar to loo but has an unusual and complex ranking system. It is especially popular in the Republic of Ireland.

**Rank in trumps**

Spades and Clubs          Diamonds          Hearts

Players Two or more people can play, but the game is best played with five or six. Each person plays for himself.

Deck A standard deck of playing cards is used. The cards are ranked, in descending order, as follows. (See diagrams opposite and below.)

**Rank in plain suits**

Spades and Clubs          Diamonds          Hearts

### Spades and clubs

Plain suits (i.e., non trump): k,q,j,a,2,3,4,5,6,7,8,9,10.

Trump suits: 5,j, a of hearts, a of spades or clubs, k,q,2,3,4,6, 7,8,9,10.

### Diamonds

Plain suit: k,q,j,10,9,8,7,6,5,4,3,2,a.

Trump suit: 5,j,a of hearts, a of diamonds, k,q,10,9,8, 7,6,4,3,2

### Hearts

Plain suit: k,q,j,10,9,8,7,6,5,4,3,2.

Trump suit: 5,j,a,k,q,10,9,8,7,6,4,3,2.

Note that the ace of hearts is always the third-best trump, regardless of suit; the 5 of the trump suit is highest; and the jack of the trump suit is second-highest.

**Objective** Each player tries to win three tricks and to prevent anyone else from doing so.

**Deal** Players draw for deal, using standard ranking with ace high and 2 low. Lowest card deals.

Five face-down cards are dealt to each player in packets of two then three, or vice versa. The next card is turned face up to indicate trumps.

The deal passes clockwise around the table.

**Pool** Each player puts an agreed number of counters into the pool. It is won by a player taking three tricks in one hand.

**Exchanging** If the face-up card denoting the trump suit is an ace, the dealer may exchange it for a card in his hand before the first card is led. This is called "robbing."

If a player has been dealt the ace of trumps he may, if he wishes, exchange any card in his hand for the face-up card.

If he does not exchange a card, he must announce that he has the ace at his first turn of play – otherwise the ace becomes the lowest-ranking trump for that round, even if it is an ace of hearts.

Play The player to the left of the dealer leads to the first trick
and the winner of each trick leads to the next.

Rules of play are the same as for whist, with the following differences.

If a card of a plain suit is led, a player may either trump
or follow suit. He may discard another plain suit card only
if he can neither follow suit nor trump.

If a card of the trump suit is led, a player must follow
suit if he can. He need not play any of the top three
trumps if the leading card was a lower trump – holding
back a card in this way is called "reneging."

Jinxing A player who wins three tricks may take the pool, and
the hand ends.

Alternatively, he may call "Jinx," implying that he will
try to win the remaining two tricks. Play continues, and if
he wins the extra two tricks he takes the pool, plus a sum
from each player equal to his original contribution to the
pot. If he does not make both tricks he loses the pool and
the hand counts as a "spoil."

Spoil is when nobody wins three tricks, or a winner fails to win
all five after jinxing. The cards are dealt for a new hand but
only the new dealer contributes to the pot. Only when the
pot is won do all the players contribute to a new pot.

## 4 VINT

A member of the whist family, vint is a game for four players playing in partnerships of two.

**Rank of cards**

Cards A standard deck of cards is used. The cards rank normally, with ace high. The suits rank no trumps (highest), hearts, diamonds, clubs, and spades (lowest).

Objective Each partnership aims to make and fufill a bid by taking tricks.

Deal The entire deck is dealt out, one face-down card at a time to each player. The deal passes clockwise around the table with each round of play.

Bidding Starting with the dealer, each player in turn bids or passes.

Each bid indicates the intention to take six tricks plus the number called, in the suit name or with no trumps. Thus the lowest bid is one spade (i.e., taking seven tricks with spades as trumps); and the highest is seven no trumps (i.e., taking thirteen tricks).

A bid is overcalled by a bid of more tricks in the same suit, or the same number of tricks in a higher ranking suit or no trumps. When a player is overcalled he may call higher when his turn comes round again, even if the only other bidder is his partner.

Play is opened by the player to the left of the highest bidder, and proceeds in a clockwise direction around the table. Each player must follow suit if able to do so; if he cannot, he either plays a trump or discards. The winner of a trick leads to the next trick.

Scoring **Each partnership records its score on a scorepad or
piece of paper divided into two sections by a horizontal
line (as in bridge, page 37).**

Game points are entered below the line. Each partnership
scores for each trick taken – whether or not the bid is ful-
filled. However, the number of tricks bid determines the
value of each trick, ranging from ten points per trick for a
bid of one, 20 points per trick for a bid of two, and so on
up to 70 points per trick for a bid of seven.

The first partnership to score 500 game points wins the
game – even if it reaches this score part way through a
hand, and regardless of whether or not it won the bidding.

Bonus points are entered above the line. They are scored as
follows:

**a** winning a game, 1000 points;

**b** winning a rubber (two out of three games), 2000 points;

**c** "little slam" (12 tricks) made but not bid, 1000 points;

**d** little slam bid and made, 6000 points;

**e** "grand slam" (13 tricks) made but not bid, 2000 points;

**f** grand slam bid and made, 12,000 points.

Honor points are scored above the line and comprise the
a,k,q,j, and 10 of trumps and the other aces. In a trump
suit, the ace is counted twice, both as an honor and as an
ace. When playing no trumps, only the four aces are honors. The partnership holding the most honors scores ten
times the trick value for each honor held in trumps, or 25
times the trick value for each honor (ace) held when playing no trumps.

For example, if the final bid is three trumps, each trick is
worth 30 points and therefore each honor is worth 300
points (10 x 3=300).

If one partnership has a majority of aces and the other a
majority of honors, those two majorities are compared,

and the partnership that has the bigger majority scores for the difference.

For example, if side A has two honors and one ace, but side B has one honor and three aces, the two honors are deducted from the three aces and side B scores for one honor, worth ten times the trick value.

But if side A has three honors and one ace, and side B has one honor and three aces, neither side scores, as the three honors and the three aces cancel each other out.

If both sides hold two aces: at no trumps, neither side scores; at trumps, the side that wins most tricks scores for its honors.

Coronet Any player holding three aces or a sequence of three cards in a plain suit – known as a "coronet" – scores 500 points, entered above the line.

If a player holds the fourth ace, he scores a further 500 points; and each extra card in a sequence also scores a further 500 points.

If the sequence is in the trump suit, or in any suit when no trumps has been declared, coronet is worth double.

Unfulfilled bids If a partnership fails to make its bid, it is penalized for each undertrick by 100 times the value of each trick (entered above the line); but it also scores game points below the line for the number of tricks it took.

**Rank of suits**

For example, if the bidding partnership made a bid of five no trumps (i.e., 11 tricks) and took only eight tricks (i.e., it failed by three tricks), scoring would be as follows:

**a** 3x50x100=15,000 penalty points;

**b** 8x50=400 game points;

**c** the opponents score game points in the usual way for the number of tricks they took, i.e., 5x50=250 game points.

## *4* WHIST

Whist evolved in the eighteenth century from an earlier game called triumph. It has since given rise to a whole family of games, including the popular contract bridge and solo whist. The rules are comparatively simple, but a great deal of skill is needed to play really well.

### Rank

Players Whist is a game for four players, two playing against two as partners. Partnerships are decided by draw (see p 12).

Players sit around a table, with partners facing each other. By convention, players are referred to by the points of the compass, with North and South playing against East and West.

Cards A standard deck of 52 playing cards is used. Cards rank normally, with ace high.

The suits are not ranked, except that one suit is designated the trump suit for each hand. A card of the trump suit beats any card from any other suit.

Objective Players aim to win tricks. A trick consists of four cards, one played by each player.

Choice of first dealer is by high cut, with ace ranking low.

Shuffle and cut Any player has the right to shuffle, but the dealer has the right to shuffle last. The player to the right of the dealer cuts the cards and passes them to the dealer.

Deal Beginning with the player to his left and going clockwise, the dealer deals out all but one of the cards, face down and one at a time.

The remaining card is placed face up on the table and its suit indicates the trump suit. The dealer adds it to his hand when it is his turn to play.

Misdeal It is a misdeal if:

a more or fewer than 13 cards are dealt to any player; or

b any card other than the last one is exposed.

It is not a misdeal if a player is dealt two or more successive cards and the dealer rectifies the error at once.

If there has been a misdeal, players may agree to accept the deal after the error has been rectified.

Any player, however, has the right to demand a new deal until the first trick is completed. After that the deal must stand. If there is to be a redeal, players throw in their cards and the deal passes one player to the left.

Play The player to the dealer's left leads by placing any one of his cards face up in the center of the table.

Each of the other players in turn plays a card to the center of the table.

If a player has a card of the same suit as the card led, he must play this card. This is called "following suit," and failure to do so is penalized (see the section below on revoking). If he does not have a card of the suit led he may play any other card.

The trick is won:

a by the player of the highest trump card, or

b if no trump cards have been played, by the player of the highest card of the suit led.

The winner of one trick leads to the next. Play continues in this way until all 13 tricks of a hand have been played.

The deal passes to the next player in a clockwise direction.

The cards are reshuffled and cut for the new deal.

Revoking is failing to follow suit when able to do so.

A player is not penalized if he corrects his error before the trick is turned over, and the partner of a player who fails to follow suit may caution him by asking if he does not have any cards of the suit led.

Once the trick has been turned over but before play to the next trick has begun, the opposing partnership may challenge and claim a revoke.

Points penalties for revoking vary with the different scoring systems for the game.

A partnership cannot win the game in any hand in which it revokes. If both partnerships revoke in the same hand, all cards are thrown in and a new deal is made.

Calling If a player exposes a card, other than when playing it to a trick, he must leave it face up on the table until one of his opponents "calls" on him to play it to a trick where it will not cause a revoke.

Scoring There are a number of ways of scoring, but the following systems are most common.

English whist uses a five-point game, including the scoring of honors. Games are grouped into rubbers.

There are three ways of scoring game points.

1 The first six tricks do not score. From the seventh trick onward, one game point is scored for each trick taken.

2 The honors are a,k,q, and j of trumps. A partnership scores four game points if it is dealt all four honors, and three game points if dealt any three.

However, if both pairs reach five game points in the same deal, the trick points from that deal take precedence over the honors points. At least one trick must be taken in the last deal before declaring game. After game, the losers' honors score, if any, is no longer counted in their game points total.

3 There are three alternative rulings concerning the penalties for revoking:
  a the revoking pair loses three game points;
  b the revoking pair transfers three game points to its opponents; or
  c the opponents gain three game points.

After each game, additional points are scored by the winners as follows:
  a three points if the opponents had no game points;
  b two points if the opponents had one or two game points; and
  c one point if the opponents had three or four game points.

A rubber consists of three games.

The winners of two out of three games score two extra points for the rubber. All points are then totalled, and the partnership with the highest score wins.

If the first two games of a rubber are won by the same pair, a third game is not played.

In America a seven-point game is usual, with two ways of scoring game points.
  1 The first six tricks played do not score. Thereafter, each trick taken scores one game point.
  2 Revoking also provides game points, as the pair that failed to follow suit transfers two of its game points to the other pair.

The first pair to get seven game points scores the difference between seven and the losers' score.

## TERMS USED IN WHIST

Finessing consists of playing the third-best card of a suit when also holding the best – trusting that the opponents do not hold the second best.

Forcing is playing a suit in which another player is void.

Long trumps are the remaining trump or trumps left in a hand after all other trumps in the deck have been played.

Loose card is a card of no value.

Quarte is any four cards of the same suit in sequence.

Quarte major is a sequence of a,k,q,j, in the same suit.

Quinte is any five cards of the same suit in sequence.

See-saw occurs when each member of a partnership is trumping a suit, and each plays these suits to the other for that purpose.

Slam is winning every trick.

Tenace consists of holding the cards immediately above and below the opposing side's best in suit, for example ace and queen when the opponents hold the king.

# Gambling Games

## INTRODUCTION

Included in this section are card games that are played primarily for gambling. This is not to suggest that some of them are any less interesting or demanding to play than some of the games included as general card games in section 1 of this book. Indeed, blackjack and poker in particular both call for high levels of skill from their players. A number of the games included here are professional games rarely found outside casinos and gambling clubs. Others are private games suitable for more general play.

Casino and gambling club games Depending on the game being played, betting in casinos and gambling clubs may be either against the house management acting as banker or against other players. As well as winning money by acting as banker in some games, managements charge players for the services of their officials and also take a percentage cut when money changes hands between players. Casino and gambling club games described in this section are: baccarat/chemin de fer, blackjack, card craps, faro, monte bank, poker, skinball, trente et quarante, and ziginette. Some of these games are also suitable for playing at home.

Private banking games In these games one player acts as banker, taking on the bets of all the others. He also has a different role from the other players in play. But unlike in casino banking games no one person is banker continuously. Instead, to equalize players' chances, the role of banker moves around – often after every hand. Private banking games included in this section are: ace-deuce-jack, banker and broker, Blücher, card put-and-take, Chinese fan-tan, hoggenheimer, horse race, lansquenet, monte bank (private version), Polish red dog, red and black, red dog (banking version), and slippery Sam.

Pool games In these private gambling games there is no
   banker. Instead all players' bets take the form of contributions to a central pool. In many games the entire pool is
   then won by a single player – usually at the end of every
   hand – but in other games the pool acts as a reservoir of
   chips, from which payments are made to players according
   to their success. Pool games included here are: bango, brag,
   injun, Kentucky derby, red dog, thirty-five, thirty-one, and
   yablon.

## NOTES ON BETTING

Betting chips When playing private gambling games, any
   counters, matchsticks, or other agreed objects may be used.
An ante is a contribution to a central betting pool made
   before a deal. It may be required from all the players or
   sometimes only from the dealer.
Odds The recognized forms in which payment odds are
   stated are:
   **a** "x to y" (e.g., 30 to 1, also written as 30-1), in which
     case the player's stake is returned in addition to the win
     payment (giving a player who staked one chip at 30 to 1
     a return of 31 chips); or
   **b** "x for y" (e.g., 30 for 1), in which case the player's stake
     is returned as part of the win payment (giving a player a
     total return of 30 chips in our example).

## 2+ ACE-DEUCE-JACK

The odds in this game are so heavily loaded that it is found only as a hustler's game. The hustler simply has to ensure that the sucker is on the wrong side of the particular version being played – in which case the sucker will on average lose his money in nearly 60 plays out of 100.

Equipment
  **1** one standard deck of 52 cards;
  **2** money for betting.

Players Two or more can play. One player is banker.

### WITH THE HUSTLER AS BANKER

Objective Players bet that none of the three cards exposed in
  play will be an ace, deuce (2), or jack.

Betting limits are agreed beforehand.

Shuffle and cut The banker shuffles. Any player has the right
  to shuffle but the banker has the right to shuffle last. Any
  player other than the banker then cuts the deck.

Preparation
  **1** The banker takes three cards face down from the bot-
    tom of the deck, making sure that no one sees their
    denominations. These three cards are ruled "dead," and
    are put to one side.
  **2** The banker then cuts two groups of cards from the
    deck, taking care that no one sees the bottom of each
    cut. He places each group face down alongside the deck,
    so that there are now three groups of cards on the table.

Bet and play Each player but the banker may place a bet. The
  banker then turns the three sections face up, exposing the
  bottom card of each section.

Settlement If any one of the three cards is an ace, deuce, or
  jack, the banker takes all bets. If none of the cards is one

Deal

Show

of these denominations, the banker pays 1 to 1 on all bets.

Continuing play All cards in the deck are collected, shuffled, and then cut for the next turn of play.

## WITH THE SUCKER AS BANKER

Sometimes the sucker wants to be banker. The hustler then suggests the following version, in which players bet on which denomination will appear. "You bank, and we'll do the guessing too," says the hustler. "You can't help but win."

On a big hustle, with a planned victim, the hustler may set up this version from the beginning.

Objective Players bet that one of the three cards exposed in play will be one of three specified denominations.

Betting limits are agreed beforehand.

Shuffle, cut, and preparation are as for the version with the hustler as banker.

Betting Each player but the banker may place a bet.

Sometimes the betting denominations are as in the first version, i.e., ace, deuce, jack.

But usually the three denominations change for each
hand, and are chosen by the players as they place their
bets.

This "guessing" process gives the banker the impression
that the odds are with him.

Play The banker turns the three sections face up, exposing the
bottom card of each section.

Settlement If none of the three cards is one of the three
denominations bet on, the banker takes all bets. But if any
one or more of the denominations appear, the banker pays
1 to 1 on all bets. (Note that he pays only 1 to 1 even if
two or three denominations appear).

Continuing play is as in the first version.

# 2+ BACCARAT/CHEMIN DE FER

Games of the baccarat and chemin de fer family originated in the baccarat that became popular in French casinos in the 1830s. In the present century they have travelled from Europe to the United States, from the United States back to Europe, and from both points to casinos throughout the world. This process has resulted in wide variations in playing rules, and what is called "baccarat" in one casino may more nearly resemble the "chemin de fer" of another. Three basic forms of play are described here.

**Card values**

1  2  3  4  5  6  7  8  9  0  0  0  0

Players At least two, but usually seven or more. Often persons without seats may also bet.

Croupier The casino provides a croupier, who assists players in making and settling bets, advises on rules and odds, and takes the casino's cut. The croupier also plays the "bank" hand when the game is banked by the casino. The casino makes an hourly charge for the croupier and his assistants, and for supervising the game.

The objective is to bet on a winning hand, i.e., on a hand with a higher point value than the other hand(s).

Hands are of two or three cards.

Cards score as follows:

**a** face (court) cards and 10s, zero;

b aces, one point;

c any other card, its numerical value.
   When scoring a hand tens are ignored – e.g., five plus seven counts as two not 12. Hence the highest possible score for a hand is nine.

The basic sequence of play is:

1 placing of bets;

2 dealing of hands;

3 receipt of another card on request;

4 comparison of hands and settlement of bets.

Equipment Several standard decks of playing cards are used. Other equipment is:

a a heavy table, padded and covered with green baize, and marked with a layout for 9 or 12 players;

b a card-holding box or "shoe," from which the cards are dealt one at a time;

c a discard box, positioned beneath a slot in the table;

d wooden palettes for distributing cards and payments to the players.

## CHEMIN DE FER

The distinctive features of the "chemin de fer" game are that: the role of banker rotates rapidly among the players; only a bank hand and one non-bank hand are dealt; bets can only be placed against the bank.

Cards Six or eight standard decks of cards are used.

The shuffle;

1 The croupier places the decks face down on the table.

2 Players and croupier take groups of cards and shuffle them, and then shuffle the groups of cards into each other.

3 The croupier gathers the cards, gives them a final shuffle in large groups, gathers them all into a single deck, and cuts the deck several times.

**Chemin de fer layout**

4 The croupier asks one of the players to make a final cut. (Often the croupier makes the actual cut, after the player has inserted an indicator (a blank or advertising) card at the point where the cut should be made).

5 Often the croupier then inserts a second indicator card into the deck, around eight or ten cards from the bottom, to give warning of the end of the shuffled cards.

6 The croupier places the deck face down in the shoe.

7 The croupier deals three or four cards from the shoe, shows them, and discards them.

First choice of banker is either:

**a** by lot;

**b** by auction, with the players bidding the amounts they are prepared to put forward as the "bank";

**c** by acceptance, the bank being offered first to the first player to the croupier's left or right (according to house rules), and then on around the table clockwise or counterclockwise, until a player accepts the bank.

The croupier passes the shoe to the first banker.

Amount of the bank On the first play of a turn as banker, the bank is:

**a** what the player bid for it if the bank was gained by auction;

**b** any figure the banker wishes to put at risk if he gained the bank by lot or acceptance.

On all subsequent plays of a turn as banker, the bank is the amount stated on the first play plus subsequent winnings.

Betting takes place before any cards are dealt.

Players can only place bets against the bank – i.e., they bet that the bank will lose.

The total of bets on a single play is limited to the amount of the bank – the banker is never liable for payment of bets in excess of this.

**Natural 8s**

**Natural 9s**

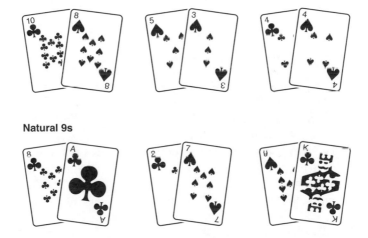

The player to the banker's right (or left, according to house rules) has first bet. Any amount of the bank he does not "fade" (bet against), may be bet against by the next player in turn. Betting passes around the table until the entire bank is covered by several bets, someone has called "Banco," or everyone has bet who wishes to. Bystanders may bet if there is part of the bank left to cover or if one of them calls "Banco."

If the bank is not completely covered, the amount not faded is safe for the hand and is kept by the banker whether he wins or loses.

"Banco" A player or bystander who wishes to bet against the entire bank makes this known by calling "Banco."

A call of "Banco" makes all other bets void.

When two or more wish to banco, a player who bancoed on the preceding hand has precedence over all others.

Otherwise, a seated player has precedence over a bystander and the order of priority among players belongs to the player who is earliest in the betting order.

Play is as follows.

1 The banker deals two hands of two cards each. The cards are dealt singly and face down, alternately to the table and to the banker himself. The "table" hand represents all players betting against the bank. It is played by whoever made the highest bet against the bank. If there are two equal bets, the player nearer the banker in the betting order has priority.

2 The player and banker examine their hands without showing them.

3 If the player's hand totals eight or nine, it is a "natural," and is immediately declared and turned face up. If it is an eight hand, the player calls "La petite"; if a nine he calls "La grande."

**4** If the player's hand is a natural, the banker shows his own cards. If only the player's hand is a natural, all bets against the bank win. If both hands are naturals, a nine beats an eight. If both hands are naturals of the same number, it is a "stand-off" and all bets are returned.

**5** If the player's hand does not contain a natural, he says "Pass." The banker then examines his own hand, and if it contains a natural he declares it immediately and wins all bets.

**6** If both hands have been examined, and neither contains a natural, the player may "draw" (request another card, face up) or "stay" (not request another card). His decision must be based on the rules of mathematical advisability (see table overleaf), except that in some games a player who has bancoed is allowed to ignore these rules.

**7** Whether the banker then draws another card or stays depends on the card that he has just given to the player (see table overleaf), except that in some games the banker is allowed the option when holding a five hand and having given a four. If a player has bancoed and is allowed to use his judgment, the banker may also ignore the rules for drawing or staying.

**8** The hands are shown. If there has been any error, the banker must reconstruct the play as it should have been.

**Winning** The hand totalling nine or nearest nine wins.

**a** If the totals are the same, all bets are returned.

**b** If the banker has won, he collects all bets less any casino levy. In most countries the casino levies a percentage (usually 5%) on bankers' winnings. Sometimes the winnings on a player's first hand as banker are exempt from the levy. (In countries where a percentage levy is illegal, all casino profits come from the hourly rate charged by the casino).

c  If the banker has lost, each player collects the amount of
   the bank that he had covered.

Keeping the bank If the banker has won a hand, he may keep
the bank for the next hand.

In this case, the new bank comprises the original bank
plus the winnings after any levy.

A player who keeps the bank is not permitted to remove
any of his winnings between hands.

If the original bank plus winnings exceeds the house
limit on bets, the excess is not at stake.

Passing the bank If the banker has won a hand but chooses
not to keep the bank, he may take his winnings and pass
the bank.

In this case:

a  the bank is offered to the players in turn until one of
   them accepts it, after which the new banker decides the
   amount of his bank; or

b  the house croupier holds an informal auction, and the
   bank passes to a player who will put up a bank equal to
   the one that has just been passed.

| **Player** | | |
|---|---|---|
| *Player holding* | *Action* | |
| 0,1,2,3,or 4 | draw | |
| 5 | optional | |
| 6 or 7 | stay | |
| 8 or 9 | face | |
| **Banker** | | |
| *After giving* | *Banker stays on* | *Banker draws on* |
| 0 or 1 | 4,5,6,7 | 3,2,1, or 0 |
| 9 | 4,5,6,7, (or3) | 2,1,0, (or3) |
| 8 | 3,4,5,6, or 7 | 2,1, or 0 |
| 7 or 6 | 7 | 6,5,4,3,2,1, or 0 |
| 5 or 4 | 6 or 7 | 5,4,3,2,1, or 0 |
| 3 or 2 | 5,6, or 7 | 4,3,2,1, or 0 |
| Player has stood | 6 or 7 | 5,4,3,2,1, or 0 |

**Baccarat baque layout**

**Losing the bank** If the banker loses a hand, the bank is offered to the players in turn – as when the banker chooses to pass the bank. (An auction is not held.)

**Reshuffling** The cards are not reshuffled until at least 5/6 of the deck has been used – and usually not until the last few cards are reached.

## BACCARAT BANQUE

Also known as baccarat à deux tables (double take baccarat), baccarat banque is the oldest European form of the game.
The distinctive features of baccarat banque are that:

a the role of the banker rotates more slowly among the players or may be held permanently by the casino or concessionaires;

b one bank hand and two non-bank hands are dealt;

c bets can be placed only against the bank.

Except when specifically described here, the rules are the same as for chemin de fer.

**Cards** Three standard decks are used.

**Banker** Sometimes the role of the banker is held permanently by the casino – or by concessionaires who pay the casino a percentage of their takings.

Otherwise the procedure is as follows.

a The bank is auctioned to the highest bidder, who pays $2^1/_2$% of his bid to the casino.

b The banker does not lose the bank if he loses a hand, but holds it until he loses the whole bank or passes.

c The banker cannot withdraw any money from the bank unless he passes – but any part of the bank not bet against on a hand is not at risk.

d When a bank is lost or passed, the bank is again auctioned. As before, the casino takes a $2^1/_2$% cut from the winning bidder.

Betting and play differ from chemin de fer in the following ways.

a The banker deals three hands – one to his right, one to his left, and one to himself.

b Bets against the bank may be placed on either the right or the left hand, or on both hands. Betting on both hands is called betting "*à cheval*" (on horseback).

c Priority for betting on the right table hand begins with the player sitting to the banker's right; for the left table hand, with the player to the banker's left. Calling "Banco" is usually allowed, but not always.

d Each hand is played by a player on the appropriate side of the table. The player playing the right hand always plays first. On the first deal, the hands are played by the players nearest the dealer on his right and left sides.

Thereafter, a player continues playing one of the table hands until he loses a hand After a player has lost a hand, the right to play that side's hand passes to the next player in rotation.

e Table players are bound by the same staying and drawing rules as in chemin de fer. The banker may stay

**Baccarat-Chemin de fer layout**

or draw on any hand, and will obviously concentrate on beating the hand on which most money has been bet.

**f** Players betting *à cheval* lose only if the bank wins both hands, and win only if the bank loses both hands. Otherwise their bets are returned.

## BACCARAT-CHEMIN DE FER (LAS VEGAS)

The distinct Las Vegas form of the game may be called baccarat, chemin de fer, or baccarat chemin de fer.

The distinctive features of the Las Vegas game are that :

**a** the role of the banker is usually held permanently by the casino, although it may rotate slowly among the players;

**b** one non-bank hand is dealt;

**c** bets can be placed either with or against the bank.

Cards Six or eight standard decks are used.

Banker When the role of banker rotates among the players, the rules for the bank are the same as for baccarat banque.

More usually the casino keeps the bank, and the procedure is as follows.

**a** The limit on bets on a hand is not the size of the bank but the house betting limit. (The house betting limit will, however, sometimes be raised when a player requests this.)

**b** There is no banco bet and no need for rules of precedence in betting.

**c** A single player can play.

**d** The casino takes a cut (usually 5%) from winning bets that have bet the bank to win.

Betting Players may bet with or against the bank.

A player betting the bank to win places his bet on the appropriate numbered section at the table center.

A player betting the bank to lose places his bet on the numbered section in front of him.

A player may also back the bank to have a natural eight or nine, and if successful, he is paid the odds of nine to one.

Play is as in chemin de fer, except that all players' and banker's options are removed to become draw plays. Thus:

**a** a player must draw if holding a hand totalling five;

**b** the banker must draw if holding a three hand when he has given a nine, or a five hand after giving a four.

# 3-9 BANGO

In this card variant of the bingo played in bingo halls, players turn over playing cards instead of covering rows of numbers on a score card.

Equipment
  **1** two standard 52-card decks, with different backs;
  **2** betting chips.

Players The game is for three to ten players.

Objective Each player aims to be the first player to turn all his face up cards face down.

Choice of first dealer is by deal: first ace to appear (see page 13).

Shuffle and cut The dealer and the player to his left each shuffle one deck of cards. Each deck is then offered separately to the player to the dealer's right to be cut as usual (see page 13).

Ante Before each deal, each player including the dealer puts an equal agreed amount into the pool.

Deal From one deck, the dealer deals five cards to each player including himself, dealing them face up and one at a time. The rest of this deck is then put to one side out of play.

Play The players arrange their cards face up in front of them. The dealer then takes the second deck of cards and deals the top card face up onto the table, stating its rank and suit as he does so.

If any player including the dealer has the identical card from the first deck face up in front of him, he now turns that card face down.

The dealer then takes the next card from the top of the second deck and deals it face up onto the table, stating its rank and suit as he does so.

Play continues in this way until one player has turned all his cards face down. He announces this by calling "Bango."

Checking The dealer checks the hand of the player who called

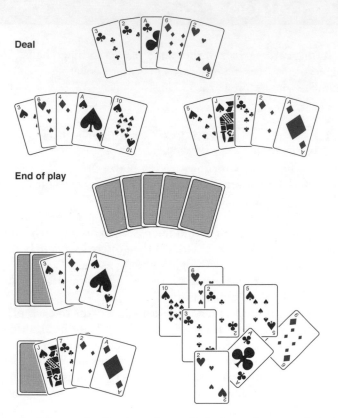

**Deal**

**End of play**

against the cards that have been dealt from the second deck, and if no mistake has been made that player wins the pool.

Change of dealer The deal passes one player to the left after each hand.

## BANGO VARIANT

In this game players take into account only the rank of the cards turned up by the dealer. The dealer calls the rank and players turn face down all cards of that rank in their hands.

# 2+ BANKER AND BROKER

This simple game has very fast betting action. Also known as Dutch bank and blind hooker, it is played in a number of slightly different ways.

Equipment:
  1 one standard deck of 52 cards;
  2 betting chips (or cash).

Players two or more.

Rank of cards is normal (ace high). Suits are not ranked.

Objective Players try to bet on a card of higher denomination than that bet on by the banker.

Choice of first banker is by high cut (see page 13).

Shuffle and cut are normal (see page 13).

Betting limits are as agreed.

Basic form of play
  1 The banker cuts a number of sections from the deck: one for himself and one for each of the other players.
  2 The other players lay bets on their sections by placing chips (or cash) beside them.
  3 The banker turns all the sections face up to show the bottom cards.
  4 The banker collects the bets on sections showing a lower denomination card than his own. He pays 1 to 1 on sections showing a card of higher denomination.

Points of variation
  1 Discarding the bottom card: either the banker removes and discards the bottom card from the deck before cutting; or he leaves an unused bottom section after cutting.
  2 Timing of bets: bets are placed either before or after the sections are cut.
  3 Number of sections cut: either the banker cuts one section for each player and one for himself (up to a limit of

**Deal**

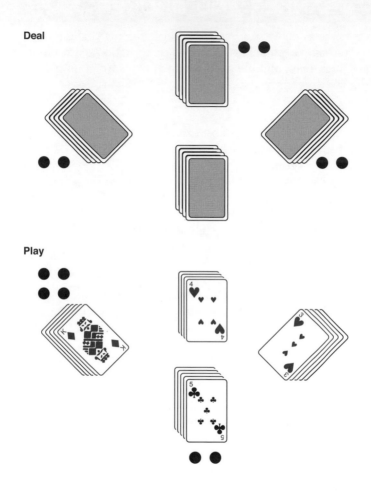

**Play**

seven), and each player may only bet on the section cut
for him; or the banker cuts three sections, two for the
players and one for himself, and each player bets at will
on either or both of the players' sections; or the banker

cuts as many sections as he likes, varying the number
from deal to deal if he wishes, and the players bet as
they please but leave one section for the banker.

4 When the banker's denomination is the same as that bet
on by a player: either the bank wins, or the player's bet
is returned.

5 Change of banker: either the bank passes one player to
the left after each deal or set number of deals; or players
cut for the bank after each deal or after a set number of
deals; or the bank is passed when a player bets on an ace
– if two players (or player and banker) both have an ace,
or if two players have bet on the same ace, the deck is
cut and the bank goes to the player with the higher card.

## 2–4 BLACKJACK

Blackjack is the world's most widespread banking card game. It is also known as BJ, twenty-one, vingt-et-un, pontoon, and vanjohn. There are two main forms: that with a "changing bank" – the usual private game; and that with a "permanent bank"– the casino game. The two forms of the game have many features in common.

**Card values**

11  10  10  10  10  9  8  7  6  5  4  3  2  1

Players Games are played by a banker/dealer and from one to six or seven or more other players (private games can have as many as 14 other players).

Value of cards Standard playing cards are used.

   **a** An ace counts as 1 or 11, at the option of the holder.

   **b** A "face" card counts as 10.

   **c** All other cards count their numerical face value.

   A joker, if used, is only an indicator card and does not enter play.

Objective Each player tries to get a higher point count in his hand than the dealer – but the value of his hand must not exceed 21. A hand whose point count exceeds 21 is immediately lost.

   A two-card hand with a value of exactly 21 (a face card, or 10, and an ace) is called a "natural" or a "blackjack."

Betting With the exception of the dealer, each player bets at the beginning of each hand. Only bets against the dealer are allowed.

At the end of each hand, the dealer pays those with point counts higher than his own.

Onlookers may be allowed to bet on any player's hand, but not on the dealer's hand.

Basic sequence of play

1 Betting, and deal of two cards to each player.
2 Receipt of further cards on request by each player in turn – with the dealer last.
3 Settlement of bets.

**Examples of 21-point hands**

**Examples of 21-point hands**

## BLACKJACK WITH A CHANGING BANK

Cards A standard deck of 52 cards (or sometimes two decks shuffled together), plus a joker that does not enter play.

Choice of first banker/dealer is by deal: usually the first ace, but in some versions the first black jack, decides (see page 13 for procedure).

Change of banker/dealer There are two alternative systems.

1 Each player has five deals as banker/dealer, after which the role passes to the next player to the left.

2 The deal passes whenever there is a hand in which a "natural" is dealt – i.e., when a player's first two cards total 21.

The player with the natural has the option of becoming the new banker/dealer on the completion of that hand.

When two or more players hold naturals, the player nearest the dealer's left has the first option.

If all players with naturals refuse the option, the present banker/dealer continues – unless he also refuses, in which case the role is offered around the table clockwise, beginning with the player to the immediate left of the present banker/dealer. If all refuse, a new banker/dealer is chosen in the same way as the original one.

Auctioning the bank Private games are occasionally run so that the banker/dealer is always decided by auction.

In all private games, however, a player who no longer wants to be banker/dealer may, between hands, put the bank and deal up for auction.

However, if there are no bids he loses the bank and deal to the first player to his left (or, if that player refuses, the bank and deal are offered clockwise around the table until accepted or until a new dealer has to be chosen in the original way).

Shuffle and cut

1 The dealer shuffles the cards. (Any player has the right to shuffle at any time but the dealer has the right to shuffle last).

2 Any other player cuts the cards. If several players want to cut, each of them must be allowed to do so.

3 The deck is placed, face down, on an upturned joker,
which acts as an indicator card. (If no joker is available,
the dealer "burns" a card – i.e., he takes the top card
from the deck, shows it to all players and places it face
up at the bottom of the deck.

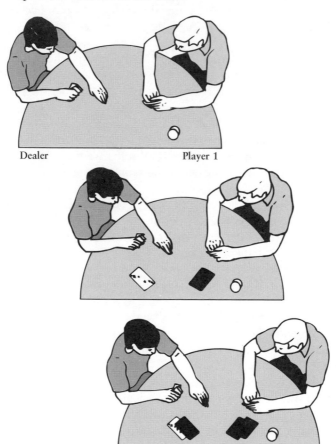

Dealer                              Player 1

An ace may not be burned, and if an ace is turned up the deck must be reshuffled and cut again.)

**Betting limits** The dealer decides the minimum and maximum allowable bets, and can alter them at will between hands.

**Bet and deal for the two forms of the private game**

The betting and dealing stage of the private game takes two main forms.

a As in the casino blackjack game, the players place their bets before they have seen any of their own cards.

b As in the pontoon game of the British Commonwealth, the players bet after looking at their own first card.

There is no standard way of distinguishing between these: American rules for private blackjack games may quote the pontoon form, while a few Americans use "pontoon" to mean standard blackjack. We have used the name "blackjack" for form (a), and "pontoon" for form (b).

**Bet and deal: "blackjack"**

1 Before any cards are dealt, each player but the dealer puts his bet in front of him in full view.

2 The dealer deals one card to each player but himself, face down, beginning with the player to his immediate left and going clockwise. He then deals one card to himself, face up.

3 A second card is then dealt to each player, including the dealer, face down.

4 If the dealer's face up card is an ace or a card worth 10 points, the dealer looks at his face down ("hole") card to see if he has a natural.

If he has, he immediately announces this and turns his cards face up. The other players then show their own cards. The dealer collects the bets of all players not having naturals; players with naturals usually have their bets returned, but in some versions of the game they also pay the dealer.

5 If the dealer's face up card is not an ace or a 10 point, or if he finds that he does not have a natural, then the player to the dealer's left commences play.

## Bet and deal: "pontoon"

1 The dealer deals one card face down to each player, including himself, beginning with the player to his immediate left and going clockwise.

Each player, including the dealer, looks at his own card.

2 Each player, except the dealer, puts his bet in front of him in full view.

The dealer may call for all bets to be doubled. Any player refusing to double drops out of the hand and loses his original bet.

If the dealer has doubled, any other player may then redouble his own individual bet.

3 The dealer deals a second card, face up, to each player including himself.

4 The dealer then considers if he has a natural, as in the "blackjack" game. If he has a natural, he collects from each player twice the amount of that player's current bet – except that from any other player with a natural he collects only that player's bet.

5 If the dealer's face up card is not an ace or a 10 point, or if he finds that he does not have a natural, then the player to the dealer's left commences play.

**First player's hand** The player to the dealer's left looks at his hand and commences play.

a If he has 21 points, he shows his cards, claims a natural, and is paid by the dealer unless the dealer also has a natural.

b If his card total is less than 21 points, he has the option of taking further cards.

If he feels that the points count he already holds is closer to 21 than the dealer is likely to achieve, then he can say "I stand," and he receives no further cards.

If he decides to attempt a total closer to 21, he can say "I draw" or "Hit me," and receives another card face up.

He can repeat this until he is satisfied with his hand, when he says "I stay." However, if his points count goes over 21 he must announce this immediately by saying "I bust."

If a player goes "bust," he turns his cards face up, the dealer collects his bet, and the player's cards are placed face up at the bottom of the deck. He is then out of the game until the next hand.

**Subsequent player's hands** Once a player has said "I stand," "I stay," or "I bust," play passes to the player to his left. This continues until all players have had the chance of drawing further cards.

**Dealer's hand** The dealer plays last.

If all players have bust, he simply discards his cards and begins the next hand.

Otherwise he turns his hidden card face up, and decides to stay or to "draw" (giving himself further cards, face up) until he is satisfied or he exceeds 21 (busts).

Once the dealer's hand is completed, all hands still in the game are shown.

**Doubling down** is a procedure allowed in the "permanent bank" game and often incorporated in the "blackjack" form of the "changing bank" game.

In his turn a player may, after looking at his first two cards, decide to "double down" – i.e., with his original two cards face up, he doubles his original bet and receives one further card only, face down. He may not look at this card until the dealer turns it up after all other players and the dealer have completed their turns of play.

(Sometimes doubling down is allowed only when the first two cards total 10 or 11.)

Buying is a procedure sometimes played in the "pontoon" form of the "changing bank" game.

At his turn, a player may "buy" a card: instead of receiving a further card face up, he adds to his original bet and receives a further card face down. The amount of the additional bet must be at least the minimum, but no greater than the original bet.

Buying can be repeated for further cards if the player wishes; or he may "twist" – i.e., draw further cards face up in the normal way. However, once a player has twisted he is not allowed to buy.

Splitting pairs is a procedure allowed in the "permanent bank" game, and often incorporated in both the "blackjack" and "pontoon" forms of the "changing bank" game.

If a player's first two cards are a pair (e.g., two 6's or two kings), they may be "split" if the player wishes – i.e., they may be treated as the basis of two separate hands.

In his turn of play, the player with the pair turns it face up – one card to his right and one to his left. He places his original bet by one of the cards and an equal amount by the other. The dealer then deals one card, face up, to the card to the player's right – after which the player plays this hand off in the normal way. When he has finished (stood, stayed, or bust), he receives another face up card, dealt to the card to his left, and then plays off this hand.

If, on splitting and receiving a new card other than an ace, a player forms a further pair, he may split the pair again if he again puts out an amount equal to his original bet. Any further pairs may also be split.

If aces are split, one card may be drawn to each split ace.

A 21 point count made in two cards after splitting does not count as a natural – it is paid off at even money and the bank does not change hands.

Irregularities

a If a player is missed on the first round of dealing, he must ask for a card from the top of the deck before the second round of dealing begins, or must stay out for that deal.

b If a player receives two cards on the first round of dealing, he has the choice of: discarding either one, or playing both hands with his original bet on each.

c If a player in the "pontoon" game receives his first card face up, he can either: bet, and receive the next card face down, or drop out of that hand.

d If a player receives two cards on the second round of the dealing, he discards either one.

e If a card appears face up in the deck, a player has the choice of accepting or refusing it.

f If a player receives a card that he did not ask for, he may either keep or discard it.

g If a player has stood on a total of over 21, he pays the dealer twice his original bet even if the dealer has bust.

(All discards are placed face up at the bottom of the deck. They may not be claimed by the next player in turn.)

Settlement If the dealer goes bust, he pays all players who have not bust.

If he does not bust, he collects the bets of all players with a lower total, and pays out to players with a higher total who have not bust.

Where a player and the dealer have the same total, rules vary. Sometimes the player's bet is returned, but often (more commonly in the "pontoon" game) the dealer collects.

All winning bets are paid off by the dealer at even money, except that a player who has beaten the bank with a natural is paid off at two to one.

Continuing play As each bet is settled, the player's cards are given to the dealer and placed face up at the bottom of the deck.

Play of further hands then continues from the same deck, without a shuffle, until the face up cards are reached. All face up cards are then shuffled by the dealer, cut by another player, and a joker or burnt card is used as an indicator as before.

Bonus payments In the "pontoon" game, a player other than the dealer can win his bet with certain special hands. These hands are declared and paid off as soon as they have been achieved.

**a** A hand with five or more cards totalling 21 or under: for a five-card hand, a player receives double his bet; for a six-card hand, a player receives four times his bet; for a seven-card hand, eight times his bet; and so on.

The win stands even if the dealer achieves a total nearer to 21.

**b** Triple 7s: for a 21 made with three 7s, a player receives three times his bet.

**c** 8,7,6: for a 21 made with an 8,7, and 6, a player receives double his bet.

None of these is a special hand if held by the dealer. They are then judged only according to their points

**Bonus payments**

count: a banker's five-card hand is beaten by a player's hand with a higher point count, and a player's win on a natural stands against a banker's triple 7s or 8,7,6. (See sample play below.)

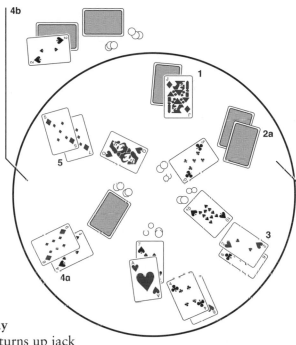

**Sample play**

1 Dealer turns up jack
2a Player 1 stands (blackjack)
2b Player 1 stands (pontoon)
3 Player 2 splits
4a Player 3 doubles down (blackjack)
4b Player 3 buys (pontoon)
5 Player 4 busts

## BLACKJACK WITH A PERMANENT BANK

Equipment:

1 a regulation blackjack table, with six or seven betting spaces on the layout;

2 a rack containing betting chips;

3 a card-dealing box ("shoe");

4 a discard receiver;

5 one, two, or four standard 52-card decks, shuffled together;

6 two blank or advertising cards to be used as indicator cards – one to cut the deck and one to mark the end of the shuffled cards.

Participants:

1 a permanent house dealer/banker;

2 one to six or seven active players.

There is also a casino observer/supervisor, who controls play and whose decision is final.

Shuffle and cut

1 Only the dealer shuffles. He may reshuffle at any time.

2 After he has shuffled, he offers the deck to a player to cut. (Casino regulations may require an "indicator card" cut, in which the dealer holds the deck and the player inserts a blank or advertising card to indicate the point where he wants the deck cut. The dealer then cuts the deck, with the indicator card going to the bottom.)

3 In many casinos, the dealer then inserts a second indicator card about 40 cards from the bottom of the deck to prevent the last cards of any shuffle coming into play.

4 If a shoe is being used, the dealer places the deck in it, face down.

5 The dealer then deals a few (usually three) cards from the top of the deck and places them to one side, out of play.

Betting limits **The casino sets the minimum and maximum bet limits. (A casino will often agree to raise the maximum at a player's request.)**

Bet and deal

1 Before any cards are dealt, each player except the dealer puts his bet on the layout in the betting space directly in front of him. If empty betting spaces are available, players are allowed in most casinos to bet on and receive more than one hand.

2 The dealer deals one card to each player, beginning with the player to his immediate left and going clockwise, and then deals one card to himself.

Then in the same way he deals a second card to each player and to himself. Whether cards are dealt face up or face down varies from casino to casino (see the section below on dealing possibilities, and page 15).

3 If the dealer's face up card is a 10 point or an ace, he looks at his face down card to see if he has a natural, exactly as in the "changing bank" game. If he has a natural, he immediately collects the bets of all players who do not have naturals; players with naturals always have their bets returned.

(In some casinos, to prevent cheating by the collaboration of a player and a crooked dealer, the dealer is not allowed to look at, or sometimes even to deal, his own face down card until all other player's hands are completed).

4 If the dealer's face up card is not a 10 point or an ace; or if he finds that he does not have a natural; or if he may not look at his face down card: then the player to the dealer's left commences play.

Dealing possibilities **The usual arrangements are listed here, and shown in the diagrams.**

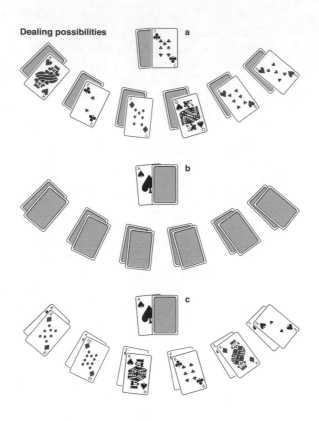

a Dealer and all players: first card received face down, second face up.
b Dealer's first card face up, second face down; players' first and second cards face down.
c Dealer's first card face up, second face down; players' first and second cards face up.
d Dealer's first card face down, second face up; players' first and second cards face up.

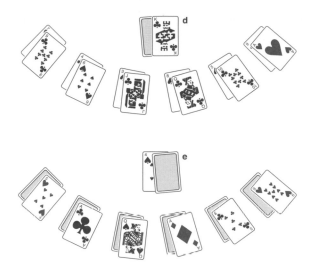

c Dealer's first card face up, second face down; players'
first card face down, second face up.

Insurance bet If the dealer's face up card is an ace, players are
in many casinos allowed to place an insurance bet against
being beaten by a dealer's natural.

Before the dealer looks at his face down card, a player
wishing for insurance puts out an amount equal to half his
present bet. If the dealer has a natural, the player gets two to
one on his insurance bet; otherwise the insurance bet is lost.

Play If a player is playing more than one hand, he must play
out the hand farthest to his right before looking at his next
hand or hands.

Play is as for the private game, with splitting and doubling down but no buying allowed.

Dealer's play In the "permanent bank" game, the dealer has
no decisions to make:

### Seven and a half: values

a  if his count is, or reaches, 17 or more – he must stay;

b  if the count is 16 or less he must draw;

c  when he holds an ace he must accept a count of the ace as 11 and not draw if this gives him 17 or more without busting. (As the dealer has no option in his play, it does not matter if he sees the players' hands. For this reason players' hands are dealt face up in some casinos.)

Settlement is as for the "changing bank" game, except that:

a  when a player and the dealer have the same total, the player's bet is always returned;

b  naturals are paid at odds of three to two, not two to one;

c  there are no bonus payments.

Irregularities are treated in the same way as in the "changing bank" game.

## VARIANTS OF BLACKJACK

There are a number of games whose basic differences from blackjack are the card values and the points count that the players are attempting to reach.

## SEVEN AND A HALF

This is an Italian-American variant of blackjack. The rules are as for blackjack with the following exceptions.

Cards The 8s,9s, and 10s are removed from a standard deck to give a deck of 40 cards. No indicator card is used.

Objective Players aim to get a total points count of $7^1/2$: non-face cards count their face value, with aces 1 point; the king of diamonds can be given the value of any card the holder chooses; other face cards each count $^1/2$ point.

Play The player receiving the king of diamonds in a preliminary deal becomes the dealer for the first hand.

The dealer decides and alters betting limits at will. A player not wishing to bet on a round can say "Deal me out."

The deal is one card face down, after which a player stands or draws one or more cards face up.

$7^1/2$ in two cards is announced and settled immediately. Unless the dealer also has $7^1/2$ in two cards, it is paid double and wins the bank. (If two or more players have $7^1/2$ in two cards, the bank goes to the player nearest the banker's left.)

Bust – 8 or more with any number of cards – is also settled immediately.

The dealer then plays, and pays surviving players with a higher total. He returns the bet of any player with the same total as himself.

The dealer shuffles the deck after every round.

## TEN AND A HALF

Ten and a half or *saton pong* is the Dutch equivalent of seven and a half. The rules are as for seven and a half, with the following exceptions.

It is played with a standard 52-card deck.

Players aim for total points count of $10^1/2$. A count of $10^1/2$

**Ten and a half: values**

is announced immediately. $10^{1}/_{2}$ in two cards is paid double.

The dealer places discards at the bottom of the deck, face up. The deal changes by passing to the left when the whole deck has been used – though the current dealer is allowed to reshuffle used cards to complete a half finished hand.

## MACAO

Macao or "three naturals" is a variant of blackjack that was popular in the 1920s and 1930s.

It is played with a standard 52-card deck.

Players aim for a total points count of 9 in one or more cards.

**Macao: values**

Card values are: zero for face cards and 10s; the face value of all other cards (with aces counting 1).

The deal is one card, face down.

A player with a 9,8, or 7 in one card announces it immediately. The dealer then shows his own card, and pays if the player's card is higher.

For a 9 in one card a winning player is paid three times his bet, for an 8 twice, and for a 7 one for one.

Players and dealer without a 7,8, or 9 in one card then draw one or more cards toward a total of 9.

The dealer then collects and then pays out on remaining bets. A player who ties with the dealer has his bet returned.

**Fifteen: values**

| 10 | 10 | 10 | 10 | 9 | 8 | 7 | 6 | 5 | 4 | 3 | 2 | 1 |

## FIFTEEN

Fifteen, also called quince, cans, or ace low, is a blackjack variant for two players with one acting as dealer.

Players aim for a points count of 15. Face cards count as 10; other cards their numerical face value (with ace as 1).

Dealer and nondealer place equal amounts in a pool before the deal.

The deal is one card face down. The nondealer stands, or draws one or more cards face up. He does not announce if he busts – he says only "I stay." The dealer then stands or draws. Both players then show their face down cards. The player nearer 15 without busting wins. If both players tie or bust, bets are left in the pool for the next deal.

The loser of one hand deals for the next.

## FARMER

This is an interesting variant of blackjack for two to eight players.

One player, the "farmer," is the equivalent of the banker/dealer in other games of the blackjack family, but in this game players also make an ante bet into a central pool or "farm." The money in the farm is won only when a player has a points count of exactly 16; other settlements are made between player and farmer after each round.

**Farmer: values**

10  10  10      6        10  9  6  5  4  3  2  1

Cards 45 cards are used, a standard 52-card deck with all the 8s and three of the 6s removed (the 6 of hearts is retained in the deck).

Objective Players aim for a total points count of 16: face cards count 10 points; other cards their face value (with ace as 1).

Choice of first farmer is as for the banker/dealer in blackjack, except that the deciding card is the 6 of hearts.

Ante bet Each player puts one unit into the farm.

Shuffle The farmer shuffles. Any other player has the right to shuffle, but the farmer has the right to shuffle last.

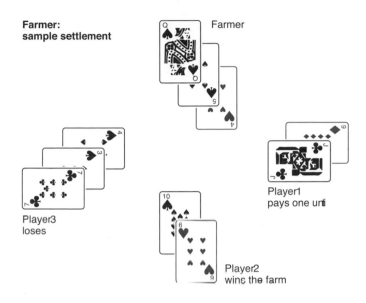

**Farmer:
sample settlement**

Farmer

Player1
pays one unit

Player3
loses

Player2
wins the farm

Cut The player to the farmer's right is offered the cut. If he does not wish to cut, any other player may do so. If no other player wishes to cut, the farmer must cut.

Deal The farmer deals one card face down to each player, including himself, beginning with the player to his left and going clockwise.

Play The player to the farmer's left begins. He looks at his card and then receives one further card from the farmer. If his total now exceeds 16, he does not announce this but says "I stay" and receives no further cards. He does not show his hand.

If his card total is less than 16, he can either stay or receive further cards as he wishes.

When he is satisfied with his hand or when his total

exceeds 16, he says "I stay," receives no further cards, and keeps his hand concealed.

Play then passes to the player to the first player's left, and play continues as described until all other players, including the farmer, have received at least one further card and had the chance to draw others.

Settlement At the end of the round, all hands are shown and settlement is as follows.

a Each player who has a count of over 16 points must pay one unit to the farmer who dealt the hand. (The farmer does not have to pay anyone if his hand exceeds 16 points).

b A player holding 16 points wins the farm (the central pool) and becomes the next farmer. If more than one player holds a total of 16, the order of precedence when deciding the new farmer is: the player with the 6 of hearts; the player with the fewest cards; the current farmer if he has 16 points; the player nearest the farmer's left.

c If no one holds a total of 16, the farm is not won. The player with the total nearest 16 then receives one unit from each player with a lower total (but not from players who have bust). If two or more players have equal totals, they divide the units won from the other players. The same farmer then deals the next hand, and all players put a further ante into the farm.

# 3+ BLÜCHER

This private banking game is named after a Prussian general who fought against Napoleon. Modified rules are given here.

Equipment:
  1 one standard deck of 52 cards;
  2 betting chips;
  3 a betting layout with areas representing each denomination of card (it can be made up of cards from another deck, or may be drawn on paper).

Players three or more.

Objective Players aim to bet on a denomination on the layout that is not matched during the hand.

   A denomination is matched when the player, having called that denomination, turns up a card of that rank.

Choice of first bank is by high cut (see page 13).

Shuffle and cut are normal (see page 13).

Betting limits are agreed beforehand.

Betting Each player but the banker places as many bets on the layout as he wishes. Each bet must be placed on only one denomination.

Play The banker turns up cards one at a time from the top of the deck to form a face up pile on the table. As he turns the first card up he says "Ace." He says "Deuce" for the second, "Three" for the third, and so on. For the eleventh, he says "Jack" for the twelfth "Queen" and for the thirteenth, "King."

   For each card, if the denomination of the exposed card matches the rank called, the bank collects any bets placed on that denomination on the layout.

   For example, if the eighth card is an 8, the banker wins the bets on section 8; if the twelfth card is a queen, he wins the bets on the queen's section.

Each time the banker wins a bet on the layout, he is paid an additional equal amount by the player who made the bet.

When the banker has counted to king he begins again from ace, still turning up a card from the deck for each rank he calls.

The players may not add to, remove, or change their bets. The banker collects bets as before, if rank and card match.

Play continues in this way until the banker has counted from ace to king four times. All the deck has then been dealt.

Doubling This occurs if at any time the banker counts from ace to king without any of the 13 cards matching the rank called.

The banker must then, with his own chips, double all players' bets that are then on the layout.

However, the bets stay on the layout and are still at risk.

This doubling only takes place once in a single deal. If the banker counts from ace to king again without any cards matching, he does not add again to the players' bets.

If the banker wins a player's bet that has been doubled, he wins all the doubled bet plus an equal amount from the player.

Final settlement Any bets still on the layout at the end of the game are returned to the players who placed them.

Continuing play Bank and deal pass one player to the left. All the cards are collected for the next deal, and new bets are placed.

## 3-12 BRAG

Brag was one of the ancestors of poker and still remains very popular in Britain. There are many forms and variants but basically the game is a form of three-card poker with no "draw."

**Hands**

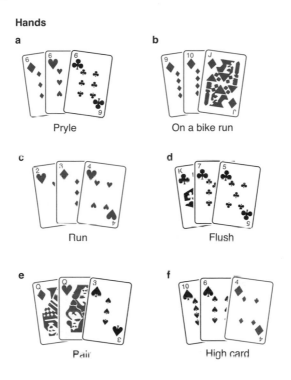

a

Pryle

b

On a bike run

c

Run

d

Flush

e

Pair

f

High card

Equipment:
1 one standard deck of 52 cards;
2 betting chips or cash.

Rank of hands A "hand" at brag contains only three cards.

Originally only threes and pairs scored but today, through poker influences, all the following are generally recognized (with the highest listed first).

a  "Pryle": three cards of the same denomination.

b  "On a bike" run: three cards in sequence from the same suit.

c  Run: three cards in sequence.

d  Flush: three cards of the same suit.

e  Pair: two cards of the same denomination and one unmatched card.

f  "High card": three unmatched cards.

Rank of cards The cards rank in normal order, with ace high, except:

a  ace can rank low to make a 3, 2, ace run or on a bike run – which then counts as the highest hand of that rank, beating ace, king, queen.

b  for pryles only, a specified denomination varying with the game played (e.g., three 3s) is ranked above three aces.

Wild cards Today brag is usually played with no wild cards, or sometimes with 2s (deuces) wild. (See diagram overleaf.)

However, the traditional wild cards for the game, listed in order of rank, are: ace of diamonds; jack of clubs; 9 of diamonds.

Hands of the same rank are valued according to the denomination of cards used – as in poker. For two special cases, see "rank of cards." Otherwise:

1  for pryles, on a bike runs, flushes, and high cards, the hand with the highest denomination card wins;

2  for pairs, the hand with the highest denomination pair wins or, if these match, the hand with the highest ranking odd card wins.

Rank of hands with wild cards A hand using wild cards is valued

## Wild cards

in the usual way (with the wild card valued according to the card it represents). However, a hand using wild cards loses to a hand that has none.

Note that a pair using a wild card loses to the same pair in natural cards even if the wild card hand has the higher odd card.

Arrangements

1 choice of first dealer is by low cut (see page 13).

2 shuffle and cut are normal (see page 13).

## THREE-CARD BRAG

This is the basic form of the game.

Players From three to 12.

The objective on each deal is to win the pool by holding the best ranking hand on a showdown or by having all the other players drop out of the betting.

Betting limits are agreed beforehand. Typical limits would be:

1 maximum one unit bet or raise;

2 one to five or one to ten units bet or raise.

Ante Sometimes rules specify that, before each deal, each
  player must contribute one unit to the pool.
Deal The dealer deals one card face down to each player,
  including himself, beginning with the player to his left
  going clockwise, and continuing until each player has three
  cards.
Play Players look at their hands and bet accordingly, beginning with the player to the dealer's left and going clockwise. Bets are placed in a central pool. Players may bet on
  any hand – bluffing is unrestricted.

  There is only one betting interval. A player cannot
"pass" and stay in the game – he must bet or drop out. If
all the players but one drop out the remaining player wins
the pool.

  Otherwise betting continues until there is a showdown,
when the player with the best hand wins. A showdown is
not allowed until all players but two have dropped out.

  Dealt cards are replaced at the bottom of the deck, face
down. The cards are reshuffled for the next hand only if a
pryle has just appeared on showdown.
Betting principles There are several alternatives:
  a  "round the table;"
  b  "bet or raise;"
  c  poker betting.
Round the table betting Each time it is his turn to bet a player
  must bet one unit or drop out.

  This continues even when there are only two players left,
but then either player may in any of his turns pay a double
amount to "see." Both players then show their cards without further betting.
Bet or raise In this system limits are agreed beforehand and
  affect only the opening bets and raises.

  In the betting interval betting is as for the round the

table system, but in any turn a player may choose to bet more than one unit.

All active players must then bet exactly the same amount each time their turn comes around – or must drop out or raise again.

Raises are therefore not like the raises in poker. Instead of players just having to "call," they set a new minimum contribution to the pool per turn.

Each player must contribute at least that full amount in subsequent turns – regardless of his previous contributions to the pool – or must drop out.

Each time the bet is raised only the increase is limited. The total bet of a player in a turn can therefore exceed the "limits."

As in the round the table system this can continue when only two players remain in until one of them pays double the amount at that time to see.

Poker betting is sometimes used (see poker, page 274). In this system the interval ends when bets are equalized.

However, unless modified, poker rules can leave more than two active players at showdown. This can be accepted, or the following rules may be observed:

**a** when there are three or more active players, a player may not call if this equalizes all players' bets (he must raise or drop out);

**b** if a player drops out and so equalizes the bets between the remaining three or more active players, the last player to raise must raise again.

"Blind" betting It is sometimes ruled that a player may bet without looking at his cards.

In this case, any player who has looked at his cards must in each turn pay double to the blind bettor if he is to stay in.

When only two active players are left an "open" bettor

cannot double his stakes to see a blind bettor. To remain in the game he must continue to bet until the blind bettor doubles his bet to see him.

When the last two active players are both blind bettors either of them can pay double to see the other.

Covering the kitty If a player runs out of money during the betting interval he places his hand face down on the pool.

Subsequent bets by other players are then placed in a side pool.

Showdown is then between three players: between the last two active players for the side pool and between these two and the player who covered the kitty for the main pool.

**Seven-card brag: pryles**

7s beat aces

## SEVEN-CARD BRAG

This version is for two to seven players.

Before each deal, players contribute equal amounts to a pool.

Each player then receives seven cards, looks at them, discards one face down, and visibly splits the remainder into two unexposed three card brag hands.

When all are ready, each player in turn exposes one hand, beginning with the player to the dealer's left.

Then each player in turn exposes his other hand, beginning with the player whose first hand was highest.

A player has complete discretion on how he splits his cards between the two hands, but he must expose the best hand first. The rank of cards is as in three-card brag, except that the highest pryle is three 7s, followed by three aces. (Three 3s rank normally – below three 4s and above three 2s.)

If the same player has the highest hand both times, he wins the pool.

Alternatively, a player whose original seven cards contained four cards of the same denomination wins the pool if he declares this at once without discarding.

Otherwise the pool is not won, but players still contribute again before the next deal.

A deal is usually one card at a time, face down. It may however, be three cards to each player, followed by another three, and then by a single card.

In the latter case, dealt cards are usually not shuffled between hands but replaced face down at the bottom of the deck with no shuffle or cut.

## NINE-CARD BRAG

This is similar to seven-card brag. A maximum of five can play, as nine cards are dealt to each player. The deal is usually in ones, but sometimes in threes.

Players divide their cards into three brag hands, exposing the highest hand first. Any player with the highest hand in all three exposures wins the pool (or, under some rules, the pool is won by a player with two out of three highest hands).

Alternatively, as in seven-card brag, the pool is won immediately by a player with four cards of a kind.

The rank of hands is as in three-card brag, except that the highest pryle is three 9s, followed by three aces. (Three 3s

### Nine-card brag: pryles

9s beat aces

rank normally – below three 4s and above three 2s ).

If no one wins the pool, players still contribute again before the next deal.

Sometimes a pool may not be won for many hours – by which time it can be very large.

## STOP THE BUS

This British students' game is a variant of three-card brag. All players start with an equal number of betting chips. An additional three-card hand – the dummy – is dealt face up onto the table. In play, each player in turn may exchange one card in his hand for one from the dummy. The discarded cards go into the dummy face up.

This continues until one player does not wish to alter his hand. All players then show their cards, and the lowest hand pays a previously agreed amount into the pool (e.g., five units).

Further hands are played until only one player has any chips remaining. He then wins the whole pool.

# 2+ CARD CRAPS

This game was created to bypass laws banning dice craps. The "shooter" deals cards instead of throwing dice.

**Cards used**

Equipment:
1 a special deck of 48 cards. It is made up of six denominations only – ace, 2,3,4,5, and 6. In each denomination there are eight cards, two in each suit. For example there are eight 6s made up of two hearts, two spades, two diamonds, and two clubs;
2 betting chips or cash.

Players Any number can play from two upward. One person is dealer and is known as the "shooter."

Choice of first shooter is by any agreed method.

Shuffle See page 13.

Cut Any player may cut; but the player to the dealer's left has the right to cut last. If he does not wish to do so, the right to cut last passes clockwise.

Basic play The shooter deals two cards from the top of the deck face up onto the table. This constitutes a "throw." The value of the two cards added together gives the score for the throw in just the same way as the two dice in dice craps. The first throw in a shooter's turn is called a "come-out" throw, as is the first throw after each time the cards win or lose.

On a come-out throw:

**a** if the shooter throws a 7 or 11, he has thrown a "natural": the cards "pass" (i.e., win) immediately.

**b** If the shooter throws a 2,3, or 12, he has thrown "craps": the cards "miss out" or "crap out" (i.e., lose) immediately.

**c** If the shooter throws a 4,5,6,8,9, or 10, he has thrown a "point": for the cards to win he must "make the point," i.e., throw the same number again before he throws a 7 – no other numbers matter.

If the shooter throws the same number again before he throws a 7, the cards pass (win).

If he throws a 7 before he throws the number again, the cards miss out or "seven out" (lose).

After a come-out throw the shooter shuffles the two cards back into the deck and he cuts the deck.

If the shooter then still has to make a point, he deals further throws but does not shuffle these back into the deck. This continues until he makes the point (wins) or sevens out (loses) – i.e., until a "decision" is reached. The entire deck is then shuffled together and cut.

If, on a point, the whole deck is used without a decision, the shooter reshuffles and cuts the deck; he then continues, trying for the same point.

Change of shooter If the shooter sevens out he must give up the cards. He may also give up the cards if:

**a** he has not made any throw in his turn; or

**b** he has just thrown a decision.

The cards pass to the next player to the left.

Change of deck When two decks are available, any player may request a change of deck at any time. The change is made immediately before the next come-out throw.

Betting and odds Players arrange bets among themselves.

Center bet On each come-out throw, the shooter places the
amount he wishes to bet in the center of the playing area.
He announces the amount, saying "I'll shoot...."

Any of the other players then "fade" (accept) whatever
part of the total they wish, by placing that amount in the
center alongside the shooter's bet.

Unless agreed at the beginning of the game, there is no set
order or amount by which players fade center bets. Players
simply place money in the center until all the shooter's bet
has been faded, or until no one wishes to place any further
amount. (However, it is sometimes agreed that any player
who faced the entire center bet on the preceding come-out,
and lost, can claim the right to fade the entire present bet ).

If the center bet is not entirely faded by the players, the
shooter may either:

a withdraw the part not faded; or

b call off all bets, by saying " No bet."

Players may not fade more than the shooter's center bet;
but if the players show eagerness to bet more, the shooter
can decide to increase the amount of his bet.

Settlement of center bet If the cards miss out (lose), the players
who faded the center bet each receive back their money
together with the equivalent amount of the center bet. If
the cards pass (win), all the money in the center is collected
by the shooter.

The center bet is therefore an even money (1 to 1) bet.
Since the probability of the cards passing is in fact 970 occa-
sions in 1,980, the shooter has a 1.414% disadvantage on
the center bet.

Other bets are known as side bets. Like the center bet, they
must be arranged before the cards are dealt.

Note that the shooter himself may make any of the side
bets he wishes, in addition to the center bet.

**Hardway bet (or gag bet)** This is a bet on whether the shooter will throw a certain number "the hard way" – i.e., as the sum of a double. Hardway bets can be placed on 4 (2+2), 6 (3+3), 8 (4+4), or 10 (5+5).

The right bettor loses if a 7 is thrown, or if the number bet on is thrown any other way before being thrown as a double.

**Double hardway** This is not a bet but a double payment made when the shooter throws a point number (4,6,8 or 10) with two cards that are pairs of the same suit, e.g., 8 with two 4s of hearts.

The payment is made by wrong bettors to those who have taken a normal "right bet" on the shooter making the point. This serves to equalize the right and wrong bettors' chances on even number points.

**Off-number bet** Two players agree to bet on any number they choose. The right bettor wins if the shooter throws the number before he throws a 7. Bettors may call off the bet before a "decision" is reached.

**Proposition** This refers to any other kind of side bet agreed upon – limited only by players' imaginations!

Such bets are always offered at odds designed to give the proposing player an advantage. There are two main categories:

**1** bets on whether the specified number(s) will appear within a certain number of throws after the bet: "one-throw bets," "two-throw bets," three-throw bets;" or

**2** bets on whether the specified number(s) will appear before other specified numbers or before a 7.

In each case, the specified number(s) bet on may be:

**a** a certain number to be thrown in any way;

**b** a certain number to be thrown in a specified way;

**c** any one of a group of numbers (e.g., a group of specified numbers, odd numbers, (numbers) before 7, etc.).

Right and wrong bets All these bets require agreement between two players.

One is the "wrong" bettor: he "lays" odds that the cards will not pass or will not make the number(s) bet on.

The other is the "right" bettor: he "takes" odds that the cards will pass or will make the number(s) bet on.

The bet and odds may be proposed by either the right or the wrong bettor; in practice, however, more experienced players tend to be "wrong" bettors and propose odds that the less experienced player will "take."

Flat bet This is a normal bet on whether a shooter's come-out throw will pass, and is made as a side bet between two players (of which one may be the shooter). Flat bets occur especially if one player has faded the entire bet.

Point bet If the shooter throws a point on his come-out throw, players may bet on whether he will "make the point." (The center and flat bets still remain to be settled in the same way.)

Come bet This is a bet on whether the cards will pass – but treating the next throw after the bet as the bet's come out throw (when in fact the shooter is throwing for a point ). If on this throw the shooter throws a 7, he sevens out on his point – but for the come bet the cards "come," because a 7 on a come-out throw is a natural.

Similarly, 11 is a natural for the come bet, but 2,3, or 12 is craps – the cards "don't come." (But all of these leave the center bet undecided, because they are neither the point number nor a 7.)

If the shooter throws a point number on the come-out throw for the come bet, this number becomes the point for the come bet. The outcome then depends, in the usual way, on whether the point or a 7 appears first.

If the shooter makes the point on his center bet without

**Table 1: True odds for bets on or between single numbers**

| Number | A Single throw | B Before a 7 | C Comparative odds |
|---|---|---|---|
| 12 | 35-1 | 6-1 | 12 |
| 11 | 17-1 | 3-1 | 2-1  11 |
| 10 | 11-1 | 2-1 | 3-1  3-2  10 |
| 9 | 8-1 | 3-2 | 4-1  2-1  4-3   9 |
| 8 | 31-5 | 6-5 | 5-1  5-2  5-3  5-4   8 |
| 7 | 5-1 | — | 6-1  3-1  2-1  3-2  6-5   7 |
| 6 | 31-5 | 6-5 | 5-1  5-2  5-3  5-4  1-1  5-6   6 |
| 5 | 8-1 | 3-2 | 4-1  2-1  4-3  1-1  4-5  2-3  4-5   5 |
| 4 | 11-1 | 2-1 | 3-1  3-2  1-1  3-4  3-5  1-2  3-5  3-4   4 |
| 3 | 17-1 | 3-1 | 2-1  1-1  2-3  1-2  2-5  1-3  2-5  1-2  2-3   3 |
| 2 | 35-1 | 6-1 | 1-1  1-2  1-3  1-4  1-5  1-6  1-5  1-4  1-3  1-2  2 |

**Table 2: Hardway bets**

| Bet | Odds against hardway | Payment on double hardway |
|---|---|---|
| 10 | 8.1 | 4.1 |
| 8 | 10.1 | 12.5 |
| 6 | 10.1 | 12.5 |
| 4 | 8.1 | 4.1 |

making the come bet point, the players making the come bet can agree to withdraw the bet or to continue the number sequence into the shooter's next turn.

True odds Table 1 above gives the true odds for various bets on or between single numbers, and provides the information from which the true odds for any bet between groups of numbers can be calculated. (A player should particularly avoid accepting 1 to 1 odds on 6 to 5 bets.)

Table 2 above gives the true odds for hardway bets.

NOTES ON TABLE 1

**A** Odds against making a number on a single throw.

**B** Odds against throwing the number before throwing a 7: for point and off-number bets.

**C** Odds against making the higher number before the lower number (e.g., 12 before 4: 3-1). Reverse the odds to give odds against making the lower number before the higher (e.g., 4 before 12: 1-3).

To calculate the odds between any groups of numbers: add all ways of making the numbers in one group, and compare with the total of all ways of making the numbers in the other group.

True odds for other one-throw bets:

**a** against any specified pair (e.g., 3+3): 35-1;

**b** against any specified combination of two different numbers (e.g., 6+5): 17-1;

**c** against any craps (2,3, or 12): 8-1.

## 2–8 CARD PUT-AND-TAKE

Taking its name from the game of put-and-take played with a specially marked teetotum, this private banking card game has some features in common with red dog.

Equipment:
 1 one standard deck of 52 cards;
 2 betting chips.

Players From two to eight.

Objective On the "take" deal each player aims to hold, and on the "put" deal not to hold, cards of the same rank as those turned up by the banker.

Choice of first banker/dealer is by high cut (see page 13).

Shuffle and cut are standard (see page 13).

Deal The banker deals five face-up cards to each player except himself, dealing them one at a time in a clockwise direction.

Betting limits Payments are one to 16 chips. One chip's value is agreed beforehand.

Play
 1 Players look at their cards.
 2 The put deal is made. The banker deals five face-up cards one at a time onto the table.

 After each card is dealt, any player holding a card of the same rank must pay chips into a pool. The payment doubles with each card: one chip for the first card turned up; two for the second; four for the third; eight for the fourth; and 16 for the fifth. A player with two or more cards of the same rank as the banker's card must pay for each one.

 The banker makes no payments.
 3 The banker takes the five cards from the table and places them face up at the bottom of the deck.

**Sample play**

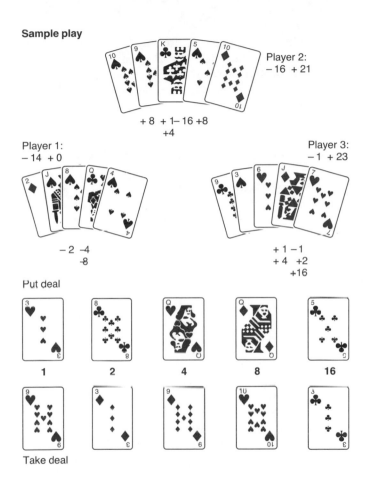

Player 2:
− 16 + 21

+ 8  + 1− 16 +8
+4

Player 1:
− 14  + 0

Player 3:
− 1  + 23

− 2  −4
−8

+ 1  −1
+ 4  +2
+16

Put deal

| 1 | 2 | 4 | 8 | 16 |

Take deal

4 The take deal is made, for which the banker deals five more cards as before. This time each player takes chips from the pool for each of his cards of the same rank. The number of chips taken increases exactly as in the put deal.

5 Any chips left in the pool after the five cards have been played go to the banker. Any chips still owing are paid by the banker from his own chips.

Change of banker/dealer After each hand the bank and deal pass to the player to the banker's left.

## VARIANTS

Ante payment Sometimes each player but the banker puts one chip into the pool before each hand.

Easy go has an additional payment and claim. Players pay – and take – one additional chip to each card that, besides being of the same rank as the card played by the banker, is also of the same color.

Red and black has an additional payment and claim for any player with three or more cards of the same suit as the card played by the banker.

Players pay – and take – one chip for the first card the banker turns up, two for the second, three for the third, four for the fourth, and five for the fifth, in addition to regular payments.

Up and down the river has a different payment and claim system. Each player pays – and takes – according to the rank of the matching cards, not according to whether it is the first, second, third, fourth, or fifth card turned up.

Payment for an ace is one chip; for a jack, 11 chips; for a queen, 12 chips; and for a king, 13. Payments on the other cards match their face value.

# 2+ CHINESE FAN-TAN

This simple game works on the same principle as the Chinese bean game of fan-tan. It was once an American gambling house game but disappeared because it gives no advantage to the banker.

Equipment:
1 one standard deck of 52 cards;
2 one joker to be used for the betting layout;
3 betting chips – preferably a different color for each player.

Players The game is for two or more players.

Objective Players aim to guess how nearly the number of cards in a section cut from the deck will be divisible by four.

Choice of first banker is by high cut (see page 13).

Betting limits Are agreed beforehand.

Bank Because each player may make more than one bet, the betting limits do not limit a bank's losses. A banker therefore places to one side, before his first hand as banker, any of his fund of chips he is not prepared to put at risk. The remainder constitutes the bank. Any winnings gained during a player's turn as banker must remain at risk in the bank until the role of banker passes to the next player.

The betting layout consists of the joker, turned face up in the center of the table. The card is placed so that one of its short sides is facing the banker.

Each of the joker's corners is allocated a number. As the banker looks at the card, the bottom left hand corner is 1, the top left hand corner 2, the top right hand corner 3, and the bottom right hand corner 4.

Bets at the corners of the joker are on one number only. Bets along the side of the joker are on the numbers of the two adjacent corners. In the example illustrated overleaf,

**Betting**　　　　　　　　　　　　**Play**

Layout

**a** bets on 3
**b** bets on 3 and 4
**c** bets on 4 and 1

bet (**a**) is on 3, bet (**b**) on 3 and 4, and bet (**c**) on 4 and 1.

A player may place as many bets as he likes, provided each bet is within the betting limits. For each bet, he puts down the number of chips he wishes to put at risk.

More than one player may make the same bet. The banker does not bet.

Shuffle The player to the banker's left shuffles the deck thoroughly and gives it to the banker.

Play The banker cuts a section of at least one third of the cards from the deck, and then counts them out face down onto the table in groups of four.

If the section divides exactly into groups of four, 4 is the winning number.

If a number of cards is left over after counting out in fours, the number left over is the winning number.

In the example illustrated, the section comprised 15 cards – three groups of cards and three over.

Settlements of bets The banker first collects losing bets and then pays winning ones.

Bets on single numbers are paid as 3 to 1 – bet (**a**) in the example illustrated opposite. Bets on two numbers are paid at evens – bet (**b**) in the example; bet (**c**) loses.

The banker first pays any winnings due to the player to his left and then those due to the other players in turn.

If the bank is emptied before all winnings have been paid, the winning bets that remain unpaid are simply returned to the bettors.

**Change of banker** Unless the bank has been emptied, bank and deal remain with one player for a set number of hands agreed beforehand. After this the banker receives all the chips then in the bank, and bank and deal pass one player to the left. The bank and deal pass immediately if a bank is emptied.

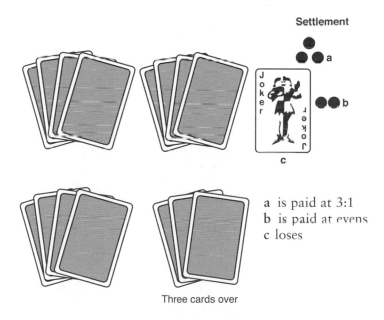

Settlement

a is paid at 3:1
b is paid at evens
c loses

Three cards over

## 2–10 **FARO**

Faro or farobank is a very old banking game. It was known as pharaon in the French court of Louis XIV. In the 1700s it was the most popular gambling house game in England. The following century it became equally popular in the United States, where it was often called "bucking the tiger."

### Equipment

1 A table covered with green baize, bearing the faro layout. The complete spades suit is usually used for the layout.
2 A dealing box from which one card can be slid at a time.
3 A casekeeper. This is a frame like an abacus used to show which cards in the deck have been played.
4 A standard deck of cards.
5 Betting chips.
6 Faro "coppers" – round or hexagonal chips of either red or black – used for betting a denomination to lose.
7 Bet markers – small flat oblongs of ivory or plastic – used to make bets over the limit of a bettor's funds.

Players Up to ten can play. House officials are a dealer, a lookout who supervises betting, and a casekeeper official. The house always banks.

Objective Players try to predict whether the next card to appear, of the denomination bet on, will be a winning or a losing card.

Cards appear in play two at a time. The first in each pair is always the losing card, the second the winning card.

Shuffle, cut and bet The dealer shuffles the cards, cuts them, and puts them in the dealing box face up. The exposed top card is called the "soda." It is ignored for betting.

Bets are now placed (see page 244).

First turn The dealer puts the soda card face up to one side to start the discard pile or "soda stack."

He then takes the next exposed card from the box and places it face up to the right of the box. This card is the losing card. The card now exposed in the box is the winning card.

Between turns Any bets on the two exposed denominations are settled. Other bets may be changed and new bets made. The casekeeper is altered to show the cards that have already appeared.

Continuing play Play continues through the deck. In each turn:

1 the dealer removes the last winning card from the box and places it face up on the discard pile;
2 a new losing card is taken from the box as in the first turn;
3 the new winning card is exposed at the top of the box.

The casekeeper has pictures of the 13 denominations, with four large wood buttons on a spindle opposite each picture.

At the beginning of the deal all the buttons are positioned at the inner ends of the spindles.

As a card is taken from the box, one of the buttons on the relevant spindle is moved along toward the outer end of the frame.

How far it is moved depends on whether it represents a winning or a losing card:

a for a losing card it is moved until it touches the outer frame or an earlier button on the same spindle;
b for a winning card a gap of about $1/2$ in is left between the button and the frame or between this and an earlier button. When the fourth card of a denomination appears, whether it is a winning or a losing card, all four buttons are pushed together against the outer frame to show that betting on this denomination is at an end.

**Casekeeper**

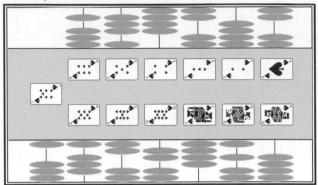

**The last turn** Three cards are left in the box for the last turn. The casekeeper shows which cards they are. The last card in the box is called the "hoc" or "hock" card.

For the last turn players may normally:

**a** bet on any one of the cards to win or lose as usual;

**b** "call the turn" – i.e., try to predict the precise order of all three cards (e.g., queen first to lose, 6 second to win, ace last). The turn is played in the usual way, except that when the winning card has been removed from the box the losing card is half slid out to confirm the denomination of the hoc card. A player's bet is returned if the card that he bet to win or lose appears as the hoc card.

**Continuing the game** After the last turn all cards are gathered and shuffled for the next deal.

**Betting** There are three kinds of bet apart from bets on the last turn: bets on a single denomination; bets on a set of denominations; bets that take action in every turn.

**Bets on a single denomination** are settled when a card of that denomination appears. To make the same bet again a player places a new stake on the layout.

Bets on a set of denominations are bets on groups of different numbers that appear close together on the layout (see placing of bets diagram and explanation). They are settled as soon as any one of the denominations bet on appears.

To make the same bet again, a player places a new stake on the layout.

Bets that take action in every turn remain on the layout until removed by the player. There are two such bets: a "high card" bet an an "even or odd card" bet.

In a high card bet the player bets that the higher denomination card of each pair will win in each turn, or, if he has "coppered" the bet, that the higher card will lose. (For this bet ace ranks low).

In an even or odd card bet the player bets that either the even card or the odd card will win in each turn. (For this bet ace, jack, and king count as odd, and queen is even.)

With these two bets the player wins or loses on every turn. Each time he loses he gives the dealer a number of chips equal to his stake. Each time he wins he receives an equal number. The actual stake remains on the table until the player stops making the bet.

Explanation of placing of bets diagram (next page):

a  bets a single denomination (5);
b  bets two denominations horizontally adjacent (2+3);
c  bets two denominations diagonally adjacent (6+9);
d  bets two denominations vertically adjacent (2+q);
e  bets 6+7;
f  bets 7+8;
g  bets two denominations horizontally adjacent and separated by one other denomination (j+k);
h  bets three denominations horizontally adjacent (8,9,10);
i  bets three denominations in a right angle (3,10,j);
j  bets 6,7,8;

**k** bets adjacent denominations in a square (4,5,9,10);
**l** bets the even denomination card in each turn (the chip
position is between the 2 and the table edge);
**m** bets the odd denomination card in each turn (the chip
position is between the 5 and the table edge);
**n** bets the higher denomination card in each turn.

Bets to win using one or several chips All bets may be made
with one chip or several chips.

If several chips are used, they are stacked vertically
except for bet (**c**). For that bet they are tilted or "heeled,"
by moving the bottom chip in to rest on the corner of one
card and tilting the remainder toward the other card.

Bets to lose using one or several chips In general these bets are
placed as for bets to win but are "coppered" – i.e., a faro
copper is placed on top of the betting chip(s).

The only exception is where bet (**c**) is made with a single

**Placing of bets**

chip. In this case the copper is placed in the usual position not far from the tip of one of the cards, with the chip on top of it tilting toward the other card.

Betting one card to win and one to lose This bet can be placed on any two adjacent denominations or on bet (**g**).

If the bet is made with a single chip, a copper is placed on the edge or corner of the lose card and the chip is tilted toward the win card.

If the bet is made with several chips, one chip is placed on the edge or corner of the lose card and the remaining chips are tilted on it in the direction of the win card.

This bet is settled as soon as one of the denominations appears as a winning or losing card.

Last turn bet: "calling the turn" The stake is placed on the card bet to lose and angled toward the card bet to win.

**a** When made with a single chip, a copper is placed on the card bet to lose on the edge nearest the card bet to win. The single chip is placed on it, tilted toward the card bet to win. Another copper is placed on top of the single chip.

**b** When made with several chips, one chip is placed on the card bet to lose on the edge nearest the card bet to win. The remaining chips are tilted on the bottom chip so that they point toward the card bet to win.

When the third card lies between the winning and losing cards, the bet is tilted toward the outside of the layout. This shows that it avoids the middle card, i.e., the middle card is bet to be the hoc card.

Last turn bet: "cat hop" The stake is placed as for calling the turn.

Bet markers are used when a player wants to place on the layout at one time more bets than he has funds for. For each marker placed on the layout the player must have staked an equal value in chips elsewhere on the layout. If one of the player's bets loses, the dealer takes payment in chips. The player must then withdraw his marker bet unless the value of his chips on the layout still exceeds the value of the markers he has used.

If one of the player's bets wins, the player wins an equivalent amount in chips.

A "split" occurs in a turn when a single bet has covered both winning and losing cards.

   **a** A split on a single denomination occurs when two cards of the same denomination appear in a turn. The house takes half of any bet on that denomination; the other half is returned to the bettor.

   **b** A split on a set of denominations occurs when two cards of a group bet on by a player appear in a single turn. The bet is returned to the bettor.

   **c** A split on bets that take action in every turn occurs when both cards in a turn are of the same denomination or are both odd or both even. The bet remains on the table and the bettor neither makes nor receives any payment.

Betting on "cases" When only one card of a denomination is left in the box, this is called "cases" – e.g., "cases on the queen." Most houses forbid a player to bet on cases until after he has bet on a denomination that could be split.

"Cat hop" bet On the last turn the casekeeper may show that the three cards left are not all of different denominations. "Calling the turn" is then replaced by the "cat hop" bet. It may be made on denominations or colors.

   **a** If two of the three cards are of the same denomination, a player may make a cat hop on denominations, predicting the order of denominations as usual – e.g., 10,6,10. (A player may still bet one denomination to win or lose as usual.)

**b** If all three cards are of the same denomination, a player may make a cat hop on color, predicting the order of suit colors – e.g., red, black, red.

Cat hop bets are placed in front of the dealer according to whatever temporary regulations he states.

Settlement A player who calls the turn successfully is paid at 4 to 1. A player who makes a successful cat hop bet is paid at 2 to 1. All other bets are paid at even money (1 to 1).

## 2+ HOGGENHEIMER

A game of pure chance in which the settlement of bets depends on how soon the banker turns up a joker.

Equipment:
1. one standard deck of 52 cards from which the 2s,3s,4s,5s, and 6s have been removed.
2. one joker (or any discarded card if a joker is not used);
3. betting chips.

Players The game is for two or more players.

Objective Players try to bet on a card (or cards) exposed before the joker is exposed.

Choice of first banker is by high cut (see page 13).

Shuffle and cut are normal (see page 13).

Dealing the layout The banker deals four rows of eight cards face down, and the 33rd card face down to one side. He takes care that no card's face is seen during the deal.

Betting limits are agreed beforehand.

Betting Each player except the banker places as many bets as he likes. The card bet on is shown by the bet's position on the layout. The top row represents spades, the next hearts, the next diamonds, and the bottom row clubs. The column farthest to the right represents 7s, the next 8s, and so on; the column farthest to the left represents aces.

Examples of betting are shown in the illustration opposite:
- **a** is a bet on the jack of hearts;
- **b** is on the king of diamonds;
- **c** is on two adjacent cards – the 7s of spades and hearts;
- **d** is on two adjacent cards – the 9 and 10 of spades;
- **e** is on four cards in a square – the 8s and 9s of hearts and diamonds;
- **f** is on a column of cards of a single denomination – all the 10s;

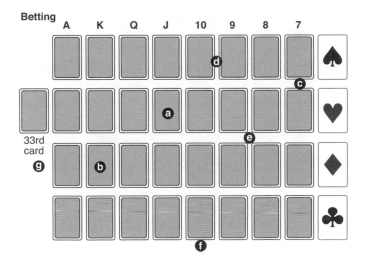

**g** is on a row of cards of the same suit – all the diamonds.

Play The banker turns the 33rd card face up.

If it is a joker the deal ends and the banker collects all bets.

If it is any other card the banker places it face up in its correct position on the layout.

Any bet on that position is replaced on top of the card.

The face-down card that was in that position is removed, turned face up, and placed in its correct position in the layout. Play continues in this way until the joker appears. (See diagram overleaf)

Settlement A player's bet wins if all the cards bet on are turned up before the joker. The banker collects all other bets.

In the example illustrated: bets (**a**),(**c**), and (**d**) win; bets (**b**), (**e**), (**f**), and (**g**) lose.

Bets on single cards are paid 1 to 1. Bets on two cards

are paid 2 to 1. Bets on four cards in a square or column are paid 4 to 1.

Bets on eight cards in a row are paid 8 to 1.

Continuing play The bank and deal pass one player to the left. All cards are collected for the next hand.

**Play**

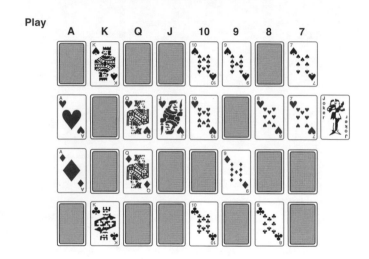

# *3+* **HORSE RACE**

An exciting game emulating the thrills of the racetrack. Bets are laid on cards that are moved like horses toward the finish line.

Equipment:
  **1** one standard deck of 52 cards;
  **2** betting chips.
Players The game is for three or more players.
Objective Player try to "win the race" by betting on the first suit to appear eight times in a deal.
Choice of first banker is by high cut (see page 13).
The "horses" The banker takes the four aces from the deck and lines them up in any order.
Shuffle and cut are standard (see page 13).
The "course" After the shuffle and cut, the banker deals seven face-up cards in a line at right angles to the horses. (See diagram overleaf.) If five or more of the cards dealt are of the same suit, the banker takes them all up, reshuffles, and deals the course again.
Betting limits are decided by the banker for each race.
Betting The banker declares the odds on each horse (suit), taking into account the cards that were dealt to form the course. If one suit has appeared predominantly in the course, there will be fewer cards of that suit to appear in the race.

The table gives an example of the odds that a banker might offer. He will choose odds that give him some degree of advantage; it is up to each player whether or not to place a bet at those odds.

The players then state their bets, placing their stakes in front of them. The banker makes a note of how much each player bets on each horse and what the odds are.

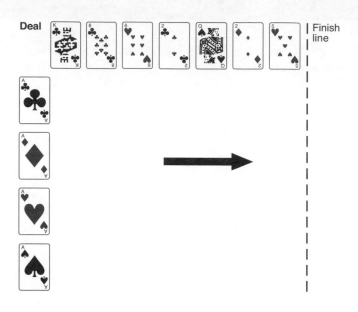

**Deal**

Finish line

The "race" The banker deals the top card from the deck face up onto the table. The horse (ace) of the same suit as the dealt card is then moved up the course one space. The banker then deals another card face up on top of the first,

### Betting odds

| Number of cards of suit in course | Odds offered on suit |
|---|---|
| 0 | Evens |
| 1 | 2-1 |
| 2 | 3-1 |
| 3 | 5-1 |
| 4 | 10-1 |
| 5 or more | Layout redealt |

**Play**

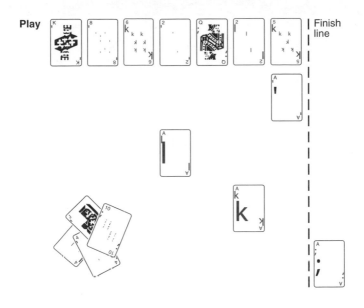

and again moves the horse of the corresponding suit one space. This continues until one horse has passed the end of the course. This horse is the winner. (See diagram opposite.)

Settlement of bets The banker collects all bets placed on the losing horses. He pays at the quoted odds each bet on the winning horse.

Change of banker After each hand, the bank and deal pass one player to the left.

## 2–15 **INJUN**

This fast, amusing game is very simple to play. But it can see a lot of money change hands very rapidly, and offers opportunities for skilful judgment to anyone familiar with mathematical odds. Bets are placed in a central pool; there is no banker.

Equipment:
  **1** one standard deck of 52 cards;
  **2** betting chips or cash.
Players from two to about 15.
Rank of cards The cards rank in normal order, with ace high.
  The suits are not ranked.
The objective is to bet on holding a higher ranking card than any other player.
Choice of first dealer is by deal: first ace to appear (see page 13).
Shuffle and cut are normal (see page 13).
Ante Before each deal, each player, including the dealer, puts an equal amount into the center of the table to form a pool.
Deal The dealer deals one card face down to each player including himself, beginning with the player to his left and going clockwise.
Play Players are not allowed to look at their own cards. Each picks up his own card and puts it against his forehead.
  He holds it there, face outward, so that all the other players in the game can see the card.
  Players should watch carefully at this stage of play to check that no player glimpses his own card.
Betting begins with the player to the dealer's left, and goes clockwise.
  Each player bets according to his judgment of whether his own card, which he cannot see, is likely to be higher in rank than all the others players' cards – which he can see.
  A player must bet to stay in the game. If he drops out at

any time, he places his card face down on the table in front of him.

All bets are placed in the pool.

**Betting principles** There are two alternatives:

**a** poker betting;

**b** brag betting.

**Poker betting** In this alternative each player in turn bets, calls, raises, or drops out until the bets are equalized. When this happens, betting ends and there is a showdown between all active players.

**Brag betting** In this alternative, betting is as in the "round the table" system in brag. Each player in each of his turns contributes one unit to the pool, or drops out.

No one can raise and betting continues until all but two players have dropped out. These last two active players then continue to put bets of one unit each into the pool, until:

**a** one of them drops out leaving the other player the winner; or

**b** one of them pays two units to "see the other" and there is a showdown between these two players.

**Showdown** On showdown all active players look at their own cards. The player with the highest card wins the play and takes the pool. Ties for highest card divide the pool.

**"Covering the kitty"** If a player runs out of money during betting he places his card face down on the pool – allowing all players to remind themselves of its rank before he does so. Subsequent bets of other players are then placed in a side pool. Showdown is then between three players: between the last two active players for the side pool, and between these two and the player who covered the kitty for the main pool.

**Continuing play** After the pool has been won the deal passes one player to the left and all players ante for the next play.

# 3–9 KENTUCKY DERBY

Also called pasteboard derby, this pool betting game has a varied race and simple betting.

Equipment:
  1 one standard deck of 52 cards;
  2 betting chips or cash.

Players three or more.

Objective Players try to bet on the winning "horse."

Choice of first dealer is by high cut (see page 13).

Shuffle and cut The four aces are removed from the deck. The rest of the deck is shuffled and cut as usual (see page 13).

The "course" After the shuffle and cut, the dealer forms the course by dealing seven face down cards in line.

The "horses" The four aces are the horses – they can be given the names of favorites. These cards are lined up just below the first course card, in the order: hearts, diamonds, spades, clubs.

  To make judging easier, the two red aces are put to one side of the course and the two black aces to the other.

  The player to the dealer's left lines up the aces and moves them during the race.

Ante Before the game, each player including the dealer puts an equal agreed amount into the pool.

Betting Each player decides which horse he will back. A player may bet only on one horse; more than one player may bet on the same horse.

  A horse still runs even if no one bets on it.

  It is best to write down the selections if there are several players. This is done by the player to the dealer's right. He also has charge of the pool and pays out the winnings at the end.

Starting the race The dealer deals the top card from the deck face up onto the table just behind the ace of hearts.

The player to the dealer's left moves the ace of hearts the appropiate number of spaces up the course, if any (see moves table, page 261).

The dealer then deals a card behind the ace of diamonds, and so on.

**Running the race** How far a horse moves depends on the card dealt. The dealer deals one card to each ace in turn, in the order: hearts, diamonds, spades, clubs, and then starts again. Further cards dealt to each ace are placed face up on top of the cards first dealt, forming four discard piles.

**Finishing the race** A horse finishes when it passes the last course card.

But the winner is only decided when all horses have had an equal number of turns. The winner is then the ace that has gone farthest over the finishing line.

If the second place horse is to be decided too, and only the winning horse has crossed the finishing line, then the winner's discard pile is turned face down, and play continues with the remaining aces.

**Splitting "dead heats"** Sometimes two aces have gone an equal distance over the finishing line on the same turn.

Each is then dealt a further card from the deck. This continues until, with an equal number of cards dealt, one horse has gone farther past the post than the other.

**Settlement: winning horse only** With fewer than six players, races are run for first place only. The pool is won by the player or players betting on the winning horse. If there are two or more sucessful bettors, the pool is split equally between them. If the pool does not divide equally, any chips over stay in the pool for the next race.

**Settlement: winner and second place** With six or more players, races may be run for first and second places. Bettors on the second place horse receive back their ante from the pool.

The remainder of the pool is won (and divided if necessary) by the player(s) who bet on the winning horse.
Preparing for the next race The deal passes to the player to the

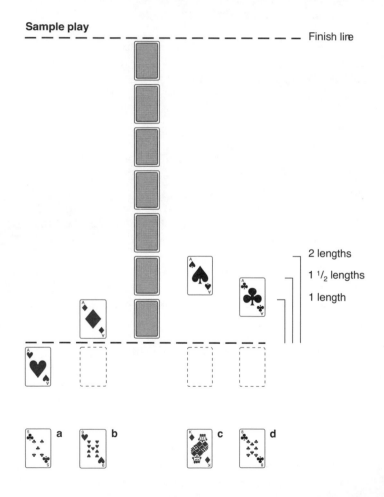

**Sample play**

Finish line

2 lengths

1 ¹/₂ lengths

1 length

dealer's left. He collects all the cards (except the aces) and reshuffles them.

The player to the new dealer's left controls the horses, and the player to his right the bets.

**The moves**

|  | *Card played* | *Distance moved* |
|---|---|---|
| **Ace moves forward** | king | 2 lengths |
|  | queen | 1½ lengths |
|  | jack | 1 length |
|  | 7,8,9,or 10 same color as ace | 1 length |
|  | 3,4,5, or 6 same color as ace | ½ length |
|  | Any card dealt of the same suit as ace adds ½ length |  |
| **Ace moves back** | 2 same color as ace | ½ length back |
|  | 2 not same color as ace | 1 length back |
| **No move** | 2 dealt while ace still on starting line |  |

# 2+ LANSQUENET

This private banking game is said to have been popular with German mercenaries in the 1600s. Its name derives from Landsknecht, the German word for mercenary. It is closely related to ziginette and skinball.

Equipment:
  **1** one standard deck of 52 cards;
  **2** betting chips.
Players two or more.
Objective Players aim to bet on a card that has not been "matched" by the time the banker's card is matched.
  A card is matched when a card of the same denomination is dealt from the deck.
Choice of first banker is by deal: first ace to appear (see page 13).
Shuffle and cut are normal (see page 13).
Dealing the layout Provided that none of the cards dealt for the layout matches, the procedure is as follows. The banker deals the top two cards from the deck (the "hand" cards) face up onto the table. He then deals one card face up to himself (the "banker's card"), followed by another one face up (the "players' card").
Matching cards in the layout The following procedure must be observed if matching cards are turned up for the layout.
  **1** If the card dealt for the second hand card matches the first, it is placed on top of it. A further card is then dealt as the second hand card. If necessary this process is repeated until the hand cards do not match.
  **2** If the card dealt as the banker's card matches one of the hand cards, it is placed on top of that card and a new banker's card dealt. This process is repeated if necessary until the banker's card is of a different denomination than the hand cards.

3 If the card dealt as the players' card matches one of the hand cards, the procedure is as for the banker's card. If the players' card is the same denomination as the banker's card, the deal is void and a new deal made.

Betting limits are decided by the banker for his hand's duration.

Betting Each player places his bet alongside the players' card.

If all chips are of the same color, the bets may be placed at different corners of the card to distinguish them.

First turn The banker deals one card from the top of the deck face up onto the table.

If the dealt card does not match any card on the layout, it is placed face up next to the players' card. It is now a further players' card, on which players may place bets.

If the dealt card matches one of the hand cards, it is placed on top of the matched card. This denomination is now out of play.

The hand cards have no effect, except to remove two denominations from the betting.

If the dealt card matches the players' card, the banker wins the players' bets. There is then no further betting on the matched denominations for the rest of the deal.

The matched and matching cards are dead, but are left on the layout, on top of each other, as a reminder that this denomination is out of play. Any further cards of that denomination are placed on top of the matched cards.

If the dealt card matches the banker's card, the banker pays all bets at even money, i.e., each winning player receives his stake plus an equal amount from the bank. Play on this deal then ceases and the bank and deal pass one player to the left.

Continuing play If the banker's card is not matched immediately, play continues in the same way until it has been matched – when the banker pays all outstanding bets.

A card is dealt in each turn – and either matches a card on the layout or becomes a new players' card.

Each time one of the players' cards is matched, the banker collects the bets on that card.

Between turns, players may place new bets on the players' cards. But a bet that has once been placed may not be removed or transferred to another card.

## Explanation of play diagram

**a** The 8 was dealt first, and became a players' card.

**b** The king was dealt, matching a hand card and having no effect on play.

**c** The 6 was dealt. It matches the banker's card – so players win all bets and the deal ends.

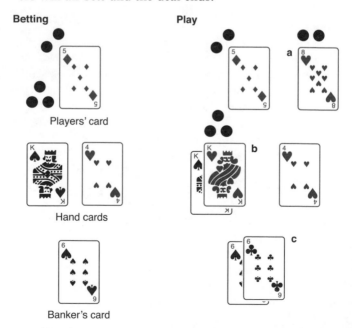

**Betting**

**Play**

Players' card

Hand cards

Banker's card

# 2+ MONTE BANK

Monte bank is the major banking card game of illegal gambling clubs. It is also called monte or Spanish monte.

## CASINO VERSION

Cards a standard deck with the 10s, 9s, and 8s removed.

**Cards used**

Players From two to as many as can get around the gaming table. One of the players is banker.

There is also a non-playing house official called a "cutter." He assists the banker and collects a 25% cut from certain bets.

When the bank passes, the amount collected by the cutter is divided equally between the house and the retiring banker.

The objective for a player is to bet on the layout card or cards that will first be matched in play.

Normally a card is "matched" when another card of the same denomination appears at the top of the deck.

Choice of first banker/dealer is by low cut.

Bank The banker places in front of him, in cash, the total amount he wishes to put at risk. The banker does not have to pay out an amount greater than this on any one hand. If the result of a hand presents a banker with losses exceeding the bank total, he pays off the highest bet first, then the next highest, until the bank is exhausted. Other bets are then void and are returned to the players.

Betting limits The minimun bet is governed by house rules. The

**Sample layouts**

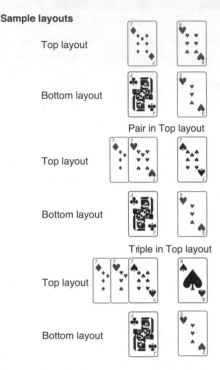

Top layout

Bottom layout

Pair in Top layout

Top layout

Bottom layout

Triple in Top layout

Top layout

Bottom layout

maximum bet is the amount of the bank. A player betting the maximum on a hand does not prevent other players betting because his bet may lose.

Shuffle and cut The dealer shuffles. Any other player may claim the right to shuffle before the cut but the dealer shuffles last. The dealer then places the cards in front of the player to his right. Any other player may claim the right to cut, but the player to the dealer's right must cut last.

Dealing the layout Holding the deck face down, the banker deals two cards from the bottom. He places them face up on the table, slightly apart. These form the "top layout."

He then deals two cards from the top of the deck and places them face up on the table just below the first two cards and slightly apart. These form the "bottom layout."

Pairs and triples If the two cards of the bottom layout are of the same denomination, the deal is void. The cards are collected and reshuffled.

The same applies if two cards, one in each layout, are of the same denomination.

If the two cards of the top layout are of the same denomination, the dealer places them on top of the other and deals another card alongside.

If this card is also of the same denomination, it is placed with the others and a further card is dealt.

If this card is the fourth of the same denomination, the deal is void.

The cards are collected and reshuffled.

Betting involves predicting which of two cards or two groups of cards on the layout will be matched earliest.

Players back a certain card or cards to be matched before another specified card or cards. Normally a card is "matched" when another card of the same denomination appears at the top of the undealt portion of the deck.

**Types of bet**

a  Circle
b  Crisscross
c  Doubler (top before bottom)
d  Doubler (right before left)

**Matching with pairs**

Same color:    Other color:
no match      match

Bets are placed in cash on the layout. The position of a bet shows the card(s) bet and the card(s) bet against. There are four types of bet:

**1** circle bet;
**2** crisscross bet;
**3** doubler bet;
**4** Monte Carlo bet.

Circle bet The player bets that a specified card will be matched before any of the other three cards on the layout (**a**).

A successful circle bet is paid at 3 to 1.

Crisscross bet The player bets that a specified card will be matched before another one specified card on the layout (**b**).

A successful crisscross bet is paid at evens (1 to 1).

Doubler bet The player bets that one of the cards (unspecified) in the top layout will be matched before either one of the cards in the bottom layout (**c**), or vice versa.

Alternatively, he bets that one of the cards (unspecified) to the dealer's right will be matched before either one of the cards to the dealer's left (**d**), or vice versa.

A successful doubler bet is paid at evens (1 to 1).

Monte Carlo bet This is a combination of the other three types of bet.

**Matching with triples**

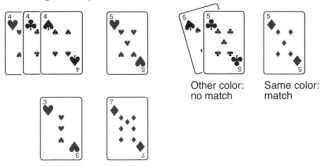

Other color:
no match

Same color:
match

Matching with pairs and triples in the layout When cards of the
same denomination have been dealt to the top layout, they
are placed together (see sections on pairs and triples).

A pair or triple is matched as usual when a further card
of the same denomination appears from the undealt part of
the deck.

But other cards on the layout are not necessarily matched
when a card of their own denomination appears. To give all
cards an equal chance, the color of the cards appearing at
the top of the deck is taken into consideration.

Matching with pairs in the layout When a denomination in the
top layout has been paired, then another card on the layout is matched only by a card which is of its own denomination and of a different color.

Matching with triples in the layout When a denomination on the
layout has been tripled, another card on the layout is
matched only by a card which is of its own denomination
and of the same color.

Crisscross bets An unmatched pair or triple will be involved in
some way in all bets on a layout, with the exception of
those crisscross bets in which neither of the two cards bet
is the pair (or triple).

Such crisscross bets are settled as soon as one of the two cards involved is matched in the normal way, i.e., by the appearance of any card of its denomination.

For other purposes the card is not considered matched.

**Play** After bets have been placed the cutter says "That's all."

The dealer then turns the deck face up, showing the bottom card only.

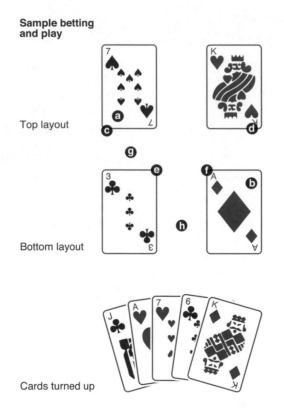

**Sample betting and play**

Top layout

Bottom layout

Cards turned up

If the card matches any of the cards on the layout, all bets involved are settled and the matched card is removed from the layout.

If the card does not match any card on the layout, or if there are still other bets unsettled, the dealer removes the bottom card and places it to one side, exposing the next face-up card. This continues until all bets have been won or lost, each exposed card being added to the discard pile.

The deal is complete as soon as the last bet on the layout has been settled. (This will happen before all cards on the layout have been matched.) The dealer then gathers all cards and shuffles them for the next deal.

**House cut and banker's cut** When a player wins because the card he has backed is matched by the very first card exposed, the house takes a 25% cut from the player's winnings.

When the bank passes, the total collected is divided equally between the house and the retiring banker.

House cuts are collected by the cutter.

**Change of banker** A banker may hold the bank for as long as he wishes or he may be limited to a set number of deals agreed by players beforehand. However, a banker may pass the bank at any time when there are no unsettled bets on the table. He indicates that he is passing the bank by saying "Aces."

If the bank becomes exhausted, the role of the banker passes immediately.

The role of the banker always passes to the next player to the left.

**Variant** Sometimes the dealer adds unmatched cards from the deck to the layout. Players may place further bets on them as in ziginette.

**Sample betting** (see diagram overleaf)

a  bets 7 of spades;
b  bets ace of diamonds;

    **c** bets 7 of spades against 3 of clubs;

    **d** bets king of hearts against ace of diamonds;

    **e** bets 3 of clubs against king of hearts;

    **f** bets ace of diamonds against 7 of spades;

    **g** bets left layout;

    **h** bets bottom layout.

Sample play with pairs Cards turned up:

    **1** jack of clubs, no action;

    **2** ace of hearts, bet (**d**) loses (crisscross bet not involving pair); all other bets undecided;

    **3** 7 of hearts, bet (**a**) wins, paid 3-1; bets (**c**) and (**g**) win, paid evens; bets (**b**), (**f**) and (**h**) lose; bet (**e**) undecided;

    **4** 6 of clubs, no action;

    **5** king of diamonds, bet (**e**) loses.

## MONTE BANK: PRIVATE

This is a simple version of the gambling club game.

Cards are matched by suit, not by denomination.

Equipment:

    **1** one standard deck of 52 cards with all 10s, 9s, and 8s removed to leave a 40-card deck;

    **2** betting chips.

Players The game is for two or more players.

Objective Players bet that one of two cards on a "layout" (pair of cards) will be matched.

    A card is matched when the next card exposed from the deck is of the same suit.

Choice of first banker/dealer is by low cut (see page 13).

Shuffle and cut are normal (see page 13).

Dealing the layouts Holding the deck face down, the banker deals two cards from the bottom. He places them face up on the table, slightly apart. These form the "top layout."

    He then deals two cards from the top of the deck and

places them face up on the table, slightly below the first two cards.

These form the "bottom layout."

The deal is valid whatever suits appear – even if all four cards are of the same suit.

Betting Each player except the banker may bet on the top or the bottom layout or on both. A bet on a particular layout is shown by placing the chips between that pair of cards.

Betting limits are agreed beforehand.

Play The banker turns the deck face up, exposing the bottom card. This card is known as the "gate."

If the gate card's suit matches one (or both) of the cards in a layout, the players win any bets on that layout.

If the gate card matches cards in both layouts, the players win their bets on both layouts.

If no layout card is matched all bets are lost.

Settlement The banker collects all losing bets.

Winning bets are paid at 1 to 1, even if both cards in a layout were matched.

Continuing play The banker collects together the layout cards, and places them to one side to form a discard pile.

He then turns the deck face down, takes the next gate card from the bottom of the deck and puts it on the discard pile.

He then deals the layout cards for the next hand. There is no shuffle or cut.

Change of banker Bank and deal remain with one player for a previously agreed number of hands (up to a maximum of six).

At least 10 cards of the deck should remain unplayed to prevent players calculating which suits remain.

The bank and deal then pass one player to the left. All cards are collected, and the deck shuffled and cut as before. If the bank is emptied at any time, bank and deal pass.

## *2–8+* **POKER**

Poker is played all over the world. It has been called the national card game of the United States, where it developed its present form. Poker ranks with blackjack among card games. Although the betting element is central to both games, they also allow for great skill; it is this that sets them apart from most pure gambling games.

Equipment:
1  One standard deck of 52 cards (see also the section on arrangements page 288).
2  One or two jokers as "wild" cards if desired (see also the section on wild cards page 278).
3  Betting with chips or cash.

Players Two to eight or more. Certain forms of poker can be played by up to 14 people. No alliances are allowed; a player may play only for himself.

Basic terms The usage of some poker terms is not standard. In the following text a "hand" means the cards, or the particular combination of cards, held by a player.

A single game, from one shuffle to the next, is here called a "play" (rather than a "hand").

Objective Each player tries to maximize his winnings.

On each play all bets are put into a common pool (the "pot").

One player wins the pool on a play if:
a  he holds a higher-ranking hand than anyone still betting at the end (the "showdown"); or
b  all other players drop out of the betting before the showdown in the belief that they cannot win.

Rank of cards Cards rank in the normal order. Ace usually ranks high, except in the 5, 4, 3, 2, ace sequence; in a "high-low" game it may rank either high or low (see page 305).

**Rank of hands**

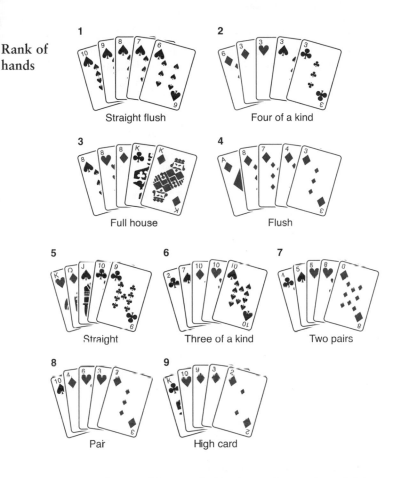

1 Straight flush

2 Four of a kind

3 Full house

4 Flush

5 Straight

6 Three of a kind

7 Two pairs

8 Pair

9 High card

Sometimes low-ranking cards (2s, 3s, and even 4s and 5s) are removed from the deck to speed up the game.

The suits are ranked.

Poker hands In standard poker all hands must, for scoring (showdown) purposes, contain five cards, although fewer or more than this may be held at different stages of the game. The following hands are universally recognized. Each hand loses to the one listed before it, and defeats the one listed after it. This order derives from the mathematical probabilities involved.

1 Straight flush: five cards in sequence of the same suit. (a,k,q,j,10, of the same suit is known as a "royal flush").

2 Four of a kind or "fours": four cards of the same denomination, and one unmatched card.

3 Full house: three cards of one denomination, and two cards of another denomination.

4 Flush: five cards of the same suit, but not in sequence.

5 Straight: five cards in sequence, but not of the same suit.

6 Three of a kind or "threes": three cards of the same denomination, and two unmatched cards.

7 Two pairs: two cards of one denomination, two cards of another denomination, and one unmatched card.

8 One pair: two cards of the same denomination, and three unmatched cards.

9 High card: five unmatched cards.

Other hands are sometimes accepted locally (e.g., a "blaze" denotes any five court cards). Their inclusion and their ranking should be agreed before the game begins.

Hands of the same rank When poker hands are of the same rank, the winning hand is decided by the rank of the cards involved.

The following rules apply where no wild cards are used.

1 Straight flush: the highest ranking card in a sequence decides the best hand. Thus a royal flush is the highest when there are no wild cards. Note that the ace in a 5,4,3,2, ace sequence ranks low, so this hand would be beaten by 6,5,4,3,2. The same rule applies to straights.

2 Four of a kind: the hand with the highest ranking matched cards wins.

3 Full house: the hand with the highest ranking "three of a kind" wins.

4 Flush: the hand with the highest ranking card wins. If the highest cards are the same denomination, the next highest are compared. This continues down to the lowest, until a difference is found.

5 Straight: as for straight flush.

6 Three of a kind: as for four of a kind.

7 Two pairs: the hand with the highest ranking pair wins. If the higher pairs in two hands are the same, the lower pairs are compared. If both pairs in two hands are the same, the hand with the best-ranking unmatched card wins.

8 One pair: the hand with the highest ranking pair wins. If the pairs in two hands are the same, the highest unmatched cards are compared. If these are the same, the next highest are compared. This continues down to the lowest, until a difference is found.

9 High card: as for flush.

Hands tie if they contain exactly the same denominations: the suits are irrelevant. Hands that tie as highest in a showdown divide the pool between them. If the pool is not exactly divisible, the amount left over goes to the player who was "called" (i.e., the player who first made the highest bet).

Wild cards Sometimes players agree at the beginning of a game to designate certain cards "wild." A wild card is one that may represent a card of any denomination.

Any card or group of cards may be agreed on, but the following are popular choices: the joker (or two jokers); the "deuce" (2 of spades if no joker is available); all the deuces; all the deuces and "treys" (3s); red 10s.

**Wild cards**

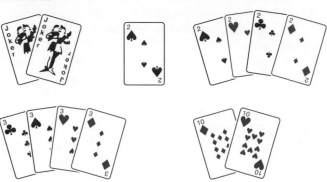

In some forms of the game, a card that occupies a particular position in the game may count as wild, for example each player's "hole" (concealed) card in some stud poker games.

Two alternative rules govern the use of a wild card. The holder may either:

**a** use it to represent any card (denomination and suit) he does not hold; or

**b** use it to represent any card even if he holds that card.

    In either case, a wild card ranks the same as the card it represents.

    If a joker is used as a wild card, it may be used either like any other wild card, or alternatively as a "bug." The bug may be used to represent only an ace or any card the player needs to complete a straight or a flush. Again, the use of the joker as the bug may or may not be limited to cards not held by the players.

Hands with wild cards Wild cards rank exactly the same as the cards they stand for, so when comparing hands of the same rank, ties are possible between same-denomination fours, full

**Hands with wild cards**

Five of a kind

Double ace high flush

houses, and threes. With fours and threes, the rank of the other cards in the hands decides the winner where possible.

If hands with wild cards are of identical rank, the hand with no or fewer wild cards win. If there are the same number of wild cards, the hands tie.

Where wild cards are used for any card (even one held by the player) two new hands are possible.

1 Five of a kind: five cards of the same denomination. This ranks as highest hand, above a straight flush.

2 Double ace high flush: flush including two aces. This ranks above flush and below full house.

Sometimes, a wild card may be used only to make five of a kind – but not to make double ace high flush. This must be decided before the start of play.

Prohibitions A player may not:

a attempt to make a private agreement with any other player (e.g., divide the pool without a showdown);

b waive his turn as dealer, unless physically unable to deal;

c look at the discards (either before or after showdown),

**Example of a
betting interval**

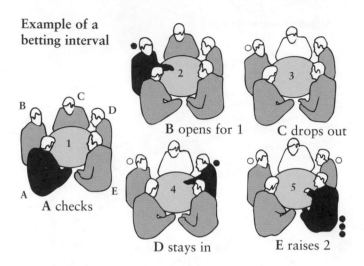

B opens for 1

C drops out

A checks

D stays in

E raises 2

at undealt cards, at another player's hand, or at a hole card (in stud poker);

d take chips or money from the pool during play, except as correct change for a verbally stated bet;

e leave the table taking his cards with him (he should ask another player, preferably a non-active one, to play his hand for him – if he fails to do so and misses his turn, his hand is dead).

Bluffing is allowed (i.e., trying to mislead other players by statements, actions, or manner). Bluffing may include: making announcements out of turn about one's hand or plan of play that are not true or are not subsequently kept to; playing so as to make one's hand seem weaker than it is.

Sarcasm, heckling, and derision are allowed – help is not!

Betting intervals In a single play there will be at least one betting interval, and normally two or more.

These always follow receipt of cards by players, but the

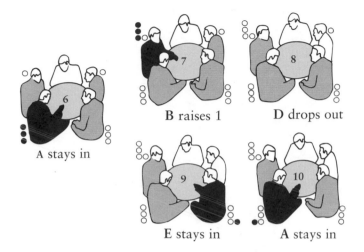

A stays in

B raises 1

D drops out

E stays in

A stays in

precise number and when they occur depend on the form of poker being played.

In each betting interval, a certain player will have the right to bet or not to bet first. (How he is chosen depends on the form of the game.)

Thereafter players bet or do not bet in clockwise rotation.

**Principles of betting** All bets on a play are placed together near the center of the table to form a pool. One player bets first ("opens the betting"). Thereafter each player in turn must either "drop out," "stay in," or "raise."

In his turn, a player announces what he is doing before he places any chips in the pool.

For a first bet or a raise, he also announces the amount of the bet or raise.

A bet is not considered made until the bettor has removed his hand from the chips bet: until then it can be withdrawn.

## Example of a betting interval

| Player bet | Bet | Action | Total bet |
|---|---|---|---|
| A | 0 | checks | 0 |
| B | 1 | opens for 1 | 1 |
| C | 0 | drops out | (0) |
| D | 1 | stays in | 1 |
| E | 3 | raises 2 | 3 |
| A | 3 | stays in | 3 |
| B | 3 | raises 1 | 4 |
| D | 0 | drops out | (1) |
| E | 1 | stays in | 4 |
| A | 1 | stays in | 4 |

The betting interval ends. The only three players still active have bet equal amounts; B may not raise the betting again.

a Drop out (or "fold"): the player discards his hand and gives up his chance of winning the pool on this play.

A player may drop out at any time, even if he has previously bet on this play in an earlier interval or in this interval; but any chips he has already bet remain in the pool and go to the pool winner.

A player who has dropped out is no longer "active," and may not take further action in this play.

b Stay in (or "call" or "see"): the player puts in just enough chips to make the total he has bet so far in this play exactly equal to the total bet by the player with the highest total bet.

c Raise (or "up" or "go better"): the player puts in enough chips to stay in, plus an additional number. The additional amount is that by which he "raises the last bet."

Every other player in the game must then either stay in (by bringing his total bet up to the raised amount), drop out, or raise again ("reraise").

Checking is allowed in many games of poker. A player who checks at the beginning of a betting interval stays in the game for the moment without making a bet. If all active players check, the betting interval ends.

But if one player bets, the interval continues as usual: all other players (including those who have checked) must now stay in, drop out, or raise. To stay in, a player who has checked must equal the highest bet made so far.

If all players check on the first betting interval, the play is void and ends. The next player in turn deals the next round (see the section on the pattern of play, page 291).

A betting interval ends when either:

a all players have checked;

b only one player is still active (and therefore wins), all the others having dropped out; or

c the bets of active players are equalized. This happens when all players still active have put equal amounts in the pool, and the turn has come round again to the last person to raise (or, if no one raised, to the person who opened the betting): he may not then raise again. As long as the bets are unequal any player may raise, but as soon as the bets are equal, no one may raise.

Passing may mean either:

a to drop out; or

b to check (where checking is allowed).

In games where checking is allowed, a player who says "Pass" is assumed to be checking, if checking is available to him. (A player shows that he is dropping out by discarding his hand.)

Games in which no checking is allowed are referred to as "pass and out" (or "pass out" or "bet or drop").

Sandbagging is poker slang for either:

a checking to disguise a good hand – this is sometimes

considered unethical, but is better accepted as a regular part of bluffing; or

**b** constant raising and reraising by two players, forcing a third along with them if he wishes to stay in play.

Raising to force out other players is an essential part of poker, but beyond a certain point it can spoil the game's character.

Two optional rulings can keep it in check: limiting raises, and freezing raises.

A limit on raises is often agreed beforehand. Possible limits are:

**a** three (or sometimes two) by one player in one betting interval;

**b** a total of three by all players in one betting interval.

Freezing the raise is becoming accepted procedure. If there have been two or more raises (whether by one or several players) in a single betting interval, any player who has not raised in that interval may "freeze the raise."

In addition to betting sufficient to stay in, he bets a previously agreed amount, usually two to five times the normal maximum bet (see the section below on betting.)

Other active players must then drop out or stay in by equalling his bet.

The action only freezes the raise for that betting interval.

Side bets are sometimes made between players. For example, in a "high card bet" in stud poker, players bet on who will have the highest first upcard.

Bonuses It is sometimes agreed before play that, on showdown, a player holding a royal flush, straight flush, or four will receive a payment from each player, whether active or not. The amount agreed is usually three to five times the maximum bet.

Betting prohibitions A player may not:

**a** bet for another player;

b borrow money or chips from another player during play;
c take back a bet after it has been placed in the pool and the bettor's hand been removed. An inadequate bet must be added to, otherwise it is lost and the player's cards are dead.

**Betting limits** The system to be used must be decided upon before play. The betting limits are also the raise limits. Note that a player forced to bet, for example, the maximum amount to stay in, may still in that turn raise by the maximum (or by any lesser amount).

**Specified limits: fixed** Minimum and maximum amounts are specified before play starts. Sometimes it is agreed that either:
a any amount between the limits is acceptable as a bet or raise;
b only specified amounts between the limits are acceptable as a bet or raise; or
c no amount between the limits is acceptable as a bet or raise.

**Specified limits: varying** The minimum and maximum limits change during a play; for example, limits for the final betting interval are always twice the earlier limits.

**Last bet limit** The opening bet is governed by agreed limits. Thereafter, the maximum bet or raise is the amount put in the pool by the previous bettor's action.
Players must decide that either:
a each betting interval recommences at the original limits; or
b continuous growth is allowed over a single play.

**Pot limit** The opening bet is governed by agreed limits.
Thereafter, the maximum bet or raise is the total amount in the pool at that time. To calculate this, a player wishing to raise may include in the pool total the sum needed for him to stay in. Agreement on an absolute maximum is still necessary.

Table stakes Before the session, each player puts any amount
of money he wishes onto the table, or buys chips to that
amount.

(A minimum is agreed beforehand, and sometimes a
maximum too.)

Any amount a player wins is added to his table amount.
He may also, from his own pocket, increase his table
amount – but not during play, and only by at least the
agreed minimum.

During a play, a player may not: borrow from, or owe
money to, the pool; decrease his table amount or withdraw
chips from it; sell chips back to the bank until he with-
draws from the game.

The maximum betting limit for a player is his table amount
at the time (the minimum is the amount agreed beforehand).

If a player's table amount is used up in a play, he has the
right to remain in for the main pool showdown. Any
amounts bet by other players, above the amount he has
bet, are put into a side pool.

No limit A player can bet or raise any amount. He may borrow during a play, if he can, but he may not put IOUs in
the pool.

To stay in, he must equal the highest bet.

In the old no limit games, a player had 24 hours to raise
money for a bet. No limit games have now virtually disappeared.

Freeze out This can be played with any limits system except
table stakes.

Before the session, each player puts an equal number of
chips on the table in front of him. Winnings are added to
this amount, but no players may add new chips, lend chips,
or remove chips from the game.

As soon as a player has lost all his chips, he drops out.

The session continues until one player has won all the chips.

Jackpot This ruling can be played with any limits system.

It applies if all other players drop out in a play, after one player has opened the betting. In the next play and before the deal, the others must each "ante" (put) into the pool an amount equal to a single bet made in the previous play.

The new maximum limit (for this play only) is the total amount now in the pool before play starts (providing that this is higher than the normal maximum).

The minimum is as usual.

Whangdoodle This ruling can be played with any limit system.

After the appearance of any very good hand (e.g., full house or better), the usual or opening limits are doubled for the next play.

Sometimes the special limits hold for the next round of play, i.e., one deal by each player.

Example of table stakes

In the example shown overleaf: of three active players, player B has only 30 units left on the table.

a Player A bets 40 units: 30 go into the main pool; 10 start a side pool.

b Player B bets his 30 units, if he wants to stay in the main pool.

c Player C bets 50 units: 30 go into the main pool, the rest into the side pool.

Betting between A and C then continues until their side pool bets have been equalized.

B makes no further bets, and there are no further payments into the main pool, on this or any further betting intervals in this play.

At the showdown, B wins the main pool if he has the best hand.

The side pool can only be won by A or C.

**Example of table stakes**

## ARRANGEMENTS

Banker poker is not a banking game. Bets are made as contributions to a pool. The "banker" simply supervises the supply of betting chips. He records how many have been issued to each player, including himself, and keeps the payments and the unissued stock to one side.

Players must not make exchanges or transactions among themselves. A player needing more chips must purchase them from the banker's stock; a player with surplus chips may sell them back into stock.

The banker is either the host or any player chosen by lot (e.g., high cut) or agreement.

The kitty is a fund for buying new cards or refreshments, set up by agreement before the game starts.

Usually, one betting unit is contributed to it from any

pot in which there has been more than one raise or, alternatively, where the winner holds a hand of a specified rank or better.

The banker arranges all this.

Any chips in the kitty at the end of the game are divided equally among those still playing. (A player who leaves before the end loses the right to any part of the kitty.)

Betting chips are almost always used rather than cash. Usually different colors represent different values; for example: white, one unit; red, five units; blue, 10 units; yellow, 25 units.

A game with seven or more players needs about 200 chips.

The best value distribution depends on the maximum betting limit.

At the start of play each player buys chips to the same total value, for example 50 units.

A player's stock of chips must always be kept in full view of the other players, and not be taken from the table except for cashing.

Two decks of cards with contrasting backs are usually used in club play. At the end of one play, one deck is collected and shuffled by the player who dealt last, while the other is dealt into play by the new dealer.

New deck(s) may be called for by any player at any time.

Seating at the start of a session is random, unless a player demands a reseating after the first dealer has been chosen but before play begins.

On reseating, the first dealer has first choice of a seat. He then shuffles the deck, has it cut by the player to his right, and deals one card face up to each player in rotation, beginning with the player to his left.

The player with the lowest ranking card sits to the

dealer's left, the player with the next lowest card to that player's left, and so on. Of two cards of the same denomination, that dealt first ranks higher.

The dealer then gathers the cards and has them shuffled and cut for play.

After play starts, or after a reseating, no one may demand a reseating for at least half an hour, provided no one joins or leaves the game.

If a player joins the game after it starts and someone questions the seat he takes, the dealer, between plays, deals a card to each existing player, and the new player takes his seat to the left of the player with the lowest card. This is done separately for each player joining.

If a player replaces another player, he must take the seat vacated, provided no one objects.

Two players may exchange seats just before any play, provided no one objects.

Time limit The time at which the game will end should be agreed before play starts, and be strictly observed.

Any player who then wishes to continue can do so, but should set a new time limit.

Time limit for a decision by a player during play (e.g., how many cards to draw, how to bet) is five minutes. This is important in a high-limit game. If a player fails to act within this time, his hand is dead.

Rules to be agreed before the start of the game (best written
down) are:

a the form of game to be played;
b wild cards and their use;
c any special hands and rulings;
d the value of chips;
e betting limits and checking;
f limits on raises and/or payment for freezing a raise;
g bonus payments and payments to the kitty.

Club and casino poker The management supplies table, chips,
cards, dealer and/or inspector. It takes a cut – usually a
direct charge on the winner of each pool, but sometimes an
hourly charge for tables and officials.

Irregularities Because poker can be played for very high stakes,
innumerable rules govern irregularities of play, both acci-
dental and deliberate. It is impossible to treat all of these
here. The reader who wishes to play poker for high stakes
should consult an advanced book on the subject.

PATTERN OF PLAY
Rotation of play is clockwise. No player acts until the active
player nearest to his right has acted.
Choice of first dealer is by deal: the first jack to appear.
Shuffle and cut See page 13.
The deal is clockwise to active players only, beginning with
the active player nearest the dealer's left.
Play varies from one form of poker to another.
Showdown After the final betting interval, players still active
expose their hands (in draw poker) or hole card(s) (in stud
poker), beginning with the player being called, and in a
clockwise direction.
     Each player announces the rank of hand he is claiming.
In any discrepancy the cards "speak for themselves" – this

includes giving the hand a higher rating than claimed, except if there are wild cards (when the player's announcement cannot be improved on).

The hand of highest rank wins.

Tied hands divide the pool equally.

Change of dealer After each play, the deal passes one player to the left of the previous dealer.

## FORMS OF POKER

Closed and open poker are the two main forms.

1 Closed poker, usually played in the form of draw poker.
Players receive their cards face down. After a betting interval, they discard the cards they do not want, and receive replacements from the deck.

A second betting interval is followed by a showdown if more than one player is still active.

2 Open poker, known as stud poker. This is a faster game than draw poker and allows for more skill. As there is no exchange of cards, the average rank of winning hands is lower than in draw poker.

Players receive some cards face down, some face up. Betting intervals interupt the deal. After the deal, players cannot receive replacements, but (in versions where more than five cards per player are dealt) each chooses only five cards to form his final hand.

A final betting interval is followed by a showdown if more than one player is still active.

Choice of form The form to be played may be decided by the host or by club rules; but if a decision has to be made, two factors should be taken into account.

1 Numbers of players. The best games for a particular number of players are as follows: four or under, stud poker; five to eight, any form of poker; nine or ten, five

card stud; more than ten any variant with fewer than five cards per player – or split into two tables.

2 **Relative experience** If some players are considerably more experienced than others, it is best to choose one of the less common variants in which the element of skill is lower.

Dealer's choice If it is agreed to play "dealer's choice," the dealer chooses the game to be played: a standard form, a known variant, or any new and easily explained variant he can devise.

He designates any wild cards. He may not, however, alter the betting limits, add cards to or remove them from the deck, or alter basic poker rules.

His choice of game holds by agreement, either:

a for his deal only; or

b for a complete round of dealing. The next dealer in turn then chooses for the next complete round.

Sometimes, a play or round of dealer's choice is played whenever a very good hand appears (e.g., full house or better).

**Play rotates clockwise**

**Deal passes to left**

## STUD POKER:
## STANDARD GAME (FIVE-CARD)

Players Up to ten may play.

Ante Usually, a small compulsory bet is made by all players.

Opening deal One card is dealt face down to each player (the "hole" card), then one card face up. Each player examines his hand.

First betting interval The player with the highest ranking face-up card must open or drop. A wild card is considered higher than an ace. If two players hold equal-ranking cards, the player nearest the dealer's left opens.

After the opener, each player drops, stays in, bets, raises or reraises in the normal way until betting is equalized.

Continuing play Further rounds of dealing one card face up to each player alternate with betting intervals, until the end of the fourth interval (when each player has one face down and four face-up cards). On these deals, the dealer leaves the deck resting on the table and takes cards one at a time from the top. On the betting intervals, the player with the right to open is the one with the highest ranking completed

**Five-card stud:
end of betting**

Player 3
dropped out

hand in exposed cards – the dealer announces that player and also announces exposed hands, possible flushes and straights, and the last deal.

The showdown follows the fourth betting interval; all active players expose their hole cards.

Additional rules

1 If all the players check, the betting interval ends and the play continues.

2 If a player drops out, he turns all his cards face down and does not reveal his hole card.

3 If on any betting interval only one active player is left, he wins and the play ends. He need not show his hole card.

4 A "four flush" is often ruled a ranking hand in stud poker, i.e., four cards of the same suit plus one other. At showdown (and in deciding the start of a betting interval) it beats a pair but loses to two pairs.

## STUD POKER: VARIANTS

Six-card stud This is like five-card stud, except that after the fourth betting interval each player receives a sixth card face down. This is followed by a fifth (final) betting interval.

At the showdown, each active player chooses five cards from his six to form his final hand.

Seven-card stud (or seven-toed Pete or down the river). This game is for two to eight players.

The opening deal is of three cards: two hole cards, then one face up. Betting intervals and rounds of dealing face-up cards then alternate as usual, until active players have seven cards (including the two hole cards).

After a final betting interval, each active player chooses five cards from his seven to form his showdown hand.

Seven-card stud: low hole card wild As above, but each player's

**Seven-card stud:
end of betting**

Player 3
dropped out

lower ranking hole card is wild – as, for him, is any other
card of that denomination. Sometimes players are allowed
to choose either one of their hole cards (and its denomination) as wild.

Mexican stud is like five-card stud, except that all cards are
dealt face down.

After the second and each subsequent betting round,
each player turns up any one of his face-down cards, leaving one chosen card as hole card.

Sometimes a player's final hole card is ruled wild,
together with any other cards of that denomination that he
holds.

Other five-card stud variants

1 Last card down: the last card is dealt face down, giving
   two hole cards.
2 Last card optionally down: a player may turn up his
   hole card before the last dealing round and receive his
   fifth card face down.

Low-hand stud The lowest hand wins the pool. The lowest
exposed hand begins each betting interval. Other rules are
as for the form of stud being played.

## DRAW POKER

The basic pattern of the game is as follows:

1 Ante: a small compulsory bet is made by all players.

2 Deal: five face-down cards are dealt to each player in the normal way. Players count their cards, then look at them.

3 First betting interval: the player to the dealer's left has the right to bet first: if he does not bet, the other players may bet in turn.

4 Draw: each active player in turn may discard one or more cards and receive from the dealer the same number, face down, from the undealt part of the deck. A player need not draw – he may "stand pat."

5 Second betting interval: the player who made the first bet in the first interval has the right to bet first. If he has dropped out, the first active player to his left may bet.

6 Showdown takes place if more than one active player is left at the end of the second betting interval.

**Draw poker: sequence of play**

Deal    Betting    The draw

Betting    Showdown

## DRAW POKER: STANDARD GAME

Players Up to ten may play. No more than six should play in
high-betting games, since with more players it may be necessary to use discards to complete the draw.

Ante Either:

a each player puts an equal agreed amount into the pool; or

b only the dealer antes ("dealer's edge").

  The ante amount is usually the same as the minimum bet.

First betting interval There are two forms:

1 "Jacks or better." A player may not open the betting
  unless he holds a pair of jacks or any better hand.
  (Before betting is opened, players may check.) After betting has opened, a player may bet on any hand, and
  must bet or drop out. At the end of the play, the opener
  must show the cards he opened on.

2 "Pass and out" (or "pass out" or "bet or drop"). A
  player may open the betting on any hand. Each player
  must bet or drop out; no one may check. In either case,
  the player to the dealer's left is the first to "speak."

  Once the betting has opened, it proceeds in the normal
  way. If no one opens, all players ante again, and the next
  dealer deals for the next play.

The draw occurs if more than one player is still active after
the first betting interval. The dealer offers the draw to each
player in turn in normal rotation, beginning with the
player to his left and ending with himself.

  Each player in his turn either:

a states the number of cards he requires and places that
  number from his hand face down on the table in full
  view – the dealer then gives him the same number from
  the undealt part of the deck; or

b says "I stand pat," or knocks on the table, to indicate
  that he wishes to keep the hand that he has.

In his turn, the dealer also either states the number of cards he has drawn (exchanged), or indicates that he is "standing pat." Normally it is ruled that a player may draw one, two, or three cards at his discretion.

With four or fewer players, four and five card draws are sometimes allowed.

A player may use the draw to bluff in any way he wishes about the value of his hand.

The dealer must answer truthfully how many cards he himself drew. No other question need be answered truthfully by anyone.

The bottom card of the deck is not used. If further cards are required, the bottom card and the cards discarded so far are shuffled together and cut to allow the draw to continue. The usual rules apply, but the player due to draw next cuts last. No other shuffling or cutting on the draw is allowed. Sometimes, in "jack or better," the opening bettor discards one of his "openers" (i.e., one of the cards that gave him the right to open). If he does so, he must state this, and the discarded opener is kept to one side to be inspected at the end of the play. It is not used if the discards are reshuffled.

**Second betting interval** This follows the usual rules. All players may check, even if "pass and out" was enforced for the first interval. If all the players check, the interval ends. If all players except one drop out, that player wins without showing his hand (except for showing his openers in "jacks or better," if he opened the betting).

**Showdown** Each active player in turn must place all his five cards face up on the table, to be seen by all players (active or otherwise). At the same time he announces the value of his hand – he must do this even if he sees he is beaten.

If all players checked in the second betting interval, the opener shows his hand first, but if bets were placed in the second betting interval, the player who was called shows first. In either case, other active players then follow in normal rotation.

Dropping out In draw poker a player indicates that he is dropping out by placing his cards face down on the table when his turn in the betting interval arrives.

As long as a player wishes to remain in the game he must keep his cards in his hands, above table height, unless he is forced to put down the cards temporarily for some reason, in which case he must state this.

## DRAW POKER: VARIANTS

"Jacks or better" variants

1 Progressive openers: if no one opens on a play, two queens or better are required to open on the next play. If again no one opens, two kings or better are required on the next play; then two aces or better; then back down to two kings or better, two queens or better, and two jacks or better.

Each time, players must ante again; and sometimes the limits are doubled. Once a player opens, the next play reverts to jacks or better (and limits go back to normal).

2 "Jack or bobtail" to open. This is like "jacks or better" but a player may also open on a "bobtail" (four cards of the same suit plus one other card) or a "bobtail straight" (four cards in sequence plus one other card – but the sequence may not be: a,k,q,j, or 4,3,2,a).

These hands have no showdown value.

Blind opening (or "blind tiger" or "blind and straddle"). In this variation, players bet "blind," i.e., before receiving their hands. Before the deal:

1 the dealer antes only one chip;

2 the player to his left bets one chip blind ("edge");

3 the next player raises him, betting two chips blind ("straddle").

After the deal, the next player after the blind raiser has the first voluntary bet. He may call (two chip), drop out, or raise (three chips). The betting interval then proceeds as normal. The maximum raise before the draw is one chip. (Note that the dealer's ante does not count toward staying in, but the two players' blind bets do.)

In the second betting interval, the bet and raise limit is two chips. Betting begins with the first blind bettor or the (still active) player nearest his left. Players may check until a bet is made.

Sometimes, in the predeal betting, up to three voluntary blind bets – each doubling the last bet – are allowed after the blind raise. These bets count toward staying in the game in the first interval.

Shotgun Play as in the standard game, except for an additional (first) betting interval during the deal, after each player has received three cards.

Any hand can open. There is no checking.

Stormy weather Each player receives four cards. Three face-down cards are dealt to the table, one each after the second, third, and fourth dealing rounds.

There is then a betting interval. A player may open on any hand. There is no checking.

In the draw, each player may change up to four cards. After the draw, the dealer turns up the table cards one at a time, with a betting interval as each one is turned up.

At the showdown, a player uses any one of the table cards as his fifth card. None of the table cards is wild.

Lowball is often played during "jacks or better" sessions. When no one has openers for "jacks or better," lowball is played for that play only.

**Stormy weather: deal**

player2

player1

player3

Dealer

In lowball the lowest hand wins. Rules as for the standard game, with the following exceptions.

1 Ante: the dealer and the player to his left (sometimes also the second player to his left) ante.

2 First betting interval: the player to the left of the last player to ante must open or drop out. No checking is allowed. The limit is the ante amount. Antes count toward staying in.

3 Draw: before the draw the dealer "burns" (exposes and then discards) the top deck card.

4 Second betting interval: this begins with the active player nearest the dealer's left. Checking is allowed, but a player who checks cannot later raise on that play.

   Limits are agreed beforehand.

5 Showdown is won by the lowest hand.

**Lowball:
lowest hand**

Ace always counts low, and straights and flushes do not count. Therefore 1,2,3,4,5 (known as a "bicycle") counts as five low cards and is the lowest hand – regardless of suits.

The joker can be used for any card not in the player's hand.

Spit in the ocean There are many versions of this; some are given in the section on closed poker games, page 304.

1 Basic game: each player receives four cards. The next

**Spit in the ocean:
deal**

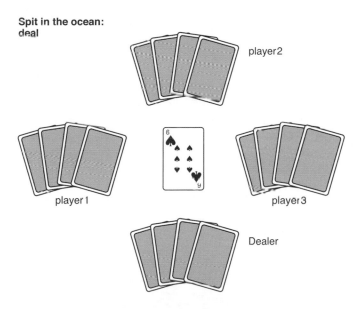

player 2

player 1

player 3

Dealer

card is dealt face up to the center. The game proceeds as usual, but at showdown each active player must count this table card as the fifth card in his hand.

2 Pig in the poke: as above, but the face-up card and all the others of the same denomination are wild (or sometimes only cards of the same denomination as the face-up card, but not the face-up card itself).

## CLOSED POKER GAMES

These are variants in which there is no draw.

Showdown straight poker (or cold hand poker) There is one betting interval before the deal. The deal is normal, but the cards are dealt face up and the best hand dealt wins.

Double barrel shotgun Each player receives five face-down cards. Beginning with the player to the dealer's left, all the players then expose any one of their cards.

Betting intervals then alternate with further rounds of exposing one card each. On the fifth and final round of exposure, the best hand wins.

Spit in the ocean variants

1 Crisscross (or X marks the spot): each player receives four cards. Five cards are then dealt face down to the center of the table in the shape of a cross.

Players examine their hands. The dealer then turns up any one of the table cards except the one at the center of the cross. A betting interval follows.

Exposure of the cards in the cross alternates with betting intevals until all but the center card of the cross have been exposed.

After the fourth betting interval the center card is exposed; showdown follows immediately.

The center card of the cross is wild, as are all the other cards of the same denomination.

Each player mentally selects his final five-card hand from any cards in his hand and the table cards. (Sometimes, he is only allowed to choose table cards from any three that form a straight line in the cross.)

2 Cincinnati: five cards are dealt to each player, and the next five cards are dealt face down to the center of the table.

The game is the same as crisscross, but without the cross pattern. None of the table cards is wild; a player may use any of the table cards in his final hand.

3 Lame-brain Pete: this is played like Cincinnati, but the lowest-ranking table card is wild, as are all the other cards of that denomination.

Three-card poker Each player receives three face-down cards, and there is a betting interval after each round of cards is dealt. Showdown follows immediately after the third interval.

The rank of hands (with the highest given first) is: three's; three-card straight flush; three-card flush; three-card straight; pair; high card.

Two-card poker (usually played with wild cards) comprises: a deal of two face-down cards to each player; a single betting interval; and a showdown. Pairs and high cards are the only hands.

## HIGH-LOW POKER

Almost any standard game or variant, draw or stud, can also be played as a high-low game. Especially popular is seven-card high-low stud.

At showdown, the highest and lowest hands split the pool.

Usually a player must declare, just before showdown, whether he is competing for the highest hand, lowest hand, or both.

**High-low: lowest hand**

It is possible to declare for both in any game where a player has more than five cards from which to select his final hand, for he is then allowed to select two different hands.

Rank of cards is as usual.

If a player is competing for the lowest hand, ace ranks low; if competing for the highest hand, ace is high or low, as he wishes; if competing for the highest and lowest hands, ace can be both high and low as he wishes.

Rank of hands is as usual. Hence the lowest possible hand without wild cards, is 6,4,3,2,a in different suits (5,4,3,2,a would be a straight).

The usual rules for comparing hands apply – highest card first, then the next highest, until a difference is found. Thus 9,7,6,5,4 ranks lower than 9,8,4,3,2.

Wild cards A wild card can only be given one denomination and a suit at showdown.

If declaring for the lowest hand, a wild card ranks the same as a low ace, without pairing any ace in the hand. Thus 4,3,2, a, wild card becomes the lowest possible hand.

Declaring follows the last betting interval. There are two methods.

a Beginning with the player to the dealer's left, each active player in turn declares himself as competing for the highest hand or lowest or both.

b Each player takes one of his chips in his hand, without revealing its color. He takes a white one if declaring low, a red one if declaring high, or a blue one if declaring both.

When all the players have decided, they show their chips.

The highest hand and lowest hand divide the pool equally (if an exact division is impossible, the highest hand receives any odd chips).

A player can only win the part of the pool for which he has declared. If more than one player has declared the same way, the player with the best hand wins that part of the pool.

If all the players have declared the same way, the player with the best hand wins the whole pool.

If a player has declared for both high and low, he must at least tie each way at showdown, or his hand is dead and he receives nothing.

## 2–10 **POLISH RED DOG**

Also known as stitch and Polish pachuk, this game was played by Polish immigrants to the United States.

Equipment:
  1 one standard deck of 52 cards;
  2 betting chips (or cash).
Players The game is for two to ten players.
Rank of cards is normal, with ace high. The suits are not
  ranked.
Objective Players aim to hold a card in the same suit but of a
  higher rank than the banker's card.
Choice of first banker is by deal: the first ace to appear. (See
  page 13).
Shuffle and cut are normal (see page 13).
Bank The banker places in the center of the table the amount
  he wishes to put at risk. A minimum is usually agreed
  before the game.

**Deal**

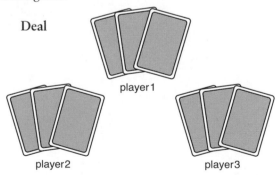

player1

player2                    player3

Deal The banker deals three face-down cards to each player
  except himself, dealing one card at a time.
Play Players bet wihout looking at their cards. Play begins

**Play**

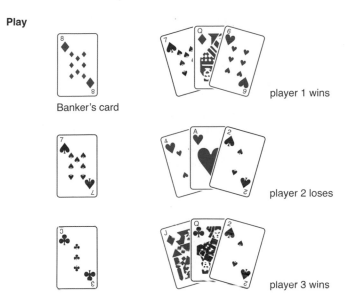

Banker's card

player 1 wins

player 2 loses

player 3 wins

with the player to the banker's left. He places his bet in front of him: this may be any amount up to half the total of the bank. The banker then "burns" the top card of the deck, i.e., he turns it face up, shows it to all players, and places it face up at the bottom of the deck. He then turns up the next card and this becomes the banker's card.

The first player then turns his own cards face up. If he holds a higher ranking card of the same suit as the banker's card, he wins; if not, he loses.

If he has won, he receives back his bet and twice that amount from the bank.

If he has lost, his bet is added to the bank.

His cards are then placed face up at the bottom of the deck. Bet and play then pass one player to the left. After

the player has bet, the banker burns one card before exposing a new banker's card.

Change of banker If the bank is emptied at any time, the bank
and deal immediately pass one player to the left and a new
round is begun.

If the bank is not emptied at the end of a round, the
same banker continues to deal.

If, at the end of any round, the bank has increased to
three or more times the size it was when the present
banker began, then the banker declares a "stitch round."
He deals one more round, and, at the end of this, collects
anything left in the bank. Bank and deal then pass one
player to the left.

A player must continue to act as banker until the bank is
emptied or a stitch round has been completed.

# 2+ RED AND BLACK

This is a private banking game derived from the casino game of trente et quarante.

Equipment:
   **1** two standard decks of 52 playing cards;
   **2** betting chips.

Players Two or more.

Objective Each player tries to forecast correctly whether he will hold more red or more black cards in his hand.

Choice of first banker is by high cut (see page 13).

Shuffle and cut are standard (see page 13) – with the two decks shuffled together to form a single deck.

Betting limits are agreed beforehand.

Betting Each player bets on red or black. He bets any amount within the limits. A player bets on black by placing his bet in front of him to his left; he bets on red by placing it in front of him to his right.

   (Alternatively each player may be given two colored tokens: one red and one black. He places one of these beside his bet.)

Play The banker deals five cards, one at a time, face up, to the player to his left. He deals them directly in front of the player, so that it is clear whether the player's bet lies to the right or left. If the first four cards consist of two red and two black cards, the player may double his bet before he receives his fifth card. After the first player's bet is settled, the banker deals to the next player to the left. He continues dealing until all players but himself have received a hand.

Settlement of bets A player wins from the banker if he is dealt three or more cards of the color bet on. If he has three of that color, he wins the amount of his bet. If he has four, he doubles his bet. If he has five, he wins four times his bet.

A player loses to the banker if he is dealt three or more cards of the color not bet on. If he has three, he loses his bet. If he has four, he pays the banker twice his bet (his original bet and a further payment equal to it). If he has five cards, he pays four times his bet (his original bet plus a payment equal to three times his bet).

**Change of banker** After the banker has dealt a hand to all the other players, the bank and deal pass one player to the left.

## 2-10 **RED DOG**

This fast betting game, also known as high-card pool, is very popular among American news reporters. It needs little skill and is usually played for low stakes.

Equipment:
  **1** one standard deck of 52 cards;
  **2** betting chips (or cash).
Players From two to ten.
Rank of cards is normal (ace high). Suits are not ranked.
Objective Players aim to hold a card in the same suit but of higher rank than a card dealt from the deck.
Choice of first dealer is by deal: first ace to appear. (See page 13).
Shuffle and cut are normal (see page 13).
Ante Before each deal, each player, including the dealer, puts an equal amount (known as the "ante") into the pool.

**Deal**

player2

player1

Dealer

player3

Deal The dealer deals five face-down cards to each player including himself, beginning with the player to his left and going clockwise.

   (Four cards each are dealt if players prefer or if more than eight are playing.)
Betting All players look at their cards. Play begins with the

**Play**

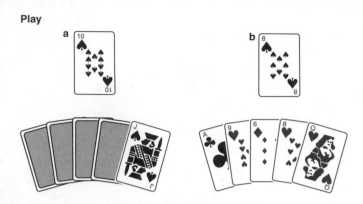

player to the dealer's left. He must bet if he wants to stay in the game. To bet he places his stake in front of him, near the pool. The minimum bet is equal to the ante. The maximum bet is equal to the total in the pool at the time. The dealer must keep note of all bets.

If a player does not wish to stay in the game, he must pay a forfeit equal to the minimum bet but may then place his hand face down on the table without showing it.

Play The dealer deals the top card from the deck face up onto the table in front of the bettor.

If the player holds a card of higher rank in the same suit, he wins; if not, he loses. If he has won, he shows the winning card only (a), and receives back his bet and an equal amount from the pool. If he has lost, he shows all his hand (b), and his bet is added to the pool.

In either case, his hand is then placed face down in front of him.

Bet and play then pass one player to the left.

When all players including the dealer have had a turn of play, the deal passes to the next player to the left. Any money in the pool remains, but all players ante again before the next deal.

Empty pool If the pool is emptied during a round, all players ante again to allow the round to continue. They must still ante again before the next round begins.

Division of the pool Sometimes the pool becomes too large for the level of betting. It is best if a limit for the pool is agreed beforehand. If the pool passes that limit, it is divided among the players at the end of that round.

Irregularities

1  If a player receives no hand, or too many cards in his hand, he may not take part in the round. The dealer is not penalized.

2  If a player receives too few cards in his hand, he may bet if he wishes, or he may discard his hand without showing it and without betting or paying a forfeit. The dealer is not penalized.

3  If the top card of the deck is accidentally exposed, it is discarded.

4  Once a player has stated his bet, he cannot alter it. A bet paid into the pool in error cannot be returned. A bet received from the pool in error cannot be taken back once the top card for the next player has been dealt.

## VARIANTS OF RED DOG

Burning card version The dealer "burns" a card from the top of the deck before each card that he exposes to settle a bet. That is, at each bettor's turn, the dealer discards the topmost card after turning it face up and showing it to all the players. The next card is then turned up to decide whether the bettor has won or lost.

Banking version Red dog can also be played as a banking game. The current dealer acts as banker. He does not deal to himself. Before the hand, the dealer places in front of him the money or chips he wishes to put at risk. This can be any amount he wishes. The players do not ante.

Each player in turn, excluding the banker, bets any amount he wishes up to the total then in the bank.

Any amount left in the bank at the end of the hand is returned to the banker. The bank and deal then pass on to the left. If the bank is emptied before all players have had a turn, the hand ends and the bank and deal pass at once.

## SIX-SPOT RED DOG: POOL VERSION
In this version there is no banker; players ante into a pool.

Equipment:

**1** one standard deck of 52 cards;

**2** betting chips or cash.

Players The game is for two to 15 players.

Rank of cards is normal (ace high).

Objective Players aim to hold a card in the same suit but of higher rank than the pool card.

Choice of first dealer is by deal: first ace to appear (see page 13).

Shuffle and cut are normal (see page 13).

Ante Before each deal, each player including the dealer puts an agreed equal amount into the pool.

Deal The dealer deals three face down cards to each player including himself, beginning with the player to his left and going clockwise.

The dealer then deals one card fron the top of the deck face up to the center of the table. If it is a 6 or lower (6,5,4,3 or 2) it becomes the pool card. If it is a 7 or higher, it is discarded and the next card from the top of the deck is dealt face up onto the table. This procedure is repeated until a 6 or lower card is dealt to become the pool card. If there is no such card left in the deck, the hand is redealt.

**Deal**

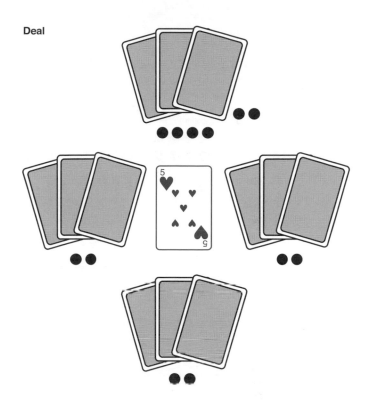

Betting All players including the dealer bet immediately without looking at their cards. The minimum bet is one chip
(or a previously agreed sum of money); the maximum is
the amount in the pool. More than one player may bet the
maximum.

Play Players then turn their hands face up. (See diagram overleaf.) If a player has a card of the same suit but ranking
higher than the pool card, he has won. If not, he has lost.

Settlement of bets is supervised by the dealer. He first adds to

**Play**

the pool the bets of all players who have lost. Then he pays out to those players who have won, beginning with the player to his left and going clockwise. Winning bets are returned together with an equal amount from the pool.

If the pool is emptied before all winning players have been paid, the remaining players receive back only their bets. If anything remains in the pool after all bets have been settled, this amount is carried over to the next round.

The deal then passes one player to the left, and all players ante again to begin the next round.

## SIX-SPOT RED DOG: BANKING VERSION

In this version the dealer acts as banker, he does not bet.

Bank Before the hand, the banker places in front of him any amount he wishes to put at risk. The players do not ante.

Deal The banker deals to the players as usual but excludes himself. He then deals one card at a time to the table in the usual way, until a 6 or lower card is dealt. This is now referred to as the banker's card.

Betting begins with the player to the banker's left. He may bet ("cover") any amount up to the total of the bank. Subsequent players may only bet against any amount of the bank that has not yet been "covered." The total of bets against the bank cannot therefore exceed the amount in the bank.

If all the bank has been covered before all players have bet, the remaining players are not allowed to bet on that hand.

Any part of the bank that is not covered when all players have bet is not at risk in that hand.

Play and settlement of bets takes place in the usual way. When all bets have been settled, any amount left in the bank is returned to the banker. The bank and deal then pass one player to the left.

# 3+ SKINBALL

Skinball is a very fast action game played in gaming houses in the American South and Midwest. It is very similar to ziginette and seems originally to have been a black American version of that game. It is also called skin or skinning.

Equipment
1  one standard deck of 52 cards;
2  a card box that allows only one card to be removed at a time.

Players The game is played by three or more people. One person is banker.

There is also a house official who keeps a watch on proceedings, transfers dead cards to the discard pile, collects and pays bets for the banker, and takes the house's percentage cut. (The house never banks the game.)

The objective is for a player not to have his card matched before the banker's card has been matched. Also, if the player has made side bets, he aims not to have his card matched before the card of any player that he has bet against has been matched.

A card is "matched" when another card of the same denomination is dealt from the card box.

Choice of first banker is by deal – the first ace to appear.

Shuffle and cut (see page 13). After the cut, the banker places the deck face down in the card box.

Betting limits are decided by the banker and can be altered by him at will.

Opening play The banker slides the top card from the card box and deals it face up to the first player to his right.

The player may accept the card or refuse it for any reason.

If a player refuses a card he is out of the game until the

next turn of play. The card that has been refused is offered to the next player to his right.

As soon as a player accepts this first card, the banker deals a second face up card from the box to himself: this is the banker's card.

Opening bet The player who has accepted the card states his bet. This may be for any amount within the betting limits.

Even if the bet is within the limits, however, the banker need not accept it. He may reduce it to any amount he chooses. If the banker does this, the player must accept the decision; he cannot withdraw.

Whichever bet the banker accepts, he places the corresponding amount of money in the center of the player's card.

The player then makes his bet by literally "covering" the banker's money with his own.

Next card in play The banker deals a third card from the box.

If this card's denomination matches either the banker's or the player's card, then the bet involved is settled.

If the card matches the banker's card, the amount on the player's card is won by the player.

If the card matches the player's card, the amount on his card is won by the banker.

If the third card does not match either of the earlier cards, it is dealt to the next player in turn. He may accept or refuse it. If he refuses it, it is offered to the next player in turn. Once the card is accepted, a bet is placed against the banker in the usual way.

Bets between players When more than one player has a card, bets may be made between them.

A player bets that the other player's card will be matched before his own.

Either of the two players may suggest the bet; the other player must be in agreement for the bet to take place.

Money involved in bets between players is stacked to one side.

Matched cards Each time a card is matched, the houseman takes both cards and puts them in a discard pile. The other two cards of the same denomination still in the deck are not allowed to enter play. When one appears it is put directly into the discard pile and a further card is dealt.

Continuation of play As long as the banker's card is not matched, the deal and betting continue as above until each player has been offered a card.

The banker then continues to deal further cards (one at a time and face up) to the table. Any card that appears that does not match either a player's card, a discarded card, or the banker's card is called a "fresh" card.

If there is a player without a card – either because he refused an earlier card or because his card has been matched – he is offered the first fresh card to appear.

If there is more than one player without a card, the fresh card is offered first to the player without a card who is nearest the banker's right.

If he refuses it, it is offered to the next player to his right without a card.

Any fresh cards that appear when every player is holding a card are placed face up in the center of the table. A player may accept any one of them as soon as the card he holds has been matched.

Each time a player accepts a card, he makes a bet against the banker in the usual way. A player with a card will often have side bets against every other player, but he must bet against the banker first.

Banker's card matched Whenever the banker's card is matched, all the players betting against him at the time win the amounts on their cards.

If there are no unsettled side bets, the bank passes to the next player to the right. All cards are collected and shuffled for the next deal.

If there are unsettled side bets, the banker chooses either:

a to continue to deal for the betting players only – he does not enter into any further bets himself and does not give out any fresh cards; or

b to take the first fresh card dealt from the deck as his new banker's card.

Any player's cards that are matched while the banker has no card become dead without the players losing their bets.

After the banker has a new card, players without cards may take fresh cards as they appear, and place new bets. Although players with outstanding side bets may make new bets against the banker, they are not obliged to do so.

When the bank is exhausted, the bank must pass.

House percentage The house takes either:

a 25% of the last winning bet of each deal; or

b 2% from each bet won by a player against the banker, plus 2% of the banker's winnings, if any, at the end of his deal.

## 2–8 **SLIPPERY SAM**

This is a private banking game related to red dog. It is popular in parts of America's Midwest.

Equipment:
    **1** one standard deck of 52 cards;
    **2** betting chips or cash.

Players Ideally six to eight, but two or more can play.

Rank of cards is normal (ace high). Suits are not ranked.

Objective Players aim to hold a card in the same suit but of a higher rank that the banker's card.

Choice of first banker is by high cut (see page 13).

Shuffle and cut are normal (see page 13).

Bank The banker places in the center of the table the amount he wishes to put at risk. This is any amount above an agreed minimum.

Deal The banker deals three cards to each player, dealing them one at a time and face down. He then deals one card face up to himself.

Play Players bet without looking at their hands. Play begins with the player to the banker's left. He may agree or refuse to bet against the exposed banker's card.

    **1** If he agrees, he bets any amount he chooses, above an agreed minimum, up to the total amount in the bank. He then looks at his cards. If he holds a card in the same suit but of higher rank than the banker's card, he wins; if not, he loses.

    **2** Alternatively, he refuses to bet against the exposed banker's card. In this case he says "Deal me another card." For this privilege he may pay into the bank an amount equal to one fifth of the bank (or, under alternative rules, he pays a previously agreed amount).

      The exposed banker's card is then discarded and

another card dealt from the top of the deck face up onto the table.

This becomes the new banker's card. The player either bets against this card in the usual way, or pays again for a new banker's card to be dealt.

**Deal**

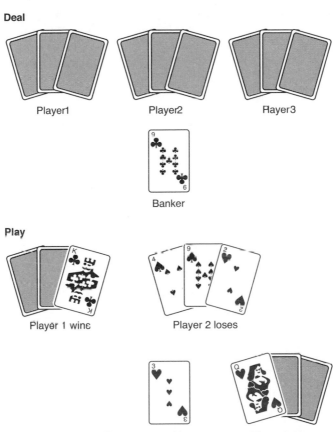

Player1

Player2

Player3

Banker

**Play**

Player 1 wins

Player 2 loses

Banker's new card

Player 3 wins

A player may reject the banker's card up to three times on a single hand, paying the same amount each time.

After the third rejection, the player may either bet in the usual way against the banker's card now exposed, or he may pass his turn without betting.

3 If the player has bet and won, he shows his winning card only. His bet is returned, plus an equal amount from the bank.

If he has bet and lost, he shows all his hand and his bet is added to the bank.

Whether he has won or lost, his hand is then added face down to a discard pile.

4 Bet and play then pass one player to the left, and continue in the same way. Each player's turn begins with the banker's card on which the last player bet or passed: a new banker's card is dealt only when paid for.

When all players except the banker have had a turn, the banker collects whatever amount is now in the bank. Bank and deal then pass one player to the left.

If the bank is emptied ("bust") before each player has had a turn, the bank and deal pass immediately.

# 2–10 **STUSS**

Stuss is a simplified form of faro with a larger percentage in the gambling house's favor.

Equipment:
1 a table with the stuss layout, usually made up of the entire spades suit;
2 a dealing box allowing one card to be removed at a time, but with a recess ("pocket") at the bottom of the box that prevents the last four cards of the deck appearing in play;
3 a standard 52-card deck;
4 betting chips of various colors.

Players Up to ten can play. House officials are a dealer and a lookout who supervises betting.

The objective is for a player to bet on a denomination that subsequently appears as a winning card before it appears as a losing card.

Cards appear in play two at a time. The first in each pair is always the losing card, the second is the winning card.

Shuffle, cut, and bet The house dealer shuffles the cards, cuts the deck, and puts it face down in the box.

Bets are then placed on the layout.

Betting A player may place as many bets as he wishes, but each bet is on one denomination only. A bet is always for a denomination to win – i.e., that the next card of that denomination to appear will be the second (winning) card in a turn.

A turn
1 The dealer removes the top card from the box and places it face up to the right.
2 Any bets on the denomination of this (losing) card are collected by the house.

3 The dealer removes the next card from the box and places it face up to the left.

4 Any bets on the denomination of this card are won by the bettors. Their bet is returned together with an equal payment by the house.

Between turns Other bets may be changed and new bets placed.

Continuing play Play continues in this way through the deck.

The two cards in play in each turn are added to those played previously, to form a winning and a losing pile.

Eventually no more cards can be dealt. There will then have been 24 two-card turns, and four cards will still remain in the pocket of the box.

Pocket cards The dealer opens the box and shows the four remaining cards. If any bets have been placed on their denominations, they are all won by the house.

Splits If two cards of the same denomination appear on a turn (a "split'), any bets on that denomination are won by the house.

Second bets are bets on a denomination of which one card has already been dealt; usually they are bet on in the normal way. Some casinos, however, do not allow second bets. In this case, the last four cards are not "pocketed" but appear for play and for betting in the normal way.

Variants

1 In a very simple form of stuss, the cards are dealt from the hand.

2 Stuss is sometimes played as a private banking game; the role of banker is taken by the player willing to put up the largest bank.

# 2–5 THIRTY-FIVE

Thirty-five is a modern version of the Italian game of trentacinque. Bets are placed in a central pool; there is no banker.

**Card values**

| 10 | 10 | 10 | 10 | 9 | 8 | 7 | 6 | 5 | 4 | 3 | 2 | 1 |

Equipment:
1 one standard deck of 52 cards;
2 betting chips or cash.

Players The game is for two to five players.

Rank of cards Face cards count 10 points; others count their numerical face value.

Objective Each player aims to hold a total of 35 points or more in one suit.

Choice of first dealer is by high cut (see page 13).

Shuffle and deal are normal (see page 13).

Ante Before each hand, each player including the dealer places an agreed equal amount in the center of the table to constitute the pool.

Deal
1 The dealer deals one card face down to each player including himself and then one card face down to the center of the table. He continues in this way until each hand, including the hand on the table, contains four cards. He then deals no further cards to the center of the

**Deal**

table, but continues dealing to each player, including himself, until each has a further five cards. Thus the hand at the center of the table contains four cards and the other hands nine cards each.

2 The remaining cards of the deck are placed to one side and do not enter subsequent play.

3 The players then examine their cards. A player who holds cards in any one suit to the value of 35 or over announces this and takes the pool. If two or more players have 35 or more, the pool is divided between them.

4 If no player claims the pool, bidding begins.

Bidding for the "buy" Betting takes the form of bidding for the table hand – the "buy."

Bidding begins with the player to the dealer's left. His opening bid may be any amount up to the total in the pool.

(If he does not wish to bid, he throws in his cards.)

Thereafter, each player may raise the bid or throw in his cards until only one player is left prepared to bid. He then takes the table hand and adds it to the nine cards he already holds.

Settlement involves only the pool and the player who has taken the table hand. If the player now holds cards to the value of 35 or over in any one suit, he declares this, shows his cards, and takes an amount from the pool equal to his bid. If his bid exceeded the amount of the pool, he takes all the pool but has no further claim.

If the player does not hold cards in one suit to the value of 35 or more, he pays into the pool an amount equal to his bid.

Division of the pool Sometimes the pool becomes too large for the level of betting. It is best if a limit for the pool is agreed beforehand. If the pool passes that limit, it is divided among the players.

Change of dealer The deal passes one player to the left after each hand.

**End of play**

Making 35 – in hearts

## 3-15 THIRTY-ONE

The name thirty-one comes from the number of points awarded to the highest scoring hand (ace, queen, 10 of the same suit) in this pool betting game. An alternative name is schnautz.

**Card values**

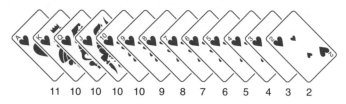

| | | | | | | | | | | | | |
|---|---|---|---|---|---|---|---|---|---|---|---|---|
| 11 | 10 | 10 | 10 | 10 | 9 | 8 | 7 | 6 | 5 | 4 | 3 | 2 |

Equipment:
  **1** one standard deck of 52 cards;
  **2** betting chips or cash.
Players From 3 to 15.
Value of cards Aces count 11, face cards 10, and all other cards their numerical face value.
Rank of cards is normal, ace high. Thus although face cards all count 10, king beats queen, and queen beats jack.
Objective Players aim to obtain the highest points count from three cards of the same suit or rank.
Choice of first dealer is by low cut (see page 13).
Shuffle and cut are normal (see page 13).
Ante Before each hand, each player including the dealer puts an agreed amount into a pool.
Deal The dealer deals one card face down to each player including himself, beginning with the player to this left and going clockwise; and then one card face up to the center. This continues until all players and the table hand (the "widow") each have three cards.

**Deal**

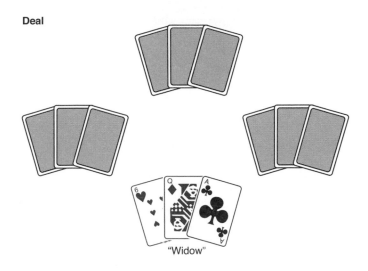

"Widow"

Play Each player examines his cards and announces immediately if he holds:

a three cards of one suit – with a points total of 31 ("31 points");

b any three cards of the same rank ("three cards");

c three cards of one suit – with a points total that he feels is high enough to win ("x points").

If a player announces immediately, all players show their hands and the highest point count wins.

If a player announces immediately, the player to the dealer's left must exchange one of his cards with any face up card on the table. (Sometimes it is agreed that two or even three cards may be exchanged in one turn). He is not allowed to pass. The next player then does the same. Cards that have been put out by a player may subsequently be picked up.

**Play**

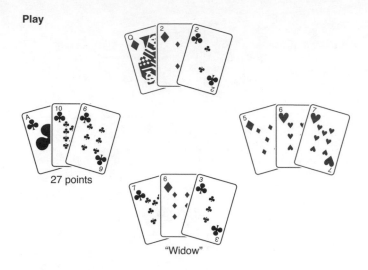

27 points

"Widow"

Play continues around the table in this way until one player has 31 points or is satisfied with his cards.

If a player has 31 points he must announce it immediately, and all exchanging ends. All players then show their hands.

If a player is satisfied with his hand, he knocks on the table instead of exchanging a card in his next turn. In this case, hands are not shown until each of the other players in turn has had the option of exchanging one more card.

The pool is won by the player who shows the best hand. The deal then passes to the next player to the left.

Scoring of hands A hand with three cards of the same rank scores $30\frac{1}{2}$; all others score their points count.

Where two or more players have hands scoring the same number of points, the hand containing the higher ranking card wins. For example: ace, king, queen beats ace, queen, jack. (Note that a score of 25 or 26 points often wins.)

## 2+ TRENTE ET QUARANTE

Trente et quarante is one of the most popular games in French and Italian casinos, although it is rarely found elsewhere. It originated in seventeenth-century Europe and is also known as rouge et noir.

**Card values**

| 10 | 10 | 10 | 10 | 9 | 8 | 7 | 6 | 5 | 4 | 3 | 2 | 1 |

Equipment:
1 regulation table with trente et quarante double layout;
2 six standard 52-card decks shuffled together to form a single deck of 312 cards;
3 an indicator card for cutting the deck.

Players Any number of people can play up to the limit that the table will accommodate.

Five croupiers operate the game: four control the bank and one acts as dealer ("tailleur"). A supervisor sits on a stand overlooking the table.

Value of cards Court cards count 10. All other cards count their face value, with aces counting one.

The objective is to bet which of two rows of cards will give a total points count near 31.

Shuffle and cut At the start of a round of play the dealing croupier spreads all six decks on the table. (If it is not the first round of play, the cards must first be taken from the discard receiver and sorted until they are all face down.)

All croupiers and players each take a group of cards and shuffle them. The croupier then gathers all the cards and gives them a further shuffle. He offers one player the whole deck to cut. The player iserts the indicator card at the point at which he wants the cards cut. The dealer cuts the deck at this point and the indicator card and all cards above it go to the bottom of the deck.

Betting All bets are placed against the bank. Before the play, players bet in one or both of the following ways, placing their bets on the layout.

a Players bet which row will win, either black (N for "noir" on the layout) or red (R for "rouge").

b Players bet whether the suit color of the very first card dealt will or will not match the color of the winning row. If they want to bet that it will match, they bet on C for "couleur" on the layout. If they want to bet that it will not match, they bet on I for "inverse."

Play The players place their bets (see the section on betting).

The dealing croupier then takes about 50 cards from the top of the deck and deals one card face up onto the table.

He then deals further cards face up, placing them alternately to the right and left of the first card. After each card he announces the total number of points now contained in the row. When the total equals or passes 31 points he stops

**Sample betting and play**

a bets black row to win
b bets red row
c bets first card will match winning row
d bets first card will not match winning row

**Black row**

33 points

**Red row**

37 points

The black row is nearer to 31, and so wins
a wins
b loses
c wins
d loses

dealing. This first row is called the "black" row, whatever the suit color of the cards it contains.

The dealing croupier in exactly the same way then deals a second row below the first. This is the "red" row. He again stops dealing when the total equals or passes 31 points.

The row with the points total nearer to 31 is the winning row.

The winning total will always be in the range 31 to 39 inclusive – i.e., between 30 and 40. It is from this that the game takes its name.

Settlement of bets After the deal the dealing croupier announces the result.

Traditionally he calls the results for red and color only, i.e., "Rouge gagne" (red wins) or "Rouge perd" (red loses), and "Couleur gagne" (color wins) or "Couleur perd" (color loses).

The croupiers collect all losing bets. All winning bets are paid off at even money (1 to 1). If both rows tie at more than 31 (a "refait"), all bets are returned.

If both rows tie at 31 ("refait de trente et un") the bank takes half of all bets and returns the remainder, or, rather than lose half his bet, a player may decide to leave his bet in "prison" (P on the layout) for the next deal. If his original bet is successful in this next deal, his bet is returned but earns no money. If it is unsuccessful he now loses all his bet. (Sometimes with a bet in prison the player may choose whether to maintain his original bet or transfer it to its opposite.)

Insurance bet Before a hand is dealt, a player can indicate that he wishes to insure against a tie at 31. The charge for this is 5% of his wager.

## 2–8 **YABLON**

This game is also called in between and ace-deuce. It is most commonly played as a pool game.

Equipment:
1 one standard deck of 52 cards;
2 betting chips or cash.

Players From two to eight.

Rank of cards is normal, ace high. Suits have no significance.

Objective Each player hopes to draw a card ranking between his first two cards.

Choice of first dealer is by deal: first ace to appear (see page 13).

Shuffle and cut are normal (see page 13).

Ante Before each deal each player including the dealer puts an equal agreed amount into the pool.

Deal The dealer deals two face down cards one at a time to each player including himself.

**Deal**

**Play**

Player wins

Consecutive cards: no bet

Player loses

Play Begins with the player to the dealer's left.

1 He examines his cards and decides whether to bet.

2 If he does not wish to bet he says "No bet," and returns his cards to the dealer to be placed on a discard pile. Play then passes to the left.

   If the next player does not wish to bet, he places his bet in front of him near the pool. The minimum bet is the same amount as a player's ante; the maximum is the total then in the pool.

3 The dealer deals him the top card from the deck, face up. This is called the player's draw card.

4 The player turns his two original cards face up.

5 If his draw card ranks between his original two cards, the player wins. For example, if he has a 5 and a 9 he must draw a 6, 7 or 8 to win; if he has a 2 and an ace

he can draw any card except a 2 or an ace to win. Note
that if a player holds two identical cards (e.g., two 6s) or
two consecutive cards (e.g., 10 and jack), he cannot win
and will not bet.

6  If the player has won, he retains his bet and takes from
the pool a similar sum. If he has lost, his bet goes to the
pool.

7  Each player including the dealer has a turn of play, with
turns passing to the left.

Continuing play After each player has had a turn, the deal
passes to the player to the dealer's left. He collects all the
cards, shuffles them and has them cut for the next hand.

Any money left in the pool remains for the next hand,
but players also ante again.

Division of pool If the pool passes a limit agreed beforehand it
is immediately divided among the players.

## BANKING VERSION

Yablon can also be played as a banking game. The dealer
acts as banker and does not deal himself a hand.

Before the hand, the dealer places in front of him the
money or chips he wishes to put at risk. This can be any
amount he wishes. The players do not ante.

Each player in turn bets any amount he wishes, up to the
amount then in the bank. The dealer does not have a turn.

Any amount left in the bank at the end of the hand is
returned to the banker. The bank and deal then pass one
player to the left.

If the bank is emptied before all players have had a turn,
the hand ends and the bank and deal pass at once.

# 2+ ZIGINETTE

Ziginette is the Italians' favorite way of seeing money change hands at cards. The rules given here are those played in American gaming houses.

**Cards used**

Equipment:
1 one standard 52-card deck from which all the 8s, 9s, and 10s have been removed, leaving 40 cards;
2 a metal card box that allows only one card to be removed at a time.

Players Two or more people can play. One person is the banker. There are also two house officials. One, the "cutter," collects and pays bets for the banker and takes the house percentage cut. (The house never banks the game). The other, the "lookout," keeps a watch on proceedings and transfers dead cards to the discard pile.

The objective is for a player to bet on a table card that is not matched by the time the banker's card has been matched. A card is "matched" when another card of the same denomination becomes visible at the top of the card box.

Choice of first bank is by deal – the first ace to appear. The cutter carries out the deal after he has shuffled the cards and has them cut by any player.

Shuffle and cut See page 13.

Any player other than the banker cuts the cards. The banker places the deck face up in the card box.

Deal The banker deals two cards from the box face up onto the table. The next card in the box is now visible: this is the banker's card.

If all three cards are of different denominations, players may now bet; if they are not, special rules govern further procedure (see the section on "playette," page 345).

Opening bet Any player other than the banker may place a bet on one or both of the table cards.

Betting limits The banker decides the minimum and maximum allowable bets and can alter them at will between stages of play.

Opening play The banker takes the banker's card from the box and places it so that one end rests beneath the card box but most of it is visible. It stays in this position for the rest of the deal.

This action exposes the next card in the box. If this card matches any card on the table (including the banker's

**Opening play**

Banker's card matches

Table card matches

card), any bets involved are settled. But if it does not match any card on the table, there is no further action in this turn, unless any player wishes to place a further bet.

Settlement of bets If at any time a card exposed in the box matches the banker's card, the banker loses all unsettled bets, i.e., he pays all outstanding bets by players on all table cards.

Settlement is at even money – a winning player gets back his stake plus an equal amount from the bank. Play on this deal then ceases and the bank and the deck pass one player to the right. If a card exposed in the box matches a table card on which bets have been placed, these bets are won by the banker and he continues to operate the bank.

The house cutter pays out the banker's loses and collects his winnings for him. He takes a 10% house cut from each bet won by the bank.

Next turn of play If the banker's card has not been matched, then any settlement of bets and placing of new bets ends the turn of play.

The exposed card is taken from the card box.

1 If the exposed card has matched a table card, then the exposed card and the table card it matched are now dead (even if the table card had no bets placed on it).

The cutter takes both cards and places them to one side out of play. They are dead for the remainder of the deal, as are the other two cards of the same denomination still in the card box. If cards appearing in the box are the same denomination as cards already matched, they are removed and added to the discard pile. The discard pile is kept fanned out so that the denominations of dead cards can be seen.

2 If the exposed card has not matched the table card, then it is placed face up on the table alongside the other table

cards. It is now available for players to bet on in the usual way at the end of a turn of play, provided it is not immediately matched by the new exposed card in the box. If it is immediately matched, both it and the matching card are transferred to the discard pile in the usual way and the other cards of the same denomination are also dead.

Summary of continuation play After the opening play, turns are as follows.

1 The top card is removed from the card box. If, on the previous turn, this card matched the table card, both are placed on the discard pile. If the top card was the same denomination as a card already matched, the top card is added to the discard pile. If the top card matched neither a table card nor a dead card, it is added to the table cards.

2 If the card now exposed in the box matches a table card, any bets involved are settled. If it matches the banker's card, the banker collects all bets and the deal ends.

3 If the banker's card has not been matched, players can bet on any card now on the table. This includes any card just added to the table, providing that this card has not been immediately matched by the new card exposed in the box.

Playette This is the term used when two cards of the same denomination appear in the opening deal. It is usually ruled "no deal." The cards are removed from the box and reshuffled. Sometimes the rule is that duplicate cards are "doubled up."

Doubling up – opening deal If two table cards match they are placed together, and the top card from the box is dealt to fill the empty table position.

If a table card and a box card match, the box card is added to the table card's position. In either case, the next card in the box becomes the banker's card.

**Doubling up — settlement of bets** When any two cards have been doubled up, whatever the denomination, no bets are settled until three cards of that denomination have appeared. For example, the bank does not win the bet on the 6s until a further 6 has been exposed; the bank does not win the bet on the queen of hearts until two further queens have been exposed; the bank does not lose until two further 10s have been exposed.

**Tripling** If all three cards of the opening deal are of the same denomination, then (providing "doubling up" is allowed) they are all placed together on one of the table hand positions. No decision is reached on any bet, or on the bank, until four cards of a denomination have been exposed.

**Change of banker** A banker may pass the bank at any time when there are no unsettled bets on the table.

When the banker's card is matched he must pass the bank.

All cards are collected, shuffled, and cut before the new game begins.

**Doubling up**

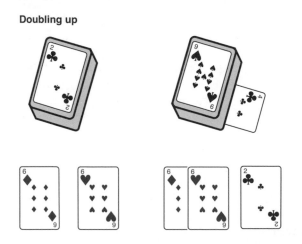

# Solitaire Card Games

## PROCEDURE AND TERMS

Patience and solitaire are general names for any card game for one player. The exact origin of such games is obscure, but they have probably existed for centuries and several hundred different games exist today. Although the outcome of many of these games depends mainly on the luck of the shuffle, others involve real skill and judgment. In addition to games for one player, this section also includes two games for two players: Russian bank and spite and malice, which share many of the features of games devised for one.

Cards Some games are played with a standard 52-card deck, others with two decks shuffled together.

Yet others are played with a "stripped" deck, from which certain cards have been discarded prior to play.

Special cards, smaller than ordinary playing cards, may be used; these are especially useful when playing in a confined space.

Certain games allow for the inclusion of a joker.

Ace, unless otherwise specified, ranks low.

Objective The object of many games is to build up sequences of cards in their suits onto base cards known as "foundations."

A second group of games involves the pairing up of certain cards.

Other games have quite a different objective, such as rebuilding the deck into a single pile, or discarding all the cards in the deck.

If a game is successful, i.e., if the game's objective is exactly achieved, it is said to "come out" or to "go through."

If a game is "blocked" this means that the cards are such that the game cannot possibly be won.

Layout At the start of most games, cards are laid out in a prescribed formation that varies from game to game. This formation or "tableau," together with any other cards dealt out at the beginning of play, forms the "layout."

Foundation cards are the first cards of certain piles onto which sequences of cards are built (the objective of many games).

In some games they form part of the layout and are set out at the beginning of a game. More often, they are not included in the layout, but are put out as they come into play.

They are usually cards of a specified rank – often aces. With rare exceptions (such as in King Albert) a card cannot be removed once it has been placed in a foundation.

Spaces (sometimes called vacancies) are gaps in the layout into which cards may legitimately be played, or places from which the cards have been removed and which may or may not be reoccupied, depending on the rules of the game.

Reserve In some games the layout includes one or more cards that may be brought into play as appropriate. This "reserve" of cards may not, however, be built onto – unlike the cards in the tableau.

The stock comprises those cards that remain after the layout has been dealt.

The stock is invariably kept face down, and may be brought into play in different ways according to the rules for particular games.

Waste pile or heap Cards from the stock that cannot immediately be played onto the layout are sometimes

## Building

a
b
c
d
e
f

placed face up in one or more waste piles, to be brought
back into the game as appropriate.

The discard pile is made up of any cards that have been set
aside during the course of play and that are not brought
back into the game.

The objective of some games is to discard all or most of
the deck.

Available cards Any card that can, in accordance with the
rules, be played onto the tableau, foundations, or spaces is
termed "available."

Sometimes the removal of a card "releases" the card next to
it; for example when the top card of a waste pile is removed
and makes the next card in the pile available for play.

Exposed cards A card is usually only available for play if it is
fully exposed, i.e., if no other card covers it either wholly
or partially.

Building is the term used for placing a card onto the tableau,
foundations, or a space in its correct sequence. This may
be done numerically, by suit or by color.

a Cards may be "built down" numerically (e.g., a 7 is built
onto an 8, a 6 onto the 7, etc).

b Cards may be "built up" numerically (e.g., a 3 is built onto
a 2, a 4 onto the 3, etc).

c Sometimes the numerical sequence may be continuous or
"round the corner" (e.g., 3,2,a,k,q), or in twos (e.g.,
7,9,j,k,2,4, etc).

d A card may only be built onto another card of the same
suit (e.g., all hearts). Or, in other games, a card may only
be built onto a card of a suit other than its own.

e A card may only be built onto a card of the same color
(e.g., all red cards).

f A card may only be built onto a card of the other color
(e.g., red, black, red, black).

# ACCORDION

Accordion, also called Tower of Babel, idle year, or Methuselah, is one of the most difficult single-deck games to get out. It is unusual in that there is no formal layout at the start of the game: the cards are merely dealt in a single row.

Cards One standard 52-card deck is used.

Objective The player aims to rebuild the deck into a single pile.

Play The cards are dealt out face up in a row, as many at a time as space allows.

Any card may be moved onto the card immediately to the left, or onto the third card to the left, provided it is of the same suit or has the same rank.

A pile of two or more cards, identified by its top card, can be similarly moved.

If a card matches both its neighbor and the card three to the left, the player may choose either move, taking into account the various possibilities.

# BELEAGUERED CASTLE

Beleaguered castle is also known by the names of sham battle and laying siege.

Cards One standard deck of 52 cards is used.

Layout Set out the four aces in a column as foundation cards. Then deal out the rest of the deck face up to form wings of six overlapping cards to the left and right of each ace; it is usual to deal columns of four cards alternately to the left and to the right of the aces.

The objective is to build up each suit in ascending numerical order, from ace through to king, on its correct foundation card.

Play Only the fully exposed cards at the ends of the rows in each wing are available for play (one card only being moved at a time). Available cards can either be moved onto one of the foundations, building suits numerically upward, or be transferred to the end of another wing, building numerically downward with no regard to suit. Spaces, created by removal of an entire row, may be filled by transferring any exposed card.

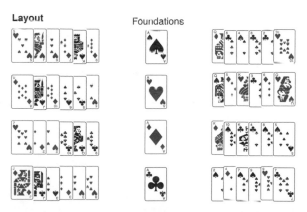

**Layout**          Foundations

# BISLEY

Kings as well as aces come into play as foundation cards in this single-deck game.

Cards A standard 52-deck is used.

Layout Set out the four aces at the beginning of the top row of the tableau. Deal nine cards to the right of the aces; then deal the rest of the deck to complete a layout of four rows of 13 cards each. In the course of play, as they become available, the four kings are put out in a row above their aces (king of hearts above ace of hearts, etc.).

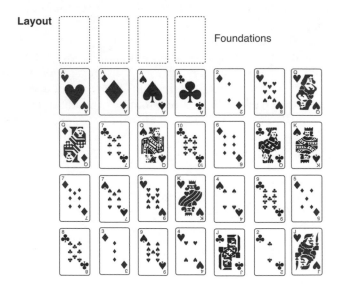

**Layout**

Foundations

Objective The aces and the kings are foundation cards, and the aim is to complete entire suits, by building up in suit sequence on the aces and building down in suit sequence on the kings.

When the two sequences meet they are put together (it does not matter at which point they meet).

Play The bottom card of each column of the tableau is available for play, either onto a foundation or onto the bottom card of another column.

Building onto the bottom cards of the columns is in ascending or descending suit sequence as the player wishes, and he may at any time reverse the order.

Spaces created in the tableau are not filled.

It is evidently important to free the kings as soon as possible, and to use every opportunity of building onto the foundations.

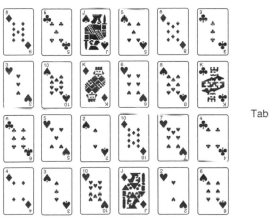

Tableau

# BRAID

Braid, or plait, is a straightforward game that gets its name from its particularly attractive layout.

Cards Two standard 52-card decks are used.

Layout Twenty cards are dealt face up in the form of a braid: the cards are laid out diagonally, and alternately pointing to right and left – each card partially covering the card beneath it (as illustrated).

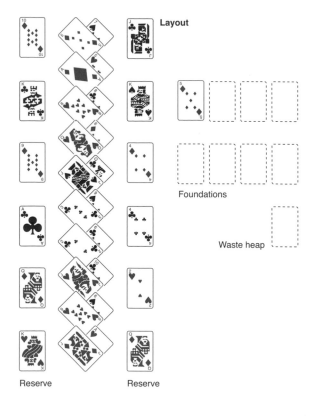

**Layout**

Foundations

Waste heap

Reserve     Reserve

Columns of six face up cards are dealt to either side of the braid; the braid and the columns together form the reserve.

The next (33rd) card is placed to the right of the reserve. It determines the rank of the other seven foundations, which are set out as they become available to make two rows of four cards.

Objective The player tries to build ascending "round the corner" suit sequences on the eight foundations (ace following king and preceding 2).

Play The bottom (fully exposed) card of the braid and all the cards in the two columns are available for play onto the foundations.

The stock is dealt one card at a time, and if the card is unplayable it is placed on a waste heap.

Any number of redeals is permitted, until the game either becomes blocked or goes through.

A space in the columns must be filled as soon as it occurs.

If the top or bottom card of a column has been removed, the vacancy may be filled by the available card of the braid, or from the top of the waste heap (which is always available).

If the vacancy is anywhere else in the column, it may only be filled from the stock.

# BRISTOL

In this game, eight fans and three waste heaps provide the cards to be transferred onto four foundations.

Cards One standard 52-card deck is used.

Layout Deal 24 cards, face up, in eight fans each of three cards. Any kings that turn up in the deal are placed at the bottom of their respective fans.

Next to this tableau, deal three more cards face up in a row to form the start of the waste heaps or reserve.

**Layout**

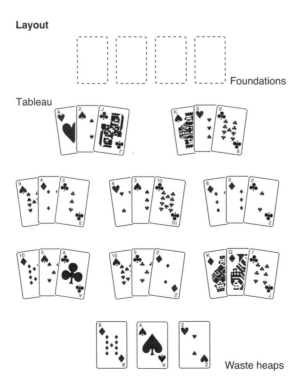

Foundations

Tableau

Waste heaps

Objective The foundation cards are aces, which are set out in a row above the tableau as they occur in play. The aim is to build four ascending sequences, ace through king, regardless of suit or color.

Play The top cards of the fans and the three waste heaps are available for play, but only one card may be moved at a time – either to a foundation or in descending sequence, regardless of suit or color, onto the exposed card of another fan.

The stock is dealt three cards at a time, one card to each of the three waste heaps.

Spaces in the waste heaps are filled only in the deal. Spaces in the tableau (caused by the removal of an entire fan) remain unfilled. Only one deal is permitted.

# CALCULATION

Calculation is an aptly named game, for it involves a considerable amount of thinking ahead. (It is sometimes called broken intervals.)

**Layout**

Foundations                    Waste heaps

**Order of building**

Cards One standard 52-card deck is used.

Layout Set out in a row any ace, 2, 3, and 4 as the foundation cards.

The objective is to build up the rest of the deck on these base cards regardless of suit or color, but strictly in accordance with the following order: On the ace: 2,3,4,5,6,7,8,9,10,j,q,k. On the 2: 4,6,8,10,q,a,3,5,7,9,j,k. On the 3: 6,9,q,2,5,8,j,a,4,7,10,k. On the 4: 8,q,3,7,j,2,6, 10,a,5,9,k.

Play Cards are turned up one at a time and either built onto the appropriate base card or placed on one of the four waste heaps immediately beside these.

Only the top card on each waste heap is available and cards cannot be moved from one waste heap to another.

Any space in the waste heaps is filled with the top card of the stock.

Much of the skill of the game lies in playing the cards to the various heaps in such a way that they are later readily available for transfer to foundations.

For example, it is best to keep kings in one waste heap or, if they come out early, at the bottom of the waste heaps. Cards of the same rank should be dispersed among the waste heaps rather than concentrated in any single heap.

Whenever possible, cards should be played to the waste heaps in reverse order to their build-up on the foundations.

# CANFIELD

Canfield is named for the nineteenth-century American gambler and art collector Richard A. Canfield; this game is one of the most popular single-deck games. It is sometimes known as demon in the United Kingdom. (Another game sometimes known as Canfield in the United Kingdom is described here as Klondike.)

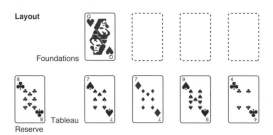

**Cards** One standard 52-card deck is used.

**Layout** Deal out a reserve pile of 13 cards face down, then turn the pile over to expose one card. Deal four more face up cards to the right of the reserve to form a tableau.

Above the first card of the tableau place the next card face up; this is the first of the four foundation cards and its rank determines the other three cards (which are laid out as they come into play).

Should one of the tableau cards have the same rank as the foundation, move it up into position and deal another card into the space left in the tableau.

**The objective** of the game is to build up the four suits on the foundation cards.

The cards rank continuously, i.e., if the foundation cards are kings, the next cards in the sequence must be aces.

**Play** The stock is turned over three cards at a time, only the exposed card of each three being in play (although cards

**Play**

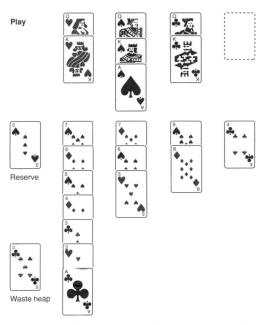

**Reserve**

**Waste heap**

below it can be played as they become available).

If there are only one or two cards at the end of the stock, they are dealt singly.

Cards are built up by suit on the foundations, and in descending alternate-color sequence regardless of suit on the columns of the tableau.

Provided the correct color and numerical sequences are maintained, an entire column of tableau can be transferred to another column.

Spaces in the tableau are filled immediately from the reserve. If the reserve is exhausted, the player may fill the space from the top of the waste heap, but he need not do so immediately.

Redeal The stock may be redealt, without shuffling, as many times as necessary until the game either blocks or is won.

# CLOCK

Although the chances of winning this game are slight, it is fun to play and very fast-moving. The name clock comes from the layout, which takes the form of a clock dial. Other names by which this game is known are sun dial, travelers, hidden cards, and four of a kind.

Cards One standard 52-card deck is used.

Layout The deck is dealt face down into 13 piles of four cards each. The cards may be dealt singly or in fours. The piles are arranged to represent a clock dial, one pile correspon- ding to each hour. The thirteenth pile is placed in the center.

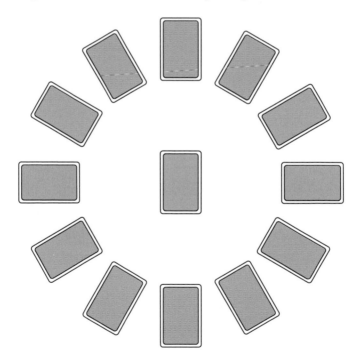

Objective By rearranging the cards, the player hopes to end up
with thirteen piles of like-numbered cards in their correct
"time" position: the four aces at one o'clock, the four 2s at
two o'clock, and so on around the dial.

The jacks represent 11 o'clock and the queens 12
o'clock. The four kings make up the thirteenth, center pile.

Play The player takes the card at the top of the center pile
and places it face up at the bottom of the pile of the same
number or "time." For example, if the card is a 7, it is put
face up underneath the seven o'clock pile.

The player then takes the top card of the seven o'clock
pile and puts it under its matching pile.

In this way the player works his way from pile to pile,
always removing the top card of the pile under which he
has just put its matching card.

If the player turns a card that happens to be on its correct
pile (e.g., a 3 is turned up from the three o'clock pile), it is
still placed at the bottom of the pile in the usual way, and
the next face down card is taken from the top of the pile.

The outcome depends on the order in which the kings are
turned up. If the fourth king is turned up before all the
other cards are face up, then the game is blocked. This
means in effect that the game can only be won if the last
card to be turned up is the fourth king. As the chance of
this happening is very small, the king may be exchanged for
any one face down card in the layout. Only one exchange is
allowed, and if the fourth king is again turned up before the
other cards are in the correct piles, then the game is lost.

# CRAZY QUILT

Crazy quilt is an unusual and interesting solitaire that gets its name from its layout of interwoven cards. It is also known as Indian carpet or Japanese rug.

**Layout**

Cards Two standard 52-card decks are used.

Layout Take an ace and a king of each suit and set them out face up in a row. These are the eight foundations.

Above them, deal out a reserve or "quilt" of eight rows of eight face up cards each, laying the cards vertically and horizontally in turn. Any card in the quilt that has one or both of its narrow sides free is available for play. For example, at the start of play four projecting cards at each side of the quilt are available.

Objective The aim is to build ascending suit sequences on the aces, and descending suit sequences on the kings.

Play Study the reserve to see if any available cards can be built onto the foundations. The removal of the reserve card releases one or more other reserve cards for play.

Spaces in the reserve remain unfilled.

Then turn up the stock one card at a time, putting the card in a waste heap if it cannot be played to a foundation. (The top card of the waste heap is always available.)

In order to release a useful card in the quilt, an available card may be played from the quilt to the top of the waste heap in either ascending or descending suit sequence.

The stock may be redealt once.

# EIGHT AWAY

Also called eight off, this game has a tableau of eight columns, none of which must ever contain more than eight cards.

Cards One standard 52-card deck is needed.

Layout Deal 48 cards face up in eight columns of six cards each. The cards in each column should overlap so that all are visible. Deal the remaining four cards face up in a row below the tableau to form the start of the reserve.

**Layout**

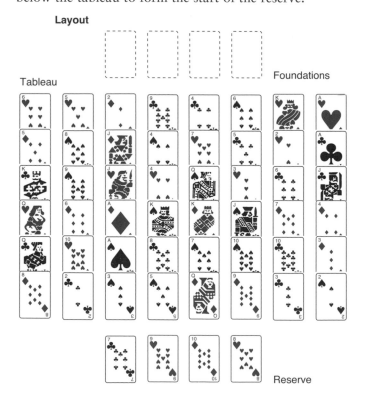

Tableau

Foundations

Reserve

Objective The player's aim is to free the aces (which are moved as they become available to form a row above the tableau), and to build on them suit sequences, ace through king.

Play The exposed cards in the tableau (those at the bottoms of the eight columns) and all the reserve cards are available for play.

They can be moved to the foundations, built in descending suit sequence on other exposed cards, or moved to the reserve – which, however, must never contain more than eight cards.

Only one card may be moved at a time. Any space that occurs in the tableau can be filled only by an available king.

# FLORENTINE

Features of this game are a tableau in the form of a five-card cross, and four foundations of which the bases are determined by the sixth card to be dealt.

**Layout**

Cards One standard deck is used.

Layout Deal five cards face up to form a cross. Deal a sixth card face up at the top left-hand corner. The rank of this card denotes the foundations; the other three cards of that rank being placed at the other corners as they come into play.

The objective is to build up ascending suit sequences on the four foundation cards.

Aces follow kings.

Play Cards from the stock are dealt one at a time. They can be played on the foundations if eligible, or packed in downward sequences regardless of suit on the four outer cards of the cross. The center card of the cross is at all times kept clear.

If one of the outer cards is transferred to a foundation card or packed on another outer card, the vacancy thus created is filled by a card from the waste heap, or by the center card of the cross (which is then replaced by a card from the waste heap).

The waste heap can be turned over and relayed once without shuffling.

# FLOWER GARDEN

In this game cards from fans, called flower beds, and cards from the hand, or bouquet, are built onto foundation cards. The flower beds are collectively called the flower garden.

Cards One standard deck is needed.

Layout Deal out 36 cards into six fans to form the flower garden. The remaining cards form the bouquet, and may be held in the hand or spread out on the table.

**Layout**

Tableau

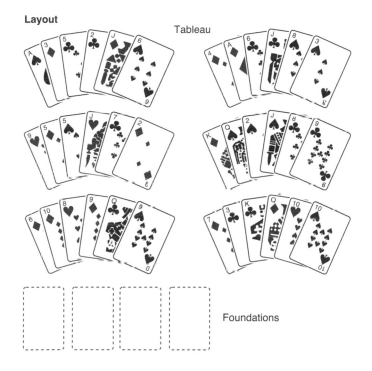

Foundations

The objective is to free the aces, which are set out below the garden as they become available, and to build onto them suit sequences in ascending order, aces through kings.

Play The exposed cards of each bed and all the bouquet cards are available for play. They may be played onto a foundation, or added to a bed in downward numerical sequence, regardless of suit.

A sequence may be transferred from one bed to another, provided that the correct numerical order is preserved. If a space is created by the removal of an entire bed, it may be filled by any available card, or by a sequence from another bed.

# FRIDAY THE THIRTEENTH

This game requires the player to establish and build upon 13 foundations, each based on a card of a different rank.

**Layout**

Foundations

Cards One standard deck is used.

Layout Set out in a row from left to right any jack, queen, king, and ace – regardless of suit. Leave enough space to the right of them for a further nine cards to be added to the row.

The objective is to establish a total of 13 foundation cards – the jack, queen, king, and ace and then any 2 through 10 as they come up in play – onto which the remaining cards (the stock) are built up four to a pile in ascending numerical order, regardless of suit or color.

Play Work through the stock, turning one card at a time face upward and building it onto one of the foundations (e.g., a queen onto the jack), or putting it out as the next foundation card. The foundations must be set out in their correct order: for example, a 3 cannot be laid out before the 2 has been established.

If a card cannot be played immediately, it is put face up on a waste heap.

Where there is a choice, it is usually better to establish a new base card rather than to build onto an existing pile. For example, if the first card turned up were a 2, it would be wiser to use it as the next base card rather than building it onto the ace.

The waste heap Any exposed card on the waste heap is available for play. When the stock is exhausted, the waste heap is turned over and may be replayed once without shuffling.

# FROG

This two deck game is also called toad in the hole. There are eight foundations based on aces, and five waste heaps.

Cards Two standard decks are used.

Layout Deal a reserve pile of 13 cards face up. If any of these cards are aces, set them out to the right of the reserve as foundations.

    If no aces are turned up, take one ace of any suit from the stock to begin the foundation row.

    The other aces are added to the row as they turn up in play, to give a complete row of eight foundations.

**Layout**

Reserve     Foundations

The objective is to build on the aces, ascending sequences from ace to king, regardless of suit or color.

Play Cards are turned up from the stock one at a time and played either onto the foundations or onto any one of five waste heaps.

The waste heaps are set out below the foundations, and cards may be added to them in any order the player chooses.

The top card of the reserve and the top cards of the waste heaps are available at all times for playing onto the foundations.

If a space occurs in the waste heaps it is filled from the stock; if the reserve is exhausted it is not replaced.

It is sound strategy to keep one waste heap for high-value cards such as kings and queens, and – if at all possible – to add cards to the waste heaps in descending numerical order so as to avoid burying low-ranking cards.

Waste heaps

# KING ALBERT

This game is named for King Albert I of the Belgians, who during World War I led his country's army against the Germans. Cards from the tableau and from the "Belgian Reserve" are built onto four foundation cards.

**Layout**

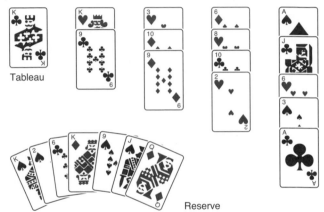

Tableau

Reserve

Cards One standard deck is used.

Layout Forty-five cards are dealt face up in rows from left to right, to form a tableau of nine columns.

The first column has one card, the second column two, and so on – the last column comprising nine cards.

The cards in each column should overlap so that all are visible.

The remaining seven cards, known as the " Belgian Reserve," may either be held in the hand or fanned out next to the tableau.

The objective is to free the four aces ( the foundations), which are placed above the tableau as they come into play.

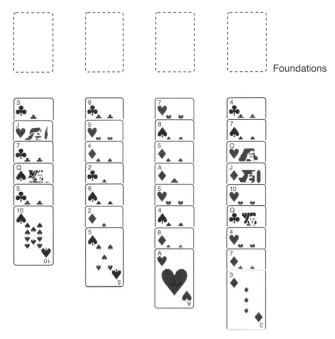

Foundations

Cards are built onto them in ascending suit sequence, from ace through king.

Play All cards in the reserve are available, as are the exposed cards of the tableau.

Only one card may be moved at a time, either onto a foundation pile or in descending, alternate-color sequence on the columns of the tableau.

If an entire column becomes vacant, the space may be filled by any available card.

If the player wishes, he may transfer cards from the foundations to the tableau, provided that they fit into the correct numerical and color sequence.

# KLONDIKE

Klondike probably owes its great popularity to its combination of judgment, luck, attractive layout, and fast-moving tempo – all ingredients of a good patience game. (In the United Kingdom this game is sometimes called Canfield.)

**Layout**

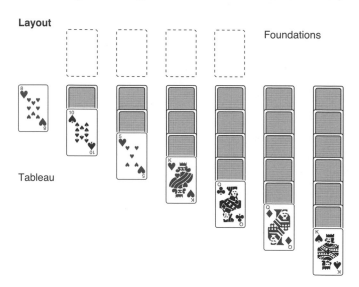

Foundations

Tableau

Cards One standard 52-card deck is used.

Layout Deal a row of seven cards, with only the first card face up. Add another row of six cards, with the first card face up on the second card of the first row, and the others face down. Deal five more rows in the same way, each row having one card fewer than the row beneath it and having only its first card face up.

Objective The four aces are the foundation cards, and they are set out above the tableau as they become available. The object is to build up the four suits on their respective aces in correct ascending order.

**Play** The hand is played one card at a time and once only.

Cards that are not immediately playable are put face up in a waste heap, the top card of which is always available.

Cards are built up in their correct suits on the foundations, or added to the columns of the tableau in descending, alternate-color order (regardless of suit).

The top (fully exposed) card of each tableau column is always available for play onto a foundation or another column.

By removing an exposed card, the face down card beneath it is turned up and becomes available.

Sequences in the tableau may be transferred from one column to another, but only as a complete unit.

Spaces created in the tableau can only be filled by kings. These may be taken (together with any cards built onto them) either from the stock or from anywhere in the tableau.

# LA BELLE LUCIE

This game has an attractive layout in which cards are arranged initially in fans of three cards each. Cards are then moved from fan to fan to free cards to be built onto four foundation piles.

**Layout**

Foundations

Tableau

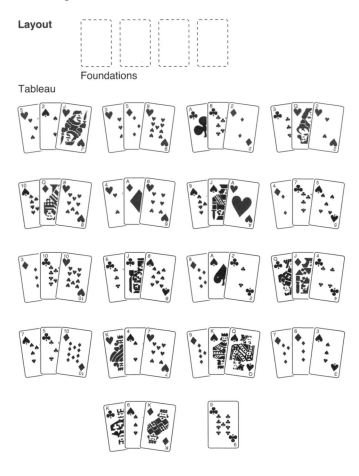

Cards One standard deck is used.

Layout The deck is dealt out into 17 fans of three cards each and one single card.

Objective The aces are the foundation cards, and they are set out in a row above the tableau as they come into play. Cards are built onto the foundations in ascending suit sequence, from ace through king.

Play The top card of each fan and the single card are available for play. One card at a time may be moved onto a foundation, or built onto another fan in downward suit sequence.

Cards may always safely be built onto the foundations, but any building down on the fans should be carefully considered, as any cards to the left of the built-down cards consequently become immobilized.

Any spaces caused by the removal of a fan are left unfilled.

Redealing Two redeals are permitted. When no further play is possible, all cards other than those on the foundation piles are gathered up, thoroughly shuffled, and redealt into fans of three cards (any one or two remaining cards forming a separate fan). After the second redeal, the player may pick out and play one card from any fan of his choice.

# LEAPFROG

Moving cards leapfrog fashion about the tableau makes for an unusual and interesting game.

**Layout**

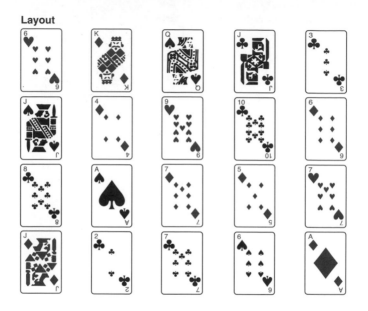

Cards One standard deck is required.

Layout Deal out 20 cards face up into four rows of five cards each.

The objective is to deal out all the remaining cards onto the table, and to end with as many spaces as possible in the layout.

Play Moves in leapfrog are very like the "jumping" moves in a game of checkers.

A card in the layout may be "leapfrogged" over an adjoining card (either horizontally, vertically, or diagonally), provided that the card onto which it lands is of the same suit or rank.

A card so played now becomes the top and identifying card of a pile, and in any subsequent leapfrogging the whole pile is moved.

A move is not limited to a single leapfrog: a succession of leapfrogs is sometimes possible.

Any card leapfrogged by another card is removed to a waste heap.

Empty spaces are filled by cards dealt from the hand whenever the player wishes. (It is better to fill the gaps as soon as they occur, in order to provide a wider choice of moves.)

# MAZE

Although maze is not one of the better known patience games, it is particularly satisfying and requires time and ingenuity to succeed at it.

**Layout**

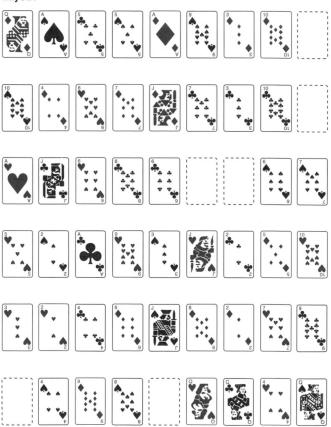

Cards One standard 52-card deck is used.

Layout The entire deck is dealt face up into two rows of eight cards and four rows of nine cards.

The four kings are then discarded, leaving a total of six spaces.

Objective By rearranging the cards one at a time, the player aims to get the four suits into their correct ascending sequence, ace through queen – one suit following the next. (The order of the suits is immaterial.)

The cards must run from left to right and from the end of one row to the beginning of the next. During play the top row is counted as following on from the bottom row.

In the final sequence, the first card must be an ace and the last card a queen.

For example, in a successful game the order might be:

ace of hearts through queen of hearts, ace of spades through queen of spades, ace of clubs through queen of clubs, ace of diamonds through queen of diamonds.

Play A card may be moved into any of the six spaces provided it is in the same suit as the card to the left or the right side of the space and that it is either: lower than the card to the right of the space; or higher than the card to the left of the space.

(For example, a 2 of diamonds may be moved into a space that either has an ace of diamonds to its left or a 3 of diamonds to its right.)

Whenever there is a space to the right of a queen, it may be filled with any of the four aces (even if there is no matching 2 on the right of the space).

## MISS MILLIGAN

In this two-deck game, cards are dealt eight at a time onto the tableau for transference onto eight foundations based on aces.

Cards Two standard decks are required.
Objective With the eight aces as the foundations, the player aims to build up the cards into ascending suit sequences.
Play Deal out eight cards face up in a row. If any of these is

**Start of play**

Foundations

First row of cards

Foundations

Cards moved into
appropriate columns

an ace, set it out above the row as a foundation. Also move any cards that can be built up on the ace in correct suit sequence, or arrranged in descending alternate-color sequence on other cards in the row.

Now deal out another row of eight cards, overlapping cards already in position or filling in any spaces as appropriate.

Once again, study the layout to see which cards may be built onto the foundations or transferred to other columns. (Several cards may be transferred together, provided they are in correct sequence.)

If at this stage a space occurs, it may only be filled by a king (plus any cards built onto it).

Continue in this way until the entire stock has been dealt – always completing all possible moves before dealing out the next batch of cards.

Weaving When no cards remain in the stock, the player may lift up any one available card or build from the tableau, and set it aside as a reserve.

Each of these reserve cards is available, and the player tries to rebuild them onto the tableau or foundations.

If he fails in rebuilding the reserve, the game is lost. If he succeeds, however, he may repeat the "weaving" process until the game goes through or is blocked.

# MONTE CARLO

Monte Carlo, also called weddings or double and quits, is a straightforward pairing game.

**Layout**

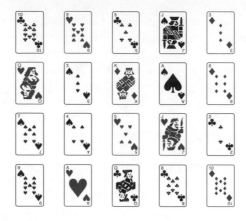

Cards One standard deck of 52 cards is used.

Layout Twenty cards are dealt out into four rows of five cards each. (Some players may prefer to deal out 25 cards in five rows of five cards each.)

Objective At the end of a successful game the player will have dealt out the entire deck and paired up all the cards, leaving an empty layout.

Play Any two cards of the same rank that touch each other top to bottom, side to side, or corner to corner are discarded.

The spaces thus made are filled by closing up the remaining cards of the layout from right to left, moving up cards from row to row as necessary, but preserving their order as originally laid out.

Extra cards are added from the stock to complete the layout, and the process is repeated until further pairing is impossible, or until the game goes through.

# NAPOLEON AT ST. HELENA

Although Napoleon was recorded as having played patience while in exile on St. Helena, it is most unlikely that he invented or even played the many games attributed to him today. The game described here is among the most interesting of this group. Its other names are forty thieves and big forty.

**Layout**

Foundations

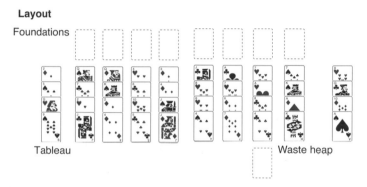

Tableau

Waste heap

Cards Two standard 52-card decks are used.

Layout Deal out forty cards into four overlapping rows of ten cards each. The bottom card in each column is available for play.

The objective is to build up suit sequences through to the kings on the eight aces, which are set out in a row above the tableau as they come into play.

Play The stock is turned over one card at a time and is either played onto the foundations, or built onto the tableau in downward suit sequence. If unplayable, cards are placed on a waste heap, of which the top card is always available.

Available tableau cards may similarly be played one at a time onto the foundations or onto another column of the tableau.

Spaces If an entire column of the tableau is cleared away, the resulting space may be filled by any one available card from elsewhere in the tableau or from the top of the waste heap.

The player should choose this card carefully, as it may give him the opportunity of releasing useful cards.

# POKER SOLITAIRE

Poker solitaire is a very challenging game that needs a mixture of luck, judgment, and practice to score well. It is a useful game for familiarizing the beginner with the scoring combinations used in regular poker.

Cards One standard deck of 52 cards is used.
Layout The tableau for poker solitaire comprises five rows of five face up cards each.

**Sample play**

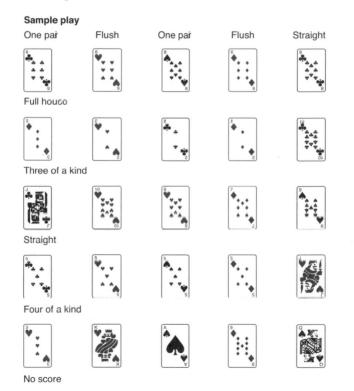

Play The cards are dealt out one by one from a thoroughly shuffled deck. Each card may be placed anywhere within the limits of the tableau.

Once in position a card may not be moved; its placing on the tableau is therefore of great importance.

Objective Each row and each column of the tableau is the equivalent of a poker hand (i.e., there is a total of 10 hands). The player tries to place the cards of each "hand" to give the highest possible scoring poker combinations.

Scoring Two different scoring systems – British and American – are given in the table below. A score of about 50 (British) or 150 (American) is considered good, and a score of about 60 (British) or 200 (American) excellent.

**Scoring table**

| Combination | British | American | Definition |
|---|---|---|---|
| Royal flush | 30 | 100 | A, k, q, j, 10 of one suit |
| Straight flush | 30 | 75 | Sequence of five cards in one suit |
| Four of a kind | 16 | 50 | Four cards of the same rank with one odd card |
| Full house | 10 | 25 | Three cards of one rank and two of another |
| Flush | 5 | 20 | Any five cards of the same suit |
| Straight | 12 | 15 | Five cards in sequence regardless of suit |
| Three of a kind | 6 | 10 | Three cards of the same rank with two odd cards |
| Two pairs | 3 | 5 | Two pairs with one odd card |
| One pair | 1 | 2 | One pair with three odd cards |

Ace can rank either high or low, but may not form part of a "round the corner" sequence (i.e., king, ace, 2 is not allowed).

Alternative rules

1 In order to improve his chance of a good score, the player may include a joker in the deal.

He can either:

a substitute the joker for one of the 25 cards before dealing them; or

b play all 25 cards in the usual way, exchanging the joker for any one card of his choice before totalling the score.

2 Another simplification of the game involves dealing out all 25 cards at the start of play in random order, and then rearranging them at will to form the best possible hands.

3 the player wishes to make the game more taxing, he may only place a card onto the tableau if it touches a previously played card either horizontally, vertically, or diagonally (rather than placing it anywhere within the confines of the tableau).

# PUSS IN THE CORNER

This game has one of the most straightforward layouts of all single-deck games

**Layout**

Foundations

Waste heaps

Cards One standard deck is used.

Layout The four aces are placed face up in a square, and then during the course of play four waste heaps are established at its corners.

The object of the game is to build up ascending sequences, ace through king, according to color but irrespective of suit.

Play Cards are played from the stock one at a time, either onto the aces (the foundation cards) or – if ineligible – onto one of the four waste heaps.

The top cards of the waste heaps are always available for play.

The player can choose onto which of the four waste heaps he wishes to put a card.

It is wise to reserve one heap for face cards, and if possible to avoid burying low-value cards under higher ones.

Redeal When the stock is exhausted, the cards in the waste heaps are collected in any order and redealt once without shuffling.

# PYRAMID

In its opening stages this game of pairing cards appears deceptively easy, and the player may think he is well on the way to winning. He will need a lot of lucky card combinations, however, for the game to go through!

**Layout**

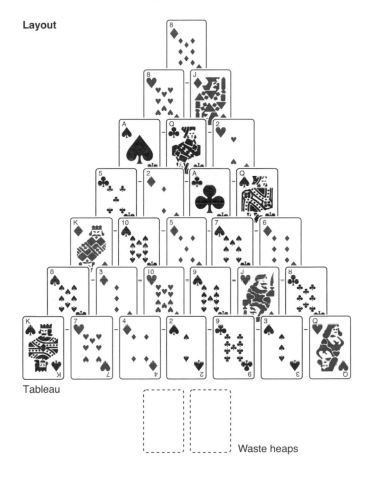

Tableau

Waste heaps

Cards One standard deck of 52 cards is used.

Layout Twenty-eight cards are dealt face up in seven rows to form a pyramid. (See diagram overleaf.)

Each card is overlapped by two other cards in the row below, except for the cards in the bottom row, which are fully exposed. Only the fully exposed cards are available for play (i.e., at the start of the game the seven cards in the bottom row).

When two cards are discarded during the course of play, the card they were overlapping becomes exposed and available for play.

The objective is to pair off the entire deck.

Play Any two available cards that together total 13 (regardless of color or suit) are paired off and placed in a waste heap.

The kings are worth 13 and may be discarded singly.

Queens are worth 12, jacks 11, and aces one.

For example, a 10 can be paired with a 3, a jack with a 2, or a 4 with a 9.

Cards in the stock are turned up one by one onto a waste heap, of which the top card is always available.

A pair may be made up of: two tableau cards; one tableau card and one card from the stock; or two stock cards (the top card from the waste pile plus the next stock card turned up).

Redeal When the stock has been dealt once and no further pairing is possible, the waste pile may be redealt without shuffling.

Some players permit two redeals; others prefer not to allow any redeal.

# ROYAL COTILLION

Named for an eighteenth-century French court dance for four couples, this two deck game uses for its foundations four aces coupled with four 2s.

Cards Two standard decks are needed.

Layout Set out face up in two columns an ace and a 2 of each suit.

　To the left of the ace column, deal 12 cards face up in three rows of four cards each.

　To the right of the 2 column, deal 16 cards face up in four rows of four cards each.

　(Some players prefer to establish the two central columns by putting out the aces and 2s as they come into play.)

The objective is to build suit sequences in the following order: on the aces, 3, 5, 7, 9, j, k, 2, 4, 6, 8, 10,q; on the 2s, 4, 6, 8, 10, q, a, 3, 5, 7, 9, j, k.

Play Only the bottom card of each column in the left wing of

## Layout

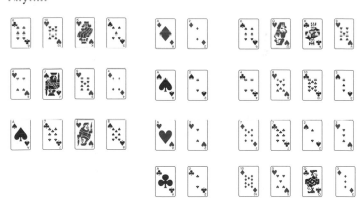

cards is available for play onto a foundation card, and the space made by such a move is not filled.

All the cards in the right wing are available, however, and spaces that occur must be filled immediately, with the top card of either the waste heap or the stock.

The stock is played one card at a time. Any card that cannot be built on a foundation or is not required for filling a space is put on the waste heap, of which the top card is always available. There is no redeal.

# RUSSIAN BANK

Also known as crapette, this patience game for two players requires a great deal of concentration. Moves are made according to a strict procedure which, if broken, may result in the player forfeiting his turn.

Cards Two standard decks are used. Each player should have his own deck with a distinctive back in order to avoid confusion.

Cards rank: k (high), q,j,10,9,8,7,6,5,4,3,2,a (low).

The objective A player's objective is to build all or as many as possible of the cards in his deck onto the foundations, the tableau, or his opponent's reserve or discard piles.

Preliminaries Each player draws a card from one of the decks: the player drawing the lower card will play first. Players then shuffle and cut their opponent's deck.

Layout To establish his reserve, each player counts out 12 cards from his deck and places them face down in a pile to his right.

Both players then deal out a column of four face up cards above their reserve: these eight cards form the tableau and are for common use.

The remaining cards in each deck are placed face down in a pile in front of each player and form his stock.

Foundations The eight aces are the foundations. They are laid out between the two columns of the tableau as they come into play. Cards are built onto the foundations in ascending suit sequence.

Building cards onto the foundations is also called building to the "center." Once a card has been built onto a foundation, it may not be removed.

Play The player who drew the lower card plays first; thereafter players take alternate turns.

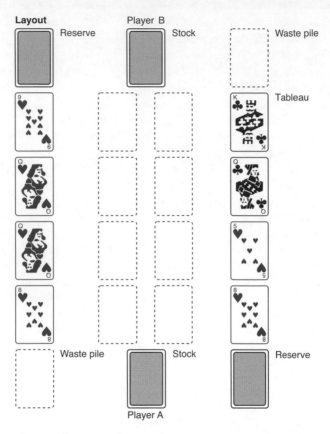

Cards must be moved according to a set procedure, as follows.

1 Both players must start their opening turns by playing any available tableau cards to the center. They must then turn up the top card of their reserve and – if possible – play that to the center. If it cannot be played to the center, it may be played elsewhere on the layout.

2 In subsequent turns, players may turn over the top card of their reserve prior to making a play.

3 Building onto the foundation always takes precedence over building elsewhere on the layout. Also, if there is a choice of cards for building onto the center, cards from the reserve must always be used before cards from the tableau or stock.

4 If no more cards can be built onto the foundation, the player may build onto the tableau in descending alternate-color sequence. He may use the top card from another tableau pile, the reserve, or the stock – there is no order of precedence.

   (Players should take every opportunity of rearranging tableau cards, so as to free blocked cards for play to the center.)

   Cards in the tableau piles should be built in overlapping rows, so that all the cards are visible.

5 A space in the tableau may be filled by the top card of another tableau pile, the reserve, or, once the reserve is exhausted, from the stock. (Spaces need not be filled as soon as they occur.)

6 If no cards can be built to the center and the top reserve card cannot be built onto the tableau, the player may turn up the top card in his stock. If this card can be played directly to the center or the tableau, the next card in the stock may be turned up, and so on until an unplayable stock card is turned up. As soon as this happens, the player must move the unplayable card face up onto a waste pile to his left. His turn then ends.

7 Cards in the waste pile cannot be played. If the player's stock is exhausted, he may, however, take the waste pile and turn it face down and unshuffled to form a new stock.

Loading Once all available cards have been played to the center, the player has the option of "loading" cards onto his opponent's reserve or waste piles in up or down suit sequence. The player must use cards from the tableau, or from his own reserve and stock.

Should the opponent's top reserve card be face down, the player may ask him at any time to turn it face up.

If an opponent has used up his reserve or waste pile (i.e., toward the end of the game) a player cannot off-load cards onto the resultant spaces.

Stops If a player thinks that his opponent has made an error in procedure, he may call "Stop," and play must immediately be halted.

If the error is proved, the wrongly moved card is returned to its former position and the offending player forfeits the rest of that turn.

Should an error not be noticed until after further moves have been made, the offender is allowed to continue without penalty.

Result The game is won by the first person who succeeds in discarding his entire deck, i.e., all the cards in his reserve, stock, and waste pile.

He scores 30 points for winning, plus two points for each card left in his opponent's reserve and one point for each left in his opponent's stock and waste pile.

If neither player succeeds in winning outright, the game is considered a draw.

Alternatively, players can evaluate their remaining cards to decide who wins. Each player counts two points for each card in his reserve and one point for each card in his stock and waste pile; the player with fewer points then scores the difference between his points total and that of his opponent.

# SCORPION

The unwary player may be caught out by the scorpion's "sting" at the tail end of the game – since delay in exposing the hidden cards may prevent the game going through!

Cards One standard deck of 52 cards is used.

Layout Deal three rows of seven cards each – the first four cards in each row face down and the remainder face up.

Below these deal four more rows of seven cards each, all face up. This makes a total of 49 cards in the tableau, and the three cards left over are put face down as the reserve.

Objective The four kings are the foundations onto which the cards are built in descending suit sequence (king through ace). The kings are not removed to separate foundation piles, but are built onto within the tableau.

Play Cards are built on the exposed cards of the layout (i.e., the bottom card of each column) in correct descending order and suit.

If, as in the example illustrated, the 6 of hearts is exposed, the 5 of hearts may be moved onto it. It may be taken from anywhere within the layout, but all the cards laid on top of it must also be moved.

Nothing may be built onto an ace.

Face down cards As each face down card is reached (by the removal of the card or cards on top of it) it is turned face up.

The sooner the hidden cards are uncovered, the better the player's chances of getting the game through. It is therefore advisable to plan moves that will clear the face down cards as rapidly as possible.

Spaces and reserve If an entire column is cleared away, the space may be filled by a king (and any cards laid on top of it).

A space need not be filled as soon as it occurs.

When no further moves are possible, the three reserve cards are turned up and added to the layout, one to the foot of each of the three left-hand columns.

Not all spaces need to be filled before using the reserve cards. It often helps to see the reserve before filling a space, and this may be done provided that all other moves have been exhausted.

**Layout**

Tableau

**Play**

Reserve

Transferring cards

# SPIDER

There are numerous versions of spider; the one described here is reputed to have been the favorite solitaire of President Franklin D. Roosevelt.

**Layout**

Cards Two standard 52-card decks are used.

Layout Deal out a tableau of four overlapping rows, each row having ten cards. Deal the first three rows face down and the fourth row face up.

Objective Cards are built onto the eight kings in descending suit sequence. Instead of setting out the kings in separate piles as they come into play, they are built onto within the tableau.

Only when a sequence is complete (i.e., king through ace in any one suit) is it discarded from the tableau.

If the solitaire comes out, all eight completed sequences will have been discarded.

Play The face up cards in the bottom row are all available, and may be built on any other available card in descending numerical sequence, irrespective of suit or color.

When a card is moved to another column, the player must also transfer all the cards built onto it.

Nothing may be built onto an ace, which ranks low and can only follow a two.

When a face down card is reached, it is turned face up and becomes available for play.

A space in the tableau may be filled by any available card or build.

Stock When there are no more moves to be made in the tableau and all the spaces have been filled, ten cards are dealt face up from the stock – one to the bottom of each column.

Play continues in the same way, a fresh batch of ten cards being dealt from the stock each time all possible moves in the tableau have been completed.

(The last deal will be of only four cards, one to be dealt to the bottom of the first four columns.)

# SPITE AND MALICE

Like Russian bank, this is a solitaire game for two players. The players' objective is to be first to get rid of all the cards from their own "payoff pile;" to achieve this end, cards are built in sequence onto stacks at the center and sides of the table.

Cards Two standard decks and four jokers are used. The decks should be distinctively backed. Ace ranks low; jokers are wild.

**Layout**

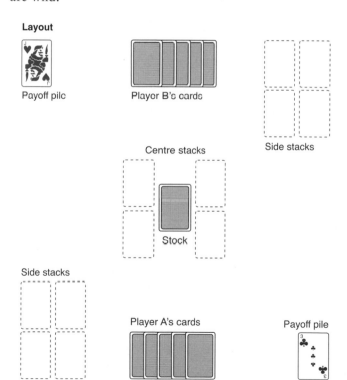

Payoff pile

Player B's cards

Side stacks

Centre stacks

Stock

Side stacks

Player A's cards

Payoff pile

The objective A player aims to get rid of all the cards on his
  payoff pile.
Preliminaries One of the decks is shuffled – without its jokers
  – and divided into two separate "payoff" piles of 26 cards,
  one for each player. The top card of each pile is turned face
  up and the player with the highest card will play first.

  If by chance the two cards have the same value, the procedure is repeated.

  The player with the lower card shuffles the second deck,
  including the four jokers. He then gives himself and his
  opponent five cards, dealing them one at a time and face
  down. The remaining cards form the stock and are placed
  face down in a pile in the middle of the table.
Play The player who had the higher card has the opening
  turn; thereafter play is alternate.
  1 Aces must be played to the center of the table as soon as
    they become available; they are the base cards of "center
    stacks" (equivalent to foundation piles).

      Available 2s must be built on the aces whenever possible.

      Cards are built on the center stacks in ascending
    sequence regardless of suit; a card from the payoff pile,
    the hand, or a side stack (see paragraph 3) may be used.

      Whenever a center stack has been built up through to
    the king, it is shuffled together with the stock at the next
    break in play.
  2 The top card of the payoff pile may be played only to
    the center stacks. Whenever this happens, the player
    may turn up the next card in the payoff pile, and so on,
    until an unplayable card is turned up.
  3 Each player may build up to four "side stacks" using
    only cards from his hand. A side stack may be started
    with a card of any value, and is built on regardless of
    suit either in descending sequence or with a card of the

same value (e.g., 7 on a 7). Only one build onto a side stack may be made in any one turn.

4 Jokers may take the place of any card except an ace.

End of turn A player may make any number of legal plays to the center stacks, but his turn ends as soon as he plays a card from his hand to a side stack.

A player may also finish his turn by saying "End" if he cannot, or wishes not to, make further moves.

Stock At the start of their second and subsequent turns, players take as many cards from the stock as they need to replenish their hand (i.e., anything up to five cards).

Result The winner is the first player to have exhausted his payoff pile. Should neither player be able to make any further moves but still have cards left in his payoff pile, the game is considered drawn.

# WINDMILL

This is a two deck game in which cards are laid out to represent the four sails of a windmill. An alternative name for the game is propeller – in which case the arms of the cross in the layout represent propeller blades.

Cards Two standard decks are used.

Layout Place any king face up at the center of the playing area. Then deal out a reserve (called the "sails") of eight face up cards: two above the king, two below it, and two to either side.

The objective is to build:

a a descending sequence of 52 cards on the central king, regardless of suit or color and with kings following aces;

b ascending sequences, ace through king and regardless of suit and color, on the first four aces that come up in play.

Play Cards are turned face up from the stock one at a time and if unplayable are put on a waste heap. The stock is only dealt once.

The first four aces to appear are put as foundation cards in the four angles of the sails.

Cards are played to the foundations from either the stock, the sails, or from the top of the waste heap (which is always available for play).

The top card of any ace foundation may be transferred to the central king foundation (building on the central pile is of prime importance if the game is to go through).

Spaces A space in the layout must be filled by the top card of either the stock or the waste heap, but it need not be filled as soon as it occurs.

This means that a space can be "saved" for a useful card – and by using his judgment in the way he fills spaces, the player can greatly increase his chances of winning.

**Alternative rule** Some players prefer the central foundation card to be an ace and the other four foundations to be kings. Should a player choose this alternative, he must build an ascending sequence on the central ace and descending sequences on the four kings.

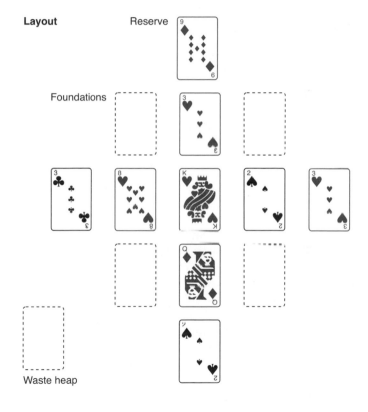

**Layout**

Reserve

Foundations

Waste heap

# Children's Card Games

## INTRODUCTION

All the games in this section are fast-moving and fun for children to play. The easiest among them – games such as slapjack, snap, and beggar my neighbor – provide an excellent first introduction to games using standard playing cards. At the other end of the scale are games like racing demon, cheat, and concentration, which are challenging enough to be enjoyed by adults and children alike.

Card recognition The simplest card games using standard playing cards involve recognizing certain cards as they appear in play. Simplest of all is slapjack, in which only the jacks must be picked out. Slightly more elaborate is beggar my neighbor, in which players must recognize face cards – kings, queens, jacks and aces.

Matching cards by rank Many card games for children depend on matching cards of the same rank. In snap, menagerie, old maid, and memory, players must watch out for pairs – for example, two 7s or two queens. In donkey and go fish, players try to collect all four cards of the same kind. Other easy games that involve matching cards by rank include go boom, cheat, and snip-snap-snorem.

Following suit Another group of simple games requires players to know the four suits – hearts, diamonds, spades, and clubs. In my ship sails, the winner is the first player to collect seven cards belonging to the same suit – for example seven spades. For other games in this group, players must also know the usual rank order of cards – from ace (low), through 2,3,4,5,6,7,8 9, and 10, to jack, queen and king (high). It is then possible to play a whole variety of games. Some of these – like card dominoes, give away, play or pay, sequence, spit, and racing demon – involve building up sequences of cards to rank order. Others – like linger longer, knockout whist, and rolling stone – serve as a useful introduction to whist and other more complex games in which tricks must be won.

# 2–6 BEGGAR MY NEIGHBOR

Beggar my neighbor is an easy and exciting game. No skill is required as the outcome depends on the luck of the deal.

Players There may be two to six players.

Cards Any deck of standard playing cards may be used, and it need not be complete. For more than three players it is a good idea to mix two decks together.

The objective is to win all the cards. But, as the game may go on for a very long time, the winner may be the player who has the most cards at the end of an agreed length of time.

Deal One player deals out all the cards in a clockwise direction – one at a time and face down. It does not matter if some players have one card more than the others.

Each player puts his cards into a neat pile face down in front of him.

Players are not allowed to look at their cards.

Play The player to the dealer's left turns up the top card in his pile and places it in the center of the playing area.

Each player in turn, in a clockwise direction, then places the top card from his pile face up on the central pile.

This continues until one player turns up an ace or face card (a jack, queen, or king).

Payment of cards The next player to the left then has to "pay" him by placing a certain number of cards on the central pile:

a  four cards for an ace;

b  three cards for a king;

c two cards for a queen;
d one card for a jack.

If, however, one of the payment cards is an ace or a face card, the payer stops turning over his cards and the player to his left then has to pay the correct number of cards.

This goes on until a player paying out cards turns over the correct number of cards with no aces or face cards.

When this happens, the last player to have turned over an ace or a face card may take the central pile and place it at the bottom of his own pile.

The player then starts a new round by playing his next card face up in the center of the playing area.

As soon as a player has no more cards, he is out.

**Payment**

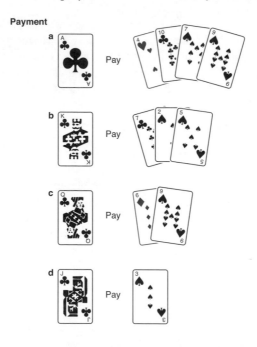

# 2+ CARD DOMINOES

This game of luck and skill is also called sevens, parliament, and fan-tan. A player can increase his chances of winning by carefully choosing the order in which he plays his cards.

**Sample play**

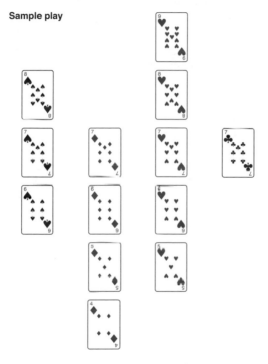

Players The game is for two or more players.

Cards One complete deck of standard playing cards is used.

Objective Each player aims to be first to play his cards onto a central pattern of cards in sequence.

Deal One player deals all the cards in a clockwise direction, one at a time and face down.

Play Each player looks at his cards and sorts them in his hand according to suit and sequence.

The player with the 7 of diamonds starts the game by putting it face up in the center. The player to his left must then try to put down either the 6 or 8 of diamonds or another 7. If he plays the 6 or 8 of diamonds he puts it respectively below or above the 7. If he plays another 7 he puts it next to the 7 of diamonds. If, however, he does not hold any of these cards he "passes" and the play then goes to the next player to the left.

Play continues in this way, with each player in turn adding a card to one of the sequences, putting down a 7, or passing.

The sequences are built up from 7 through 8,9,10, jack and queen to king, and down from 6 to ace.

End The game is won by the first player to put down all his cards, but play usually continues until every card has been played and there are four complete suit sequences.

## 3+ CHEAT

Also known as I doubt it, this game is great fun for those who like taking risks and calling people's bluffs.

Players A minimum of three people is needed to play, but the more the better.

Cards One or two decks of playing cards are used.

Objective Each player aims to be the first to get rid of all of his cards.

Deal One player deals out all the cards. Some players may have one extra card.

Play Players look at their cards. The player to the left of the dealer places one to four cards of the "same" rank (e.g., all 7s) face down in a pile in the center. He calls their rank as he does so. (In fact, the cards need not be what he claims – see cheating.)

Subsequent players must then play – or claim that they are playing – one to four cards of the rank one higher than those played by the preceding player.

**Cheating** There are at least two ways of cheating.

a instead of putting down cards of the correct rank, a player can put down any other cards, so long as he pretends that they are all the same, and of the next highest value to those just played.

If a player does not have cards of the required value, he has no alternative but to do this. It is important that a player should avoid giving the others reason to doubt him.

b A player may put down more cards than he states. Again, he should avoid drawing people's attention to this.

**Calling a player's bluff** If a player suspects another of cheating, he can challenge him by calling "Cheat" or "I doubt it" before the suspect's cards are covered by those of the next player.

The challenged player must then turn over his cards for inspection.

If the player who called "Cheat" or "I doubt it" is correct, the person who cheated picks up all the cards in the central pile and adds them to his hand.

If the player did not cheat, the challenger must pick up the central pile of cards.

The player who picks up the cards from the center starts the next round.

**End** The winner is the first person to succeed in playing his last card – i.e., either:

a he withstands a challenge from another player; or

b his cards are covered by the next player's before anyone has challenged him.

## UP AND DOWN CHEAT

The only difference between this game and ordinary cheat or I doubt it is the rank of the cards that can be played. Instead of only claiming to play cards in ascending rank, a player may also claim that he is playing cards that are either of the same rank or one rank lower than the last player's cards.

## 2+ CONCENTRATION

This card game for any number of players is also called pelmanism or memory. It is easy to play and is an excellent test of memory and observation.

Cards One or two standard decks of playing cards are used, depending on the number of players.

The cards should be clean and reasonably new, so that when they are lying face down they cannot be identified by creases, marks, or torn corners!

The playing area must be flat and as large as possible – the floor or a big table is best.

The deal One player shuffles the cards and plays them face down on the table – in all directions and so that no card is touching another.

Objective Each player tries to collect as many cards as possible by turning up pairs with the same rank (number or picture).

First player The player to the left of the dealer starts the game. He turns over two cards at random and allows the other players to see them.

If the rank of the two cards is the same, for example two aces or two kings, he takes them and may turn over two more cards. He continues in this way until he turns over two cards that do not match.

If the cards that are turned over do not match, the player

must put them face down in their original positions. His turn then ends.

Second player The person to the first player's left now turns over any two cards.

If the first card matches one that has already been turned over he must try to remember where that card is. If he is successful, he takes the pair. He continues his turn until he fails to turn over a matching pair.

Successive players Play continues with the players taking their turns in a clockwise direction, until all the cards have been collected.

The winner is the player with most cards at the end of the game.

## 3+ DONKEY

Donkey is a fast and noisy card game in which players are penalized with letters from the game's name.

Players Three or more can play.

Cards Special cards can be bought but donkey is usually played with sets of cards taken from an old deck of standard playing cards.

Each set consists of four cards with the same picture or number. The number of sets used is the same as the number of people playing. For example, if there are five players, the aces, kings, queens, jacks, and 10s might be used.

Spoons, buttons, or some other unbreakable objects should be placed in the center of the table at the start of each round.

There must be one object fewer than the number of players.

The objective is to collect a set of four cards and at the same time to avoid being the "donkey" (i.e., the first player to lose six rounds of the game).

A player is penalized with one letter from the word donkey each time he fails to pick up an object at the end of a round.

Play Keeping his cards hidden from the other players, each player chooses one card that he does not want and places it face down on the table. All the players then pass their unwanted card to the player to their left.

Each player then looks at his new card and again chooses a card to pass to his neighbor.

He may pass the new card if he wishes.

The game continues in this way, as quickly as possible, until one player has a set of four cards of the same value. When a player has a set of cards, for example four 10s, he should quietly put them face up on the table and pick up an object from the table. As soon as any player does this, the other players must reach for an object whether they have a set of four cards or not.

The player who fails to pick up an object loses the round and is penalized with a letter.

Donkey The first player to be penalized with all the letters of the word donkey loses the game and must "hee-haw" three times.

## PIG

Pig is a similar game to donkey. The number of players and the cards used are the same as for donkey, but in pig there is no need for any unbreakable objects.

The objective is to collect a set of four cards of the same value while also avoiding becoming the "prize pig."

Play is the same as for donkey, except that when a player has a set of cards he puts his finger to his nose. The last player to do so is pig for the round.

Prize pig The game is lost when one player becomes prize pig after losing ten rounds. As a forfeit, the prize pig must say "oink-oink" three times.

## 2+ GIVE AWAY

Give away is a simple game that requires players to stay alert. The faster it is played the better.

**Play**

Play to center

Play on opponent's face up card

Objective Each player aims to be first to get rid of all his cards.

Players Two or more can play this game.

Cards A standard deck of playing cards is used.

Deal One player deals out all the cards in a clockwise direction – face down and one at a time. It does not matter if some players have one card more than others.

Players do not look at their cards but put them in a neat face down pile in front of them.

Play The player to the left of the dealer turns over the top card of his face down pile.

If it is not an ace, he places if face up by his face down pile and ends his turn.

If it is an ace, he puts it face up in the center of the table and turns over another card. His turn continues until he turns over a card that he is unable to play to the center – a card may be played to the center if it is an ace or if it can be built in rank order (a,2,3,4,5,6,7,8,9,10,j,q,k) onto a center card of the same suit. When he turns over a card that cannot be played to the center he places it face up by his face down pile and ends his turn.

Each player then plays in turn. As well as playing to the center, a player may play a card onto another player's face up pile – provided that it is one higher or lower in rank than the top card of that pile.

When a player plays his last face down card onto his face up pile, he waits until his next turn before turning over his face up pile to start again.

If he plays his last face down card into the center or onto another player's pile, he turns over his face up pile immediately and continues his turn.

End The first player to get rid of all his cards wins the game.

## 2+ GO BOOM

Go boom is a straightforward game for two or more players, which can be played by quite young children.

Cards A standard deck of playing cards is used.

Objective Each player aims to be the first player to get rid of all his cards.

Deal The players cut for deal; the one with the highest card (ace ranks high) deals out the cards in a clockwise direction one at a time and face down, until each player has seven cards. Spare cards are placed face down in a neat pile in the center.

Play Each player looks at his cards and sorts them in his hand. Turns pass clockwise around the players, starting with the player to the dealer's left.

The first player chooses a card from his hand and places it face up in the center. Each of the other players in turn, making a central face up pile, plays a card that is either:

**a** of the same suit (e.g., all spades); or

**b** of the same rank (number or picture) as the card put down by the person before him.

If a player cannot follow suit or rank, he takes cards one at a time from the top of the central face down pile until he has a card that he can play onto the central face up pile. If all the cards have been taken, the player says "Pass" and play moves on to the next player.

When each player has played a card or "passed," the cards are compared for the highest card (ace ranks high) and the player of the highest card starts the next round.

If two or more players tie for the highest card, the first one to play his card starts the next round.

End The winner is the first player to get rid of all his cards and shout "Boom."

## SCORING GO BOOM

This is a variant of go boom that is made more interesting by the introduction of a scoring system. It is played in the same way as basic go boom, except that several rounds are played and points are scored for going boom.

10 points

1 point

50 points          10 points          1 point

When a player goes boom, he scores points for all the unplayed cards still in the other players' hands. Scoring is:

**a** 10 points for each king, queen, or jack;
**b** one point for each ace;
**c** the numerical face value of all other cards.

A game is won by the first player to score an agreed number of points (usually 250).

## CRAZY EIGHTS

Crazy eights is the same basic game as go boom except that the 8s are wild.

A player may play any 8 after any card, and then decides which suit should follow.

As in scoring go boom, the first player to play all his cards scores points for the unplayed cards still in the other players' hands.

Points are scored as follows:

**a** 50 points for each 8;
**b** 10 points for each king, queen, or jack;
**c** one point for each ace;
**d** the numerical face value of all other cards.

If the face down pile of cards is exhausted before any player plays all his cards, the game is blocked and the player with the lowest count in his remaining cards scores the difference in count betwen his own hand and the other players' hands.

## 2+ GO FISH

To win at this popular game, players will need a a mixture of skill and luck.

Players Fish can be played by two players, but it is better with more.

Cards A standard deck of cards is normally used, but young players may prefer to use special happy families cards.

Deal One of the players deals out all the cards. As well as dealing a hand of each player, the dealer also deals a spare hand – so, for example, five hands are dealt if there are four players.

The spare hand is placed face down in the center of the table and is called the "fish pile."

Objective Each player tries to get rid of all his cards.

Play Each player looks at his cards and sorts them into groups with the same rank (number or picture). Players must take care not to let anyone else see their cards at any time.

When all the players are ready, the person to the dealer's left asks any player, by name, for a particular card (e.g., 7 of spades). He must already possess at least one card of the same rank (e.g., 7 of hearts). If the person who is asked for a card has it, he must give it to the player who asked for it. The player who made the first request may then ask any player for another card, again provided he already has at least one card of the same rank.

A player can go on asking for cards in this way until he asks someone for a card that he does not have. The person who does not have the card then tells the player who asked for it to "go fish." The player who was told to go fish must then take one card from the top of the fish pile. The player who told him to go fish then takes over asking for cards.

Once a player collects all four cards in a group, he puts them into a pile face down in front of him.

End The winner is the first player to have no cards other than his completed groups. If two players finish at the same time, the one with most completed groups of four cards is the winner.

A group of
four 7s

## 2–7 KNOCKOUT WHIST

An easy-to-play member of the whist family, knockout whist is very popular with older children. It is a good way of learning about tricks and trumps. Players are eliminated until only one remains.

Players Two to seven people can play.
Cards A standard deck of playing cards is used.
Objective Each player aims to win all the tricks of a hand.
A trick contains one card from each player played into the center.

Except when a trump has been played, a trick is won by the highest card belonging to the suit that was led – i.e., to the same suit as the first card played in that trick.

Aces are the highest cards, followed by kings, queens, jacks, and so on down from the 10s to the 2s.

**Rank of cards**

A trump is a card belonging to the trump suit. The trump suit is determined before each game is played. A trump card beats any card belonging to the suit led.

Deal One player deals out the cards face down, one at a time, and in a clockwise direction until each player has seven cards. The remaining cards are put face down in a pile in the center. Each time the cards are dealt, the number dealt to each player is decreased by one.

Play The top card of the center pile is turned over and this determines the trump suit for the first hand.

The player to the dealer's left then starts the first trick by playing any card he chooses.

Each player in turn then plays a card, following suit if he can. If a player cannot follow suit, he may either play a trump or discard any other card into the center.

The trick is won by the player who played the highest trump card or, if no trump was played, by the player who played the highest card of the suit led.

When all seven tricks have been played, anyone who has not won a trick drops out of the game.

The dealer collects all the cards, shuffles them, and deals six cards to each remaining player.

The winner of the most tricks in the first round chooses the trump suit and plays the first card in the second hand.

Play continues in this way – with players without tricks dropping out at the end of each hand.

End The first player to win all the tricks in a single hand is the overall winner.

If play continues to the seventh hand, each player will have only one card. There will be only one trick, and the winner of this trick wins the game.

**Tricks
(four players)**

Trump suit

---

## 3+ LINGER LONGER

Linger longer is an ideal introduction to the principles of trump play that form the basis of many more complicated card games.

Players Three or more people can play. Four to six is best.
Cards A standard deck of playing cards is used.
Objective Each player tries to be the last person with cards in his hand. Players obtain new cards by winning tricks.

**Rank of cards**

**Tricks**

Trump suit

Trick won by
6 of trumps

Trick won by
ace

A trick comprises one card from each player played into the center. Unless a trump has been played, a trick is won by the highest card belonging to the suit that was led – i.e., to the same suit as the first card played in that trick.

Aces are the highest cards, followed by the kings, queens, jacks, and so on down from the 10s to the 2s.

A trump is a card belonging to the trump suit. The trump suit is determined before each game is played. A trump card beats any card belonging to the suit led.

Deal One player deals out the cards in a clockwise direction, face down and one at a time, until each player has the same number of cards as there are players. For example, if there are four players, each one of them receives four cards.

The remaining cards are placed in the center in a face down pile called the stock.

The last card dealt to the dealer is shown to all the players. The suit of this card is the trump suit for the game.

Play The player to the left of the dealer plays any card he likes face up in the center.

Each player in turn then plays one card into the center. (These cards together form a trick.) If possible, players must play a card of the same suit as the first card – this is called "following suit." If a player is unable to follow suit, he may play a trump card or any other card.

A trick is won by the player who played the highest trump card, or, if no trump was played, by the player who played the highest card of the suit led. Ace ranks high for this game. A player who wins a trick places these cards face down in front of him. He then draws the top card from the stock and adds it to the cards in his hand (no other player draws).

This player plays the first card of the next trick. Players continue playing tricks in this way as long as they have any cards in their hand – ignoring the cards in any tricks that they have won.

A player with no cards in his hand must leave the game. End The last player left in the game wins.

## 2+ MENAGERIE

This hilarious and noisy game is similar to snap. It is sometimes called animals.

Players It can be played by two, but is better with more.
Cards One or two decks of standard playing cards are used.
Objective Players aim to win all the cards.
Choosing the animals Players first choose the name of an animal with a long and tongue-twisting name.

After checking that everyone has chosen a different animal, each player is given a small piece of paper on which he must write his animal's name. (An older person can help anyone who hasn't learned to write.)

All the pieces of paper are folded and then shaken together in a bag or hat. Each player then takes one piece of paper – and the name on that paper is his animal for the game.

Players should then learn the animal names of all the persons playing.

**Deal** One player deals out all the cards in a clockwise direction – one at a time and face down. It does not matter if some players have one card more than the others.

Each player puts his cards into a neat pile face down in front of him. Players are not allowed to look at their cards.

**Play** The player to the dealer's left turns over the top card of his pile and places it face up to start a face up pile of cards next to his face down pile. The next player to his left does the same, and so on around the players until any player sees that the cards on the top of any two face up piles have the same value.

Whenever the top card on any two players' face up piles are the same (e.g., two 7s), each of these two players must call out the other player's animal name three times.

The first player to do so wins the other player's face up pile and adds these cards to the bottom of his own face down pile.

**Penalty** If a player wrongly calls out a name, he must give all his face up cards to the player whose animal name he called.

## ANIMAL NOISES

This game is played like menagerie, except that:

a players choose animals that make distinctive noises (e.g., dog, cat, or duck);

b players imitate their opponents' animal noises instead of repeating their animal names.

## 4–7 MY SHIP SAILS

An easy game for beginners, my ship sails is also great fun when played at speed by those familiar with it.

**My ship sails**

Players Four to seven people may play.

Cards A standard deck of playing cards is used.

Objective Each player aims to be the first to collect seven cards of the same suit, for example seven spades.

Deal Each player cuts the cards and the one with the highest card (ace high) is the dealer.

He deals out the cards in a clockwise direction, one at a time and face down, until each player has seven cards. The remaining cards are not used.

Play Each player sorts his cards into suits in his hand and decides which suit he will try to collect. This will probably be the suit for which he has most cards at the start of a round, but he may change his mind during the course of play.

Exchange of cards Each player takes one card that he does not want and puts it face down on the table. When all the players are ready, they pass these cards to the next person to the right. The players pick up their new cards, decide on another card to discard, and then pass it in the same way.

End Players continue to exchange cards until one person collects seven cards of the same suit. He then calls "My ship sails," and wins the game. If two players call together, the first to start calling is the winner.

# 3+ OLD MAID

Old maid is a simple card game that is a great favorite with young children. Another name for this game is pass the lady.

**Old maid**

One queen removed

Pair of queens

The old maid

Players This is a game for three or more players.

Cards One of the queens is removed from a standard deck to leave an odd queen – the "old maid."

Deal One player deals all the cards face down, one at a time, to all players. It does not matter if some players have one card more than the others.

Objective Each player aims to get rid of all his cards by discarding pairs of equal value. The player who is left with the old maid card when play ends is the loser. There are no winners in this game.

Play Each player looks at his cards, making sure that none of the other players can see them.

If he has any pairs – two matching character cards or two playing cards with the same value – e.g., two 9s or two kings – he lays them face down on the table.

A player with three cards of the same value may only put down two of them and must keep the third, but a player with four cards of the same value may put down all four in two pairs.

The players to the dealer's left fans out his cards, keeping their faces toward him, and offers them to the player to his left.

Pairs

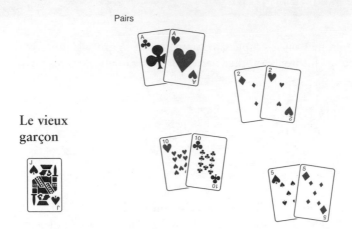

**Le vieux
garçon**

The player who is offered the cards must take any one of them. He then looks to see whether the new card pairs up with any of the cards already in his hand. If it does, he lays the pair face down on the table. If not, he adds the new card to the cards in his hand. He then fans out his cards and offers them to the player to his left.

Play continues in this way until all cards but the "old maid" have been played. The player holding the "old maid" is the loser, and all the other players call him "old maid" before a new game is started.

Variation To make the game last longer, cards may be considered as pairs only if their color matches as well as their number, for example, two red 7s or two black aces.

## LE VIEUX GARÇON

This French game is similar to old maid.

It is played with a standard deck of playing cards, with the jacks of hearts, diamonds, and clubs removed.

The game is lost by the player left with the jack of spades – called "le vieux garçon" or "old boy."

## 3+ PLAY OR PAY

This easy game, sometimes called round the corner, is fun for players learning about the rank and sequence of playing cards.

**Cards in sequence**

Players Three or more can play.

Cards A standard deck of playing cards is used.

Counters Each player starts with 20 counters.

Objective Each player aims to be first to get rid of all his cards.

Deal One player is chosen as dealer. He deals out all the cards in a clockwise direction, one at a time and face down. It does not matter if some players have one card more than others.

Play the player to the left of the dealer chooses any one of his cards and places it face up in the center.

The next player to his left then looks at his cards to see if he has the next card "in sequence."

A card is in sequence if it belongs to the same suit as the last card that was played and follows the order a,2,3,4,5,6, 7,8,9,10,j,q,k. If the last card was a king, the next card in sequence for this game is the ace of the same suit. (This is called a "round the corner" sequence.)

If the player has the next card in sequence he plays it face up onto the card in the center.

If he does not have this card, he must pay one counter into the center.

Play continues with each player in turn either playing the

next card in sequence or paying a counter.

When all the cards of a suit have been played, the player who put down the last card has an extra turn and may play any card that he chooses.

End The first player to get rid of all his cards is the winner of the round and takes all the counters from the center. Each loser must also pay him one counter for every card left in his hand. The winner of the game is the player with most counters after an agreed number of rounds.

## 2+ RACING DEMON

Racing demon is a fast and noisy game in which players race to get rid of all their cards.

Players Any number can play.

Cards One complete deck of standard playing cards is needed for each player. Old decks with different backs are recommended.

Playing area This game requires a lot of space.

Deal Each player shuffles and deals his own deck.

After shuffling, each player first deals out 13 cards, face down in a pile in front of him.

This pile is then turned over so that only the top card is visible. He then deals four cards face up, in a row alongside his pile of 13 cards.

His spare cards should be held face down in one hand.

Objective Each player aims:

a to get rid of his pile of 13 cards;

b to play as many cards as possible into the center.

Start of play One of the players is chosen to be the starter.

**Play**

Play to centre          Play on face up cards

When all the players have dealt out their cards, he starts play by shouting "Go!"

Play All the players play at the same time: there is no waiting to play in turn. Players may either play cards into the center or onto their own face up cards.

Play into the center If a player has an ace among his face up cards, he should place it face up in the center.

Once an ace has been played into the center, anyone with a face up 2 of the same suit can play this onto the ace. A face up 3 of the same suit can then be added by any player, and so on through to the 10, jack, queen, and king.

Playing on face up cards As well as building up the piles in the center, a player can build piles of cards on the four cards alongside his original pile of 13.

Cards added to these piles must be in descending order and alternately black and red (for example a black 6 can be added to a red 7 and then a red 5 added to the black 6).

Cards added to these piles may be:

**a** the top card from the player's original pile of 13;

**b** a card, or a correct sequence of cards, from one of the player's other face up piles.

Any space left by the removal of one of the four face up piles should be filled with the top card from the player's original pile of 13.

Spare card If a player is unable to play a face up card into the center or to move any of his face up cards, he turns to the cards that were spare after he first dealt out his cards.

These spare cards are turned over, three at a time, onto a separate pile, until one of them can be played into the center or onto a face up pile.

When all the spare cards have been turned over, the player picks up the pile, turns it face down, and continues play.

End As soon as any player uses up all his cards from his original pile of 13, he shouts "Out" and play ends.

Scoring The cards in the center are sorted into their separate decks.

A player's final score is the difference between the number of his cards in the center and the number of cards left in his original face up piles.

The winner is the player with the highest score.

## 4–6 ROLLING STONE

This popular game is highly unpredictable in its outcome. Just as a player is on the verge of winning he can get a new handful of cards to play. It is also known as enflay or schwellen.

Players Four, five, or six people can play.

Cards A standard deck of playing cards is used, but with cards removed so that there are eight cards per player.

The following cards should be removed before play:

a  for four players, the 2s,3s,4s,5s and 6s;

**Rank of cards**

b for five players, the 2s, 3s, and 4s;

c for six players, the 2s.

Objective Each player aims to be the first to get rid of all his cards.

Deal Each player cuts the cards and the one with the highest card (ace high) is the dealer. He deals out all the cards in a clockwise direction, one at a time and face down.

Play Each player looks at his cards and sorts them into suits in his hand.

The player to the dealer's left starts play by choosing a card from his hand and placing it, face up, in the center.

The other players, in turn, then try to play one card of the same suit.

If all the players are able to "follow suit," these cards (called a "trick") are put to one side and are out of play for the rest of the game. The player who played the highest card (with ace high) then starts the next trick by playing the next card into the center.

If any player is unable to follow suit, he must pick up the cards already played for that trick and add them to his own hand.

He then plays the first card of the next trick, but must not use any of the cards that he has just picked up.

End The winner is the first person to play all his cards.

## 2+ SEQUENCE

This game is easily learned but calls for a little skill in choosing which card to play when starting a sequence.

**A sequence**

Players Two or more can play sequence but it is best with four or five players.

Cards A standard deck of playing cards is used.

Objective Each player aims to be first to get rid of all his cards.

Deal One player is chosen as dealer. He deals out all the cards in a clockwise direction, one at a time and face down. It does not matter if some players have one card more than others.

Play The player to the left of the dealer starts by putting his lowest cards of any suit face up in the center. (2s count as the lowest cards and aces as the highest.)

The player with the next card in sequence then plays it face up onto the card in the center. A card is in sequence if it is of the same suit as the last card that was played and follows the order 2, 3, 4, 5, 6, 7, 8, 9, 10, j, q, k, a.

Play continues in this way until the ace is played and the sequence ends.

A player who ends a sequence starts another by playing any card from his hand.

When part of a suit has already been played, a sequence ends with the highest card yet to play. The following sequence is then started by the player who played the highest card.

End The first player to get rid of all his cards is the winner.

Scoring If more than one round is to be played, players may each start with 10 counters or beans.

At the end of every round each loser pays the winner one bean for every card still in his hand.

The winner is the player with most counters or beans after an agreed number of rounds.

## 2+ SLAPJACK

This is an exciting game that needs no skill. It can be enjoyed by the very young as the only requirement is that players can recognize a jack.

Players Two or more can play.

Cards Standard playing cards are used. If there are more than three players it is a good idea to mix two decks together. It does not matter if a few cards are missing.

Objective Players aim to win all the cards.

Deal One player deals out all the cards in a clockwise direction – one at a time and face down. It does not matter if some players have one card more than others.

Each player puts his card into a neat pile face down in front of him. Players are not allowed to look at their cards.

Play The player to the dealer's left turns over the top card of his pile and places it face up in the center.

Turns then pass around to the left, with each player placing his card on top of the previous player's card.

Slapping a jack When a jack is turned up, each player tries to be the first to put his hand on the card – i.e., to "slap the jack."

The successful player wins the central pile of cards and

shufffles them with his own cards to form his new face down pile.

The player to the winner's left starts the next round, placing a card face up in the center.

If more than one player puts his hand on the jack, the winner is the player whose hand is underneath.

If possible it is a good idea to appoint a referee to settle arguments.

If a player loses all his cards, he can stay in the game if he is first to slap the next jack.

If he fails to slap the next jack he must retire from the game.

Penalty If a player slaps a card that is not a jack, he must give his top card to the player whose card he slapped in error.

End The winner of the game is either:

a the first person to collect all the cards; or

b the player with the most cards at the end of the game.

## 2+ **SNAP**

Amusing and noisy, snap is among the most familiar of all children's card games.

Players Two or more can play.

Cards Special snap cards can be bought, but the game is just as much fun with standard playing cards.

It is best to use old cards in case of damage, and it does not matter if any of the cards are missing.

If there are more than three players it is a good idea to use two decks of cards.

Objective **Players** aim to win all the cards.

Deal One player deals out all the cards in a clockwise direction – one at a time and face down. It does not matter if some players have one card more than the others.

Each player puts his cards into a neat pile face down in front of him.

Players are not allowed to look at their cards.

Play The player to the dealer's left turns over the top card of his pile and places it face up to start a face up pile of cards next to his face down pile.

The next player to his left does the same, and so on around the players until any player sees that the cards on top of any two face up piles have the same value (e.g., two 10s).

Snap The first player to shout "Snap," when there are matching cards on top of two face up piles, collects both these piles of cards and puts them at the bottom of his own face down pile.

**Snap!**

Players now continue turning cards over as before, beginning with the player to the left of the last player who turned over a card.

Snap pool If two players shout "Snap" together, the matching face up piles are put face up in a pool in the center.

Players then continue to turn over cards, and the pool is won by the first player to shout "Snap pool" when the top card of any player's face up pile matches the top card of the pool.

No more cards When a player runs out of face down cards, he simply turns over his face up cards when it is next his turn to play.

Penalty There are diferent rules for when a player calls "Snap" in error:

**a** the player gives one card from his face down pile to each of the other players;

**b** the player's own face up pile is put into a central pool to be won like an ordinary snap pool.

End The game ends when only one player has any cards.

## EASY SNAP

This version is particularly suitable for very young children.

Instead of having individual face up piles, each player plays his cards onto a central face up pile. Players shout "Snap" when the top two cards are of the same value.

## SPEED SNAP

In this faster version of snap, players still turn their cards up one at a time, but all players do so together.

## 3+ SNIP-SNAP-SNOREM

A game with funny words to say, snip-snap-snorem is noisy, fast-moving, and fun to play.

Players It is a game for three or more players.

Cards A standard deck of playing cards is used.

Objective Each player aims to be the first to get rid of all his cards.

Deal Each player cuts the cards and the one with the highest card (ace high) is the dealer.

He deals out all the cards in a clockwise direction, one at a time, and face down.

It does not matter if some players have one card more than the others.

Play Each player looks at his cards without letting any other player see them, and sorts them in his hand.

Turns pass clockwise around the players, starting with the player to the dealer's left.

The first player places any one of his cards face up in the center.

If the next player has a card of the same rank (e.g., another queen, if the first player played a queen), he places this face up in the center of the table and shouts "Snip" as he plays it.

If he has another card of the same rank he keeps it until his next turn.

If he does not have a card of the same rank, he says "Pass" and play moves on around the players.

The next player with a card of the same rank shouts "Snap" when he plays it, and the player of the fourth card shouts "Snorem!"

The player of the fourth card starts the next round.

End The winner is the first player to play all his cards.

Variation If a player has more than one card of the same rank, he must play them all in the same turn, saying the appropriate words.

**Sample play**

Snip

Snap

Snorem

## JIG

This is played exactly like snip-snap-snorem except that instead of playing four cards of the same rank, a sequence of four cards is played.

For example, if the first player puts down a 5, this is followed by a 6, then a 7, and finally an 8.

The cards can be from different suits.

Players call out "Jiggety, joggety, jig" when playing the cards.

## 2 SPIT

Spit is an excellent game that calls for alertness and speed.

Players Two people can play.

Cards A complete deck of standard cards is used.

Deal All the cards are dealt out equally between the two players.

Before play starts, each player lays out a row of cards in front of him as follows:

1 starting from the left, he places three cards face down followed by a fourth card face up;

2 he places a second face down card on each of the first two face down cards and a face down and a face up card on the third;

3 he places a face down card on the first pile and a face up card on the second;

4 he places a face up card on the first pile.

Each player then places the rest of his cards face down in
5 pile to the left of his row.

Objective Each player aims to be the first to get rid of all his cards.

**Play to center**

Start of play **When both players are ready, either one of them calls "Spit!"**

Immediately both players take the top card from their piles of spare cards and place them face up, side by side, in the center.

Playing into the center **Each player then quickly plays as many cards as possible from his row of face up cards onto either of the face up cards in the center of the table.**

A card may be played into the center if it has a numerical value either one higher or one lower than a central face up card. (For example, a 9 or a jack can be played onto a 10. Either a king or 2 can be played onto an ace.) If playing a face up card into the center exposes a face down card in a player's row, this card should be turned face up.

Players continue to play cards onto the central piles in this manner until neither player can put out any more of his cards.

Spit **If neither player can play any card from his row of face up cards, one of the players shouts "Spit!"**

Both players take the top card from the piles of spare cards and place them face up on their central piles.

If possible, players then resume playing cards into the center from their face up piles.

If players still cannot add any cards from their face up rows, the other player calls "Spit!" and both players again play the top card of their spare piles. They continue in this way until either player can play a card from his row.

If a player wishes to call "Spit!" and the player's spare piles have been used up, each player takes his own central pile and turns it face down to form a new spare pile. The player then calls "Spit!" and play continues as before.

End of a round When a player has played all the cards from his face up row into the center, he shouts "Out!" and wins the round. He then picks up his spare pile.

The other player then collects both central face up piles, picks up the cards left in his row, and adds all these cards to the bottom of his spare pile.

Starting a new round Players lay out their cards as for the first round.

New rounds are played in the same way as the first round, except that if one player does not have enough cards for a spare pile he does without and both players play onto a single central pile.

End of game A game is won by the first player to get rid of all his cards.

# 2–4 STEALING BUNDLES

As soon as a player can spot that two cards have the same rank (face value), he is old enough to play stealing bundles. Other names for this game are old man's bundle and stealing the old man's bundle.

Players Two or four people can play.

Cards A standard deck of playing cards is used.

Objective Each player tries to collect as many cards as possible.

Deal One person is chosen as dealer. He deals the cards in a clockwise direction, one at a time and face down, until each player has four cards.

The dealer then places four cards face up in a row in the center.

Play The player to the left of the dealer begins.

If he has a card of the same rank as one of the cards in the center, he captures that card. He places the captured card and his matching card face up in a pile in front of him. This is the beginning of his "bundle."

If two or three center cards have the same rank as one of the player's cards he may capture them all in the same turn.

If none of the player's cards matches a center card, he must place one of his own cards face up in the center. This is called "trailing."

Each player then plays one card in turn. In place of or in addition to capturing cards from the center, he may steal another player's bundle if his card matches the top card of that bundle.

Every time a player captures cards he places them in his bundle with the matching card face up.

If none of his cards matches any face up card he must "trail" one of his cards.

Extra deals When all players have played each of the four cards in their hands, the dealer deals out four more cards to each player. No cards are dealt to the center. Play then continues as before.

End The game ends when all the cards have been dealt and played.

The winner is the player with the most cards in his bundle when play ends.

## 2 WAR

An easy game, war is a good way of introducing young children to card playing.

Players This game is for two people.

Cards A complete deck of standard playing cards is used.

Objective Each player aims to win all the cards.

Deal One player deals all the cards.

Each player puts his cards into a neat pile face down in front of him. Players are not allowed to look at their cards.

Play Both players turn over the top card of their piles, and place them face up, side by side, in the center.

The player who has played the higher card, regardless of suit, wins both cards and places them face down at the bottom of his pile.

Aces are the highest cards, followed by kings, queens, jacks, and so on down from the 10s to the 2s.

**Rank of cards**

The "war" If the two cards turned up have the same value, the war is on.

Each player puts one card face down on top of his first card in the center. He then puts another card face up on top of this.

The two new face up cards are compared, and the highest card wins all six cards in the center.

If the face up cards match again, the war continues. Each player puts out another face down card with a face up card on top. Play continues in this way until someone plays a card higher than the other.

End The winner of the game is either:

**a** the first player to win all the cards; or

**b** the player with the most cards at the end of a time limit set at the start of the game.

**"War"**

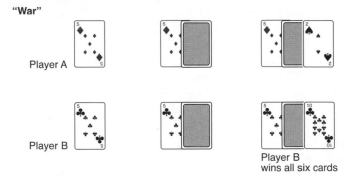

Player A

Player B

Player B
wins all six cards

## WAR FOR THREE PLAYERS

This version of war is for three players.

Deal The cards are dealt out as for war for two, except that the last card is not dealt out. (In this way, all three players begin with the same number of cards.)

Play is the same as in war for two, except that:

a when two cards of the same value are turned up, all three players engage in war;

b when three cards of the same value are turned up, the players engage in double war.

In double war each player puts out two cards face down and then one card face up. If the cards still match, the three players then continue with single war.

## PERSIAN PASHA

Persian pasha, also called pisha pasha, is a similiar game to war.

Players It is a game for two players.

Cards A complete deck of standard playing cards is used.

Objective Each player aims to win all the cards.

Deal Cards are dealt as for war.

Play Each player turns over his top card and places it on a face up pile next to his face down pile.

Players continue turning over cards until their top face up cards are of the same suit.

The player with the higher card then takes all the other player's face up pile and puts these cards at the bottom of his face down pile.

# Finding a Game

## HOW MANY PLAYERS?

This section of the book shows at a glance which games are suitable for different numbers of players. It begins with lists of games for specific numbers and ends with games for groups of two or more (page 455) and three or more (page 456) players.

### GAMES FOR ONE PLAYER

With the exception of two double solitaire games (Russian bank, and Spite and malice), all the games in Section 3 of this book are for one player.

### GAMES FOR TWO PLAYERS
*Also see games for two or more players (page 455).*

| General games | | |
| --- | --- | --- |
| All fives | Euchre, two-handed | Piquet |
| Auction pinochle | Five hundred, two-handed | Royal casino |
| Auction piquet | | Rubicon bezique |
| Bezique | Forty-five | Russian bank |
| California Jack | Gin rummy | Rummy |
| Casino | Hearts, two-handed | Seven up |
| Cribbage | Imperial | Spade casino |
| Draw casino | Kalabriasz | Spite and malice |
| Ecarte | Pinochle | |

| Gambling games |
| --- |
| Brag, nine-card |
| Fifteen |
| Thirty-five |

| Children's games | |
| --- | --- |
| Persian pasha | Stealing bundles |
| Spit | War |

## GAMES FOR THREE PLAYERS

*Also see games for two or more (page 455) and three or more (page 456) players.*

### General games

All fives
Auction pinochle
Bezique, three-handed
Calabrasella
California Jack
Casino

Cribbage, three-handed
Draw casino
Euchre, three-handed
Five hundred
Kalabriasz, three-handed
Knaves

Preference
Royal casino
Rummy
Seven up
Skat
Solo, three-handed
Spade casino

### Gambling games

Brag, nine-card
Thirty-five

### Children's games

Animal noises
Menagerie
War, for three players

## GAMES FOR FOUR PLAYERS

*Also see games for two or more (page 455) and three or more (page 456) players.*

### General games

Auction bridge
Auction forty-five
Bezique, four-handed
Boston
California jack
Call-ace euchre
Canasta
Casino
Contract bridge
Cribbage, four-handed

Draw casino
Duplicate contract bridge
Euchre, four-handed
Five hundred, four-handed
Forty-five
Gin rummy, partnership
Grand
Kalabriasz, partnership

Polignac
Railroad euchre
Royal casino
Rummy
Seven up, four-handed
Skat
Solo whist
Spade casino
Vint
Whist

## Gambling games

Brag, nine-card
Thirty-five

## Children's games

Animal noises          Rolling stone
Menagerie              Stealing bundles
My ship sails

## GAMES FOR FIVE PLAYERS

*Also see games for two or more (page 455) and three or more (page 456) players.*

## General games

Call-ace euchre
Polignac

## Children's games

My ship sails
Rolling stone

## GAMES FOR SIX PLAYERS

*Also see games for two or more (below) and three or more players (page 456).*

### General games

| | | |
|---|---|---|
| Auction forty-five | Gin rummy, | Rummy |
| Call-ace euchre | partnership | Skat |
| Forty-five | Polignac | |

### Gambling games

Brag, nine-card
Thirty-five

### Children's games

My ship sails
Rolling stone

## GAMES FOR TWO OR MORE PLAYERS

*Note that many of these games become impracticable for groups of more than seven or eight players.*
*Also see games for three or more players (page 456).*

### General games

| | | |
|---|---|---|
| Auction pitch | Nap, seven-card | Spoil five |
| Auction pitch, with | Napoleon | |
| joker | Purchase nap | |

### Gambling games

| | | |
|---|---|---|
| Ace-deuce-jack | Farmer | Red dog |
| Banker and broker | Faro | Seven and a half |
| Baccarat/Chemin de | Hoggenheimer | Six-spot red dog |
| fer | Injun | Slippery sam |
| Blackjack | Lansquenet | Stop the bus |
| Brag, nine-card | Macao | Stuss |
| Brag, seven-card | Monte bank | Tom and a half |
| Card craps | Poker | Trente et quarante |
| Card put-and-take | Polish red dog | Yablon |
| Chinese fan-tan | Red and black | Ziginette |

## Children's games

| | | |
|---|---|---|
| Beggar my neighbor | Go boom | Scoring go boom |
| Card dominoes | Go fish | Sequence |
| Concentration | Knockout whist | Slapjack |
| Crazy eights | Menagerie | Snap |
| Give away | Racing demon | |

## GAMES FOR THREE OR MORE PLAYERS
*Note that many of these games become impracticable for groups of more than seven or eight players.*

## General games

| | | |
|---|---|---|
| Black lady hearts | Heartsette | Oh hell |
| Black Maria | Irish loo | Pope Joan |
| Domino hearts | Joker hearts | Spot hearts |
| Greek hearts | Loo | |
| Hearts | Michigan | |

## Gambling games

| | | |
|---|---|---|
| Bango | Brag, three-card | Skinball |
| Blücher | Horse race | Thirty-one |
| Brag, seven-card | Kentucky derby | |

## Children's games

| | | |
|---|---|---|
| Cheat | Linger longer | Snip-snap-snorem |
| Donkey | Old maid | Up and down cheat |
| Jig | Pig | |
| Le vieux garçon | Play or pay | |

# CARD GAME VARIATIONS AND ALTERNATIVE NAMES

## VARIATIONS

*The following games are included in this book as sub-sections or variations of a game with a different name (here given in color).*

Animal noises  Menagerie
Black lady  Hearts
Black Maria  Hearts
Blind and straddle  Poker
Blind opening  Poker
Blind tiger  Poker
California jack  Seven up
Call-ace  Euchre
Chemin de fer  Baccarat
Cincinnati  Poker
Crazy eights  Go boom
Crisscross  Poker
Down the river  Poker
Easy go  Card put-and-take
Farmer  Blackjack
Fifteen  Blackjack
Gin  Rummy
Heartsette  Hearts
Jacks or better  Poker
Jig  Snip-snap-snorem
Lame-brain Pete  Poker

Le vieux garçon  Old maid
Lowball  Poker
Macao  Blackjack
Mexican stud  Poker
Persian pasha  War
Pig  Donkey
Pig in the poke  Poker
Polignac  Knaves
Railroad  Euchre
Rubicon  Bezique
Seven and a half  Blackjack
Seven-toed Pete  Poker
Shotgun  Poker
Six spot  Red dog
Spit in the ocean  Poker
Stop the bus  Brag
Stormy weather  Poker
Ten and a half  Blackjack
Up and down river  Card put and-take

## ALTERNATIVE NAMES

*The following games appear in this book under an alternative name (given here in color).*

Ace-deuce  Yablon
Ace low  Fifteen
All fours  Seven up
Animals  Menagerie
Belote  Kalabriasz
Big forty  Napoleon at St. Helena

BJ  Blackjack
Blackout  Oh hell
Blind hooker  Banker and broker
Boodle  Michigan
Broken intervals  Calculation
California loo  California jack

Cans  Fifteen
Chicago  Michigan
Chinese bezique  Six-deck bezique
Chip hearts  Spot hearts
Club  Kalabriasz
Clobber  Kalabriasz
Crapette  Russian bank
Cutthroat euchre  Three-hundred
  euchre
Demon  Canfield
Double and quits  Monte Carlo
Draw seven  California jack
Dutch bank  Banker and broker
Eight off  Eight away
Enflay  Rolling stone
Fan-tan  Card dominoes
Fan-tan  Chinese fan-tan
Farobank  Faro
Forty thieves  Napoleon at
  St. Helena
Four of a kind  Clock
Hidden cards  Clock
High-card pool  Red dog
High-low-jack  Seven up
I doubt it  Cheat
Idle year  Accordion
In between  Yablon
Indian carpet  Crazy quilt
Japanese rug  Crazy quilt
Klaberjass  Kalabriasz
Lanterloo  Loo
Laying siege  Beleaguered castle
Memory  Concentration
Methuselah  Accordion
Monte  Monte bank
Nap  Napoleon
Newmarket  Michigan
Old man's bundle  Stealing
  bundles

Old sledge  Seven up
Parliament  Card dominoes
Pass the lady  Old maid
Pasteboard derby  Kentucky derby
Pelmanism  Concentration
Penuchle  Pinochle
Pisha pasha  Persian pasha
Plait  Braid
Polish pachuk  Polish red dog
Pontoon  Blackjack
Propeller  Windmill
Put-and-take  Card put-and-take
Quince  Fifteen
Rauber skat  Skat
Rouge et noir  Trente et quarante
Round the corner  Play or pay
Saratoga  Michigan
Saton pong  Ten and a half
Schnautz  Thirty-one
Schwellen  Rolling stone
Setback  Auction pitch
Sevens  Card dominoes
Sham battle  Beleaguered castle
Skin  Skinball
Skinning  Skinball
Slippery Anne  Black Maria
Spanish monte  Monte bank
Stitch  Polish red dog
Sun dial  Clock
Three naturals  Macao
Toad in the hole  Frog
Tower of Babel  Accordion
Travelers  Clock
Twenty-one  Blackjack
Vanjohn  Blackjack
Vingt-et-un  Blackjack
Weddings  Monte Carlo

# INDEX

**A**

Accordion 350
Ace-deuce (see Yablon) 339
Ace-deuce-jack 177
Ace low (see Fifteen) 215
All fives 18
All fours (see Seven up) 147
Animal noises 428
Animals (see Menagerie) 428
Auction bridge 50
Auction forty-five 87
Auction pinochle 124
Auction pitch 20
Auction pitch, with joker 22

**B**

Baccarat 180
Baccarat banque 187
Baccarat-chemin de fer 180
Bango 191
Banker and broker 193
Beggar my neighbor 411
Beleaguered castle 351
Belote (see Kalabriasz) 102
Bezique 23
    eight-deck 30
    four-handed 31
    rubicon 26
    six-deck 28

three-handed 26
two-handed 23
Big forty (see Napoleon at St. Helena) 387
Bisley 352
BJ (see Blackjack) 196
Black lady hearts 94
Black Maria 97
Blackjack 196
Blackout (see Oh hell) 118
Blind and straddle (see Blind opening) 300
Blind hooker (see Banker and broker) 193
Blind opening 300
Blind tiger (see Blind opening) 300
Blucher 219
Boodle (see Michigan) 113
Boston 33
Brag 221
    nine-card 227
    seven-card 226
    three-card 223
Braid 354
Bridge, auction 50
Bridge, contract 37
Bridge, duplicate contract 46
Bristol 356
Broken intervals (see Calculation) 358

**C**

Calabrasella 52
Calculation 358
California jack 148
California loo (see California jack) 148
Call-ace euchre 80
Canasta 54
Canfield (see also Klondike) 360
Cans (see Fifteen) 215
Card craps 229
Card dominoes 413
Card put-and-take 236
Casino 60
  draw 64
  royal 64
  spade 65
Cheat 414
Cheat, up and down 416
Chemin de fer 181
Chicago (see Michigan) 113
Chinese bezique (see Six-deck bezique) 28
Chinese fan-tan 239
Chip hearts (see Spot hearts) 94
Cincinnati (see Poker, closed games) 304
Clab (see Kalabriasz) 102
Clobber (see Kalabriasz) 102
Clock 362
Concentration 416
Crapette (see Russian bank) 397
Contract bridge 37
Crazy eights 422
Crazy quilt 364

Cribbage 66
  five-card 72
  four-handed 73
  seven-card 73
  six-card 67
  three-handed 73
Crisscross poker (see Poker, closed games) 304
Cutthroat euchre (see Euchre, three-handed) 80

**D**

Demon (see Canfield) 360
Domino hearts 95
Donkey 417
Double and quits (see Monte Carlo) 386
Down the river (see Seven-card stud poker) 295
Draw casino 64
Draw poker 297
  variants 300
Draw seven (see California jack) 148
Duplicate contract bridge 46
Dutch bank (see Banker and broker) 193

**E**

Easy snap 442
Ecarté 74
Eight away 366
Eight off (see Eight away) 366
Enflay (see Rolling stone) 436
Euchre 77
  call-ace 80

cut-throat (see Euchre, three-handed) 80
four-handed 77
railroad 79
three-handed 80
two-handed 79

**F**

Fan-tan (see Card dominoes) 413
Fan-tan (see Chinese fan-tan) 239
Farmer 216
Faro 242
Farobank (see Faro) 242
Fifteen 215
Five hundred 81
four-handed 83
three-handed 81
two-handed 83
Florentine 388
Flower garden 389
Forty-five 84
auction 87
Forty thieves (see Napoleon at St. Helena) 387
Four of a kind (see Clock) 362
Friday the thirteenth 371
Frog 372

**G**

Gin rummy 144
Give away 419
Go boom 420
scoring 421
Go fish 423

Grand 89
Greek hearts 95

**H**

Hearts 93
black lady 94
domino 95
Greek 95
joker 96
spot 94
two-handed 96
Heartsette 96
Hidden cards (see Clock) 362
High-card pool (see Red dog) 313
High-low jack (see Seven up) 147
High-low poker 305
Hoggenheimer 250
Horse race 253

**I**

I doubt it (see Cheat) 414
Idle year (see Accordion) 350
Imperial 98
In between (see Yablon) 339
Indian carpet (see Crazy quilt) 364
Injun 256
Irish loo 112

**J**

Jacks or better 300
Japanese rug (see Crazy quilt) 364
Jig 445
Joker hearts 96

**K**

Kalabriasz 102
  partnership 107
  three-handed 106
Kentucky derby 258
King Albert 374
Klaberjass (see Kalabriasz) 102
Klondike 376
Knaves 108
Knockout whist 424

**L**

La belle Lucie 378
Lame-brain Pete (see Poker,
  closed games) 304
Lansquenet 262
Lanterloo (see Loo) 110
Laying siege (see Beleaguered
  castle) 351
Le vieux garçon 432
Leapfrog 380
Linger longer 426
Loo 110
  five-card 112
  Irish 112
  three-card 110
Low-hand stud 296
Lowball poker 301

**M**

Macao 214
Maze 382
Memory (see Concentration)
  416
Menagerie 428
Methuselah (see Accordion) 350

Mexican stud poker 296
Michigan 113
Miss Milligan 384
Monte (see Monte bank) 265
Monte bank 265
  casino 265
  private 272
Monte Carlo 386
My ship sails 430

**N**

Nap (see Napoleon) 116
  purchase 117
  seven-card 117
Napoleon 116
Napoleon at St. Helena 387
Newmarket (see Michigan) 113

**O**

Oh hell 118
Old maid 431
Old man's bundle (see Stealing
  bundles) 448
Old sledge (see Seven up) 147

**P**

Parliament (see Card dominoes)
  413
Pass the lady (see Old maid) 431
Pasteboard derby (see Kentucky
  derby) 258
Pelmanism (see Concentration)
  416
Penuchle (see Pinochle) 120
Persian Pasha 451
Pig 418

Pig in the poke (see Spit in the ocean) 303
Pinochle 120
  auction 124
Piquet 127
  au cent 133
  auction 134
Pisha pasha (see Persian pasha) 451
Plait (see Braid) 354
Play or pay 433
Poker 274
  closed games 304
  draw 297
  draw variants 300
  high-low 305
  stud 294
  stud variants 295
Poker solitaire 389
Polignac 108
Polish Pachuk (see Polish red dog) 308
Polish red dog 308
Pontoon (see Blackjack) 196
Pope Joan 135
Preference 140
Propeller (see Windmill) 408
Purchase nap 117
Puss in the corner 392
Put-and-take (see Card put-and-take) 236
Pyramid 393

**Q**
Quince (see Fifteen) 215

**R**
Racing demon 434
Railroad euchre 79
Rauber skat (see Skat) 150
Red and black 311
Red dog 313
  Polish 308
  six-spot 316
Rolling stone 436
Rouge et noir (see Trente et quarante) 335
Round the corner (see Play or pay) 433
Royal casino 64
Royal cotillion 395
Rubicon bezique 26
Rummy 142
Russian bank 397

**S**
Saratoga (see Michigan) 113
Satong Pong (See Ten and a half) 213
Schnautz (see Thirty-one) 332
Schwellen (see Rolling Stone) 436
Scoring go Boom 421
Scorpion 401
Sequence 438
Set back (see Auction pitch) 20
Seven and a half 213
Seven-card stud poker 295
Seven-toed Pete (see Seven-card stud poker) 295
Seven up 147
  four-handed 148
Sevens (see Card dominoes) 413

Sham battle (see Beleaguered castle) 351
Shotgun 301
Six-card stud poker 295
Six-spot red dog 316
Skat 150
Skin (see Skinball) 320
Skinball 320
Skinning (see Skinball) 320
Slapjack 439
Slippery Anne (see Black Maria) 97
Slippery Sam 324
Snap 441
  easy 442
  speed 443
Snip-snap-snorem 443
Solo (see Solo whist) 158
  three-handed 160
Solo whist 158
Spade casino 65
Spanish monte (see Monte bank) 265
Speed snap 443
Spider 403
Spit 445
Spit in the ocean 303
Spite and malice 405
Spoil five 163
Spot hearts 94
Stealing bundles 448
Stitch (see Polish red dog) 308
Stop the bus 228
Stormy weather 301
Stud poker 294
Stuss 327
Sun dial (see Clock) 362

**T**
Ten and a half 213
Thirty-five 329
Thirty-one 332
Three naturals (see Macao) 214
Toad in the hole (see Frog) 372
Tower of Babel (see Accordion) 350
Travelers (see Clock) 362
Trente et quarante 335
Twenty-one (see Blackjack) 196

**U**
Up and down cheat 416
Up and down the river 238

**V**
Vanjohn (see Blackjack) 196
Ving-et-un (see Blackjack) 196
Vint 166

**W**
War 449
  for three players 450
Weddings (see Monte Carlo) 386
Whist 170
  knockout 424
  solo 158
Windmill 408

**Y**
Yablon 339

**Z**
Ziginette 342